The Order of Joy

SUNY series in Psychoanalysis and Culture

Henry Sussman, editor

The Order of Joy

*Beyond the Cultural
Politics of Enjoyment*

Scott Wilson

State University of New York Press

The cover image is reproduced by permission of the Still National Osteopathic Museum, Kirksville, MO [AS 49].

Published by
State University of New York Press, Albany

For information, contact State University of New York Press, Albany, NY
www.sunypress.edu

Production by Kelli W. LeRoux
Marketing by Anne M. Valentine

Library of Congress Cataloging-in-Publication Data

Wilson, Scott, 1962–
    The order of joy : beyond the cultural politics of enjoyment / Scott Wilson.
        p. cm. — (SUNY series in psychoanalysis and culture ; 352)
    Includes bibliographical references and index.
    ISBN 978-0-7914-7449-5 (hardcover : alk. paper)   1. Joy.   I. Title.
    BF575.H27W56 2008
    128—dc22
                                                                            2007035474

10 9 8 7 6 5 4 3 2 1

for Mia

We live today under a new world order
The web which weaves together all things envelops our bodies,
Bathes our limbs,
In a halo of joy.

—Michel Houellebecq, *Atomised*

Contents

Preface

THE CULT OF JOY

I would like and I hope I'll die of an overdose [Laughter] of pleasure of any kind. Because I think it's really difficult and I always have the feeling that I do not feel the pleasure, the complete total pleasure and, for me, it's related to death. . . . Because I think that the kind of pleasure I would consider as the real pleasure would be so deep, so intense, so overwhelming that I couldn't survive it. I would die.

—Foucault, *Politics, Philosophy, Culture*

Discussing his difficulty with the "middle range pleasures that make up everyday life," Michel Foucault attempted to describe in an interview shortly before his death what, for him, constituted real pleasure. For Foucault, real pleasure lies in excess of the quotidian tastes and pleasures that ameliorate a life of work and responsibility. Real pleasure would be a pleasure over and above everyday pleasures, not necessarily an antithesis to them, but an overdose and an enhancement that could not be born by a mortal. In the interview, Foucault gives as his example the near-death experience of being hit by a car, and his use of drugs as the "mediation to those incredibly intense joys that I am looking for' (1988: 12). As James Miller shows, those intense joys were also bound up with Foucault's interest in *l'éclat des supplices*—the splendor and explosive glory of death by torture—and in S/M practices in San Francisco where that interest could be acted out and elaborated (see Miller, 1993: 212–213; 262–272).

The evocation of an intense joy before death (and even a joy *of* death) recalls the example of Georges Bataille, a writer of particular interest and importance to Foucault. In a piece written for the journal *Acéphale* in June 1939, entitled "The Practice of Joy Before Death," Bataille sketches in the main elements of what would become his method of meditation, his

xi

atheological means of placing himself at the limit of an extreme inner experience (see Bataille, 2001). "Joy before death belongs only to the person for whom there is no *beyond*; it is the only intellectually honest route in the search for ecstasy" (Bataille, 1985: 236). The practice of joy before death presupposes that there is no beyond, no transcendence, no God even as it rejects the endless deferral of a joy that will eventually come as the end or product of a work (jouissance). Joy is not a jouissance in that sense, it is joy in the immanence of imminent death—"a shameless, indecent saintliness [that] can lead to a sufficiently happy *loss of self*" (Bataille, 1985: 236–237). "Joy before death annihilates me . . . I remain in this annihilation and, from there, I picture nature as a play of forces expressed in multiplied and incessant agony" (237). Though it contemplates agony and annihilation, joy before death is essentially an affirmation of life, "the joy of existence of all that comes into the world" (239). This affirmation gives itself up, joyfully, to the play of forces that clash, constitute, and divide up the self, multiplying its potential and enhancing its range of experience in the transformative power of violent expenditures.

This is one of the main aspects that attracted Foucault to Bataille's writing, as a method and model, both of his life and his work. In an interview with Duccio Trombadori, Foucault speaks about how the example of Bataille's experience enables one to live "as close as possible to the impossibility of living, which lies at the limit or extreme . . . [which has the effect] of 'tearing' the subject from itself in such a way that it is no longer the subject as such, or that it is completely 'other' than itself so that it may arrive at its annihilation, its dissociation" (Foucault, 1991: 31). This description not only provides a model for how one may continually transform one's life, but also, since Foucault's work was inextricably bound up with his life, offers a model for his thought. He regarded the writing of his books "as direct experiences 'to tear' me from myself, to prevent me from always being the same" (1991: 32). Foucault took very seriously the idea that joy before death should be conceived as an order of practice. It was a mode of experimentation, a process without a definable end whose outcome (other than death) could not be foreseen. In his own life, Foucault used extreme erotic experiences to break down, at the level of the body, the formations of knowledge, the types of normativity and mode of subjectivity that had hitherto held it in its grip. Foucault's experiences were designed "to invent oneself" anew, make a new self "appear" (Miller, 1993: 269). Through the *épreuve* of S/M practices, something like a combination of medieval ordeal and scientific test, Foucault underwent experiments in desexualization (273). The practices broke down "the habitual dispositions of the body" by having it subjected to "wave after wave of unfamiliar sensations." In so doing, they opened up "a general economy of pleasure not based on sexual norms" (273). Foucault's general economy redistributes pleasures away from their normative focus on the genitalia, promising a new order of joy. Miller quotes an interview in which Foucault speculates about the current arid climate of sexuality being dissolved by this "great pleasure of the body in explosion" (274), so that "the incredulity currently elicited by the prospect of a life lived free of a preoccupation with penises, vaginas, and orgasms, may one day seem as myopic, and historically curious, as the Victorian dread of masturbation" (274).

In his experiments with anorganic and anorgasmic joy, Foucault felt the instincts and drives of his body turn into a teeming mass of formless pseudopods or an amoeba, decomposing into a microcosm of subhuman particles ready to merge and change shape. Summing up the experience, Foucault continued:

> There is a creation of anarchy within the body, where its hier-archies, its localizations and designations, its organicity, if you will, is in the process of disintegrating . . . This is something "unnameable," "useless," outside of all the programs of de-sire. It is the body made totally plastic by pleasure: something that opens itself, that tightens, that throbs, that beats, that gapes. (Foucault, cited in Miller: 274)

In its own way, then, joy was for Foucault a mode of scientific inquiry, "a game of truth" that enabled him to develop a technology of the self in techniques of the body and its pleasures. In such a way, Foucault developed, in conjunction with the San Francisco S/M scene, a *techne erotica* of bodies and pleasures to oppose the technology of health and pathology that characterizes the modern regime of *scientia sexualis* (see Foucault, 1980: 57, 70–71). Rather than entering into the modern discourse on the truth of sex, truth could be "drawn from pleasure itself" (1980: 57) in a pleasurable remaking of the self via the body. Placing it within a network of erotic forces, his body, Foucault claimed, disintegrated into an organ-less plane of pliability and transformation. In this laboratory, the body and soul became remodulated and reassembled as a teeming network of pseudopods humming in amoebic joy beyond all programs of desire. Always connecting the practice of desubjectification in life with the practice of writing (Foucault, 1972: 17), the development of this technology of joy continued to shape and reshape the work until, reaching its peak in San Francisco, it seemed to subsume the work itself, and a serene meditation on the ancient uses of pleasure displaced the highly combative discourse on sexuality, power, and governmentality.

Foucault's joy became the modality of his new technology of the self and aesthetics of existence. Joy provides the possibility of experiencing differently, making possible a different correlation of knowledge, decentering and dissolving norms and therefore reordering the conditions of subjectivity. This is because joy, as the affirmation of difference, both establishes the terrain and inhabits the borders of fields of knowledge; joy does not constitute a knowledge in itself, it is rather the condition and fulminating ground of knowledge, its animation and excess. Similarly, joy is not a type of normativity even though its affirmation is the precondition of any norm that can establish itself and its rule in the negativity of its own difference. And joy forms subjectivity at the very point where it swells and overflows the moment of imaginary fullness that seems to confirm it; joy tears open subjective forms into a nonsubjective space traversed by the play of forces. Experience, then, for Foucault, is not a means of self-knowledge, but a means through which the self can be modified, elaborated, and transformed, not in relation to a law or a norm or an idea, but through a process and practice of joy.

Commenting on *Discipline and Punish*, Gilles Deleuze also notes how joy is both an external shaping power of Foucault's work and an integral part of its style and manner. The book "is full of joy or jubilation that blends in with the splendour of its style and the politics of its content. It is punctuated by horrible descriptions which are lovingly rendered" (Deleuze, 1988: 23). The book is shaped by a "sense of gaiety in horror," not the "ambivalent joy of hatred," but "the joy of wanting to destroy whatever mutilates life" (23). In this tribute, Deleuze enlists Foucault as part of his philosophical "cult of affirmation and joy" presided over by Spinoza and Nietzsche (Deleuze, 2003: 144). "Spinoza or Nietzsche are philosophers whose critical and destructive powers are without equal, but this power always springs from affirmation, from joy" (2003: 144). In its affirmative power, Foucault's books are part of a Nietzschean "comedy of the superhuman" since they elicit an "indescribable joy" even when "they speak of ugly, desperate, or terrifying things" (258).

In *Foucault* (1988), Deleuze makes a subtle correlation between Foucault's life and work, as a continuous practice of joy before death, his own conception of death—"and few men died in a way commensurate with their conception of death" (Deleuze, 1988: 95). For Deleuze, Foucault sought to escape the lines of power that seem to restratify all forms of resistance by attaining "a life that is the power of the outside" (1988: 95). But "what tells us that this outside is not a terrifying void and that this life, which seems to put up a resistance, is not just the simple distribution within the void of 'slow, partial and progressive' deaths?" (95). Foucault's practice did not invoke and experience a joy before death where death, retroactively, transforms life into a destiny, a narrative, as an "indivisible and decisive" event. Rather, death becomes "multiplied and differentiated" (95). Following Bichet, Deleuze suggests, Foucault regarded death as "being coextensive with life," "something made up of a multiplicity of partial and particular deaths" (95). Foucault's practice of multiple deaths, therefore, maintained death as an immanent principle distributing new configurations of experience in a new order of joy.

NEW ORDER

A general economy of pleasure, enjoyment, and joy shapes particular orders of subjective existence. Pleasure and pain constitute a continuous fluctuating surface that provides the interior and exterior boundary of the subject in its sensitive broaching of the real. In the intermediate position between the subject and the real there are things. Useful things, nice things, terrifying things, favorite things, phantasmatic things, desirable things, vision things, epistemic things, things of nothing, real things that find their contours in the subject's negotiation with its own reality. That reality is not simply the subject's own, of course, but is shared insofar as it is symbolized and rendered sensible by vision, language, and discourse. But just as there are different languages and different formations of discourse, so there are different modalities of pleasure. There is no hierarchy in the relationship between language and pleasure, words and things. Different modalities of pleasure—including pain, suffering and misery, laughter and tears—inhabit the gaps in language and articulate the experience and knowledge of things in different ways. Pleasure silently shapes and configures the order of things.

All order is in-formed by pleasure, and historically different orders of knowledge therefore also imply different orders of pleasure, enjoyment, or joy. There is a pleasure in finding resemblance between things, in classifying them, in identifying things and differentiating them with others, in making lists, and placing things in a hierarchy. There is an enjoyment in making things, destroying them, interpreting and toying with them, consuming them. As Foucault demonstrated, there is a joy in trawling the archive and reconstituting horrors in lovingly rendered descriptions of agony and botched mutilation. Pleasure forms the basis of any discursive formation at least as fundamentally as an *episteme*, the rules, regularities, and relations that are shaped by the very pleasure that they afford.

Through reversing the hierarchy of knowledge over enjoyment in order to excavate an "arche-aesthesia" of pleasures that in-form different epistemic orders in *The Order of Things* (1986), it might be amusing to read the constitution of one or another of Foucault's archaeological layers as the expression of an archaic drive arrested, during a particular epoch, at one of Freud's stages of infantile sexuality. Following this suggestion for a moment, it could no doubt be possible to think of the Renaissance's passion for resemblance as an expression of the oral drive that seeks out similitude, running its lips over the prose-flesh of the world, its mouth mapping out the shape of a nipple in a knuckle, a thumb, a walnut, or a breast in a hillock or an apple. And one can see in the classical age's enthusiasm for representation, classification, and exchange the analytic rigor proper to anal eroticism, the anal level being the locus of metaphor. (The fact that the Marquis de Sade is located at the end point of the classical age, as its revelation and apotheosis, would then be no coincidence, of course.) The genitality of the modern age is evident in its self-conscious avowal of maturity and production, retrospectively placing itself in a teleological structure, at the end of a process of historical development, endlessly defining and redefining its normativity in relation to the perversions of nongenital, nonreproductive sexual activity.

However amusing it might be to characterize these periods in this way, it would only reinscribe Foucault's account of historical discontinuities into a rather traditional history—albeit a psychoanalytic history of libidinal development. A Foucaultian arche-aesthesia of pleasures would instead historicize jouissance itself as the basic "*stoff*" of the drive in psychoanalysis, even as it located different formations of pleasure, enjoyment, or joy as the (non)bases of epistemic order. Such formations would not necessarily mean that everyone, during a particular historical epoch, experienced pleasure in the same way. Nor would it mean that it is impossible to experience the pleasures of classification outside the classical era, or to enjoy only in the context of modernity. Rather, Foucault's epistemic divisions are a device to look at how certain experiences of pleasure shaped thought in distinctive ways. And it is arguable that, along the lines suggested by Foucault, one mode of pleasure or enjoyment took on dominance over another in its shaping of a certain field of knowledge and discursive practice. A dominant mode of pleasure-knowledge established how certain ideas appeared, the way in which science is practiced, the objects it produced, what kinds of experiences were reflected in philosophies, and so on. These modifications in pleasure and enjoyable experience are also linked to, but not determined by, technological changes that have transformed modes of human, social existence, just as they are related to various things that have, along with the empirical positivity given to them by one regime of knowledge, a certain heterogeneity with regard to that knowledge that affects the shapes, the rules, the regularities that pleasure in-forms.

The major and most common criticism of Foucault's work of this period concerns radical historical discontinuity itself, the sharp edges that separate one episteme from another. How did one space of knowledge transform into another? Moreover, how is it that Foucault himself, still writing at the edge of modernity, could describe, as if from the outside, these different systems of knowledge, including his own? Precisely, he suggests, because of the relation to 'the outside'. "Discontinuity—the fact that within the space of a few years a culture sometimes ceases to think as it had been thinking up till then and begins to think other things in a new way—probably begins with an erosion *from outside*" (Foucault, 1986: 50). An enigmatic formulation, the 'thought from outside' is given further elaboration in a contemporary essay on Maurice Blanchot (Foucault, 1987) where it is called the thought of ecstasy or joy, "born of that tradition of mystical thinking which, from the time of Pseudo-Dionysus, has prowled the borderlands of Christianity" (1987: 16). As Deleuze argued, throughout Foucault's work, he never stopped trying to open his own discourse to this exterior space, just as he sought to transform his thought through joy, submerging his own voice in the ceaseless murmuring of discourse unfolding in the void (Foucault 1971).

For Lacanian psychoanalysis, this space is the space of the Thing that is "situated in the relationship that places man in the mediating position between the real and the signifier" (Lacan, 1992: 129). The chain of signifiers is articulated along the threshold of the real that resists symbolization absolutely. Folding back from a (missed) encounter with the real, the chain of signifiers circulates around the Thing that is hollowed out in the fold, the vacuole that results though the (missed) encounter. In Lacanian terms, it could be suggested, the pleasurable modifications of order by and in which things are arranged and enjoyed takes place in the space of the Thing. Further, it is in this extimate space of the outside that is "more distant than any exterior" but is twisted, folded, and doubled by "an Inside that is deeper than any interior" (Deleuze, 1988: 110), that the relationship between exterior and interior is derived from the Thing that establishes their phantasmatic limits. It is in this space that the Thing of pleasure transmutes into the Thing of enjoyment and the Thing of joy, thereby altering the topography of the space of order in which its pleasurable objects are constituted and arranged (for a further discussion of how the transmutation of pleasures support the changes in epistemic order described in Foucault's *Order of Things*, see Wilson, 2004).

In an appendix to *Foucault* (1988), Deleuze discusses the succession of epistemic shifts outlined in *The Order of Things* and speculates on a new "Formation of the Future." After the death of man, erased like a face drawn at the edge of the sea, Deleuze wonders about the coming of the Nietzschean superman in the context of a new formation of knowledge. For Nietzsche, the superman liberates the life within man for the benefit of another form, just as language liberated itself from nineteenth-century linguistics in the sovereign form of literature. Deleuze suggests that, following language into the twentieth century, life broke free from biology, and labor from economics. To do this,

> Biology had to take a leap into molecular biology, or dispersed life regroup in the genetic code. Dispersed work had to regroup in third-generation machines, cybernetics and information technology. What would be the forces in play, with which the forces within man would then enter into a relation? (Deleuze, 1988: 131)

And indeed, what would be the mode of super-enjoyment that relates these forces with the superman—or indeed the superwoman? What joy is this? The joy that would animate the supermen and women apparently in charge of the very code that gives them the secrets of the book of life, the men and women in charge of the domain of silicon, the men and women for whom both organic and inorganic matter is at their disposal to manipulate, simulate, virtualize, fuse, and meld together in living machinic assemblages, following the trajectory of the literature that long ago liberated itself from the labor of resemblance and representation. It is this new order of joy that is the subject of what follows in this book where, in order to account for its emergence, joy will be rigorously distinguished from jouissance in a rereading of Lacan through Deleuze.

Part One

Introduction

CHAPTER ONE

The Structure of the Real

What is important is not that there are three dimensions in space. What is important is the Borromean knot and that for the sake of which we accede to the real it represents to us.

—Jacques Lacan, *Encore*

MONSTRATIONS

The publication of Gilles Deleuze and Félix Guattari's *Anti-Oedipus* in 1972 had a profound effect on Lacanian psychoanalysis. Its success pre-cipitated the publication of Jacques Lacan's seminars and established the battle lines over the development of Lacan's thought throughout the 1970s. By the end of the 1970s, and Lacan's death in 1980, Jacques-Alain Miller, Lacan's son-in-law, gained control over the legacy (Roudinesco, 1990: 564; 1997: 414). During the 1970s, Lacanianism split into the hy-perrationalist Millerian Lacanianism and the Lacanianism of Lacan him-self. As Elisabeth Roudinesco writes,

> Miller's interpretations shut [Lacan's] work in on itself . . . Lacan's gradually evolved concepts, detached from their his-tory and stripped of the ambivalence that had been their strength, were now classified, labeled, tidied up, sanitized, and above all cleansed of their polysemic complexity. (1997: 305)

Flattered by the way in which Miller applied his philosophical training to a schematization of his concepts, Lacan allowed Miller to take control of the transcription, editing, and publication of the seminars. On his death, Miller took possession of Lacan's papers and the distribution of the work. Through his editing and even rewriting, according to Roudinesco, Miller rationalized Lacan's thought to the point of turning it into a kind of dog-matism.[1] The process was already evident in the early 1970s, however, and Miller's growing influence was itself one of the reasons why Deleuze and Guattari wanted to give Lacan 'some help' in the liberation of some of his concepts from the dogmatism that was surrounding them. In a famous anecdote, Lacan apparently summoned Deleuze to his apartment, after the publication of *Anti-Oedipus*, and told him how hopeless all his disciples were except Miller. Then he said, "What I absolutely need is someone like you" (Roudinesco, 1997: 347). Deleuze acknowledges that in their book this is what he and Guattari sought to do, inspired by the creative side of Lacan's concepts. "I said to myself," recalls Deleuze, "that things would be better still if we found adequate concepts instead of using notions which are not even those of Lacan in his creative phase, but those of an orthodoxy that formed around him" (cited in Roudinesco, 1990: 494).

Perhaps symptomatic of the dual tendency in Lacanianism in the 1970s was the development of Lacan's mathemes and his exploration of the theory of knots. The increasing use and naming of mathemes in the late 1960s and 1970s undoubtedly appealed to Miller since, as the transcript of *Television* (1990) shows, he increasingly began to annotate and condense Lacan's discourse into quasi-algebraic formulas. At the same time, Lacan himself was retreating into silence and increasingly formulating his thought topographically in the form of Borromean knots. These knots replaced discourse with "monstrations" of the unrepresentable or ineffable. The term "matheme" seems to have been coined by Lacan from a combination of Levi-Strauss's *mytheme* and the Greek word *mathema*, meaning knowledge. The mathemes denoted not just meaning but the discursive demand and promise of meaning, and therefore its absence. In this sense, their mathematical incomprehensibility was partly the point, as was the implication of mathematical imcomprehension generally. Mathemes are "the writing of what is not sayable but can be transmitted" (Roudinesco, 1990: 563). For Lacan, the element of the unsayable, of incomprehension and nonmeaning, was essential if Lacanian psychoanalysis was to be taught institutionally without being turned into a discourse of the university. This is because the matheme "was not the site of an integral formalization since it presupposed a residue that permanently escaped it" (Roudinesco, 1990: 563).

Alongside the creation of mathemes, Lacan's mathematical investigations went in another direction, one not simply his own creation, but toward that of the preestablished field of topology. The shape that particularly interested Lacan was suggested by the arms/insignia of the Milanese Borromeo family. The Borromean knot names a figure in which three rings are interlinked in such a way that, if one is cut, the remaining two are set asunder. For Lacan, this figure provided a topographical means to represent the interdependence of his tripartite scheme of the Imaginary, Symbolic, and the Real, further changing its emphasis from

ISR to RSI in which the cloverleaf became "dominated by the weight of the Real." Indeed, the figure became the very structure of the Real insofar as this untranscribable structure could be rendered monstrable in the form of the knot. "It was a metaphor of the fact that everything proceeded from the one, but it also served to present that metaphor since no formalization of language was transmissable in the image of that language itself" (Roudinesco, 1990: 564). In *Encore*, Seminar XX, Lacan states that "the Borromean knot is the best metaphor of the fact that we proceed only on the basis of the One" (1999: 128), the one being the structure itself, the structure of the Real. This topology thereby "brings about a fundamental shift from symbolic to real" (Roudinesco, 1997: 359). For Roudinesco, this opposition in many ways represented the two forms of Lacanianism. She writes that

> It was thus no accident if the designation of a "dauphin" in the person of Jacques-Alain Miller occurred by way of the matheme and the transcription of the seminar, while the death of the sovereign was formulated in a Borromean idiom: nothingness, muteness, silent confinement in a topological monastery. (1990: 564)

In what follows it is the loops of the Borromean knot that inform the structure of the order of joy. This book is primarily concerned with the spaces of intersection, however, where "the web which weaves together all things envelops our bodies / Bathes our limbs, / In a halo of joy" (Houellebecq, 2001: 7). As Lacan suggests in Seminar XX, joy is the cry, the squeal, of jouissance captured, coiled, and divided in the rings of the Borromean knot (1999: 111). But to discuss this further, and how it relates to the topology that provides the structure of the Real, we must first differentiate joy from jouissance.

FROM JOUISSANCE TO JOY

There is a certain philosophical tradition, starred by the names of Spinoza, Nietzsche, Deleuze, and Foucault, that constitutes a sort of cult of joy. To this lineage perhaps could be added Georges Bataille, although he would occupy a very marginal space. Bataille's notion of joy before death of course informs Foucault, but is regarded with suspicion by Deleuze. Joy can also be located in the margins of Lacan's teaching, but not in the form of that teaching given to it by Jacques-Alain Miller. Joy needs to be strictly differentiated from jouissance, particularly in the way it has been conceptualized by Miller and his followers.

Jouissance, for Lacan, is a highly fluid notion that is elaborated differently and continually modified in the 1950s, 1960s, and 1970s in relation to Freud, Hegel, Sade, and Bataille. In the early seminars, it seems to be synonymous with pleasure, but by the late 1950s and early 1960s, the notion of jouissance is developed in contradistinction to pleasure. Later, in the 1970s, jouissance seems to be a substance infusing bodies and signifiers, split into male and female varieties, that articulates and differentiates restricted and general economies, in Bataille's terms.

In Seminar I (1953–54), jouissance is defined in a reading of Hegel's master-slave dialectic mediated through the seminars of Alexandre Kojève in the 1930s. Lacan explicates the master-slave myth in terms of the imaginary and symbolic registers. The structure of jouissance in the interhuman bond, as it is outlined by Hegel, remains crucial for Lacan, and particularly some of his followers, even as the substance of jouissance changes.

> Beginning with the mythical situation, an action is undertaken, and establishes the relation between pleasure [*jouissance*] and labour. A law is imposed on the slave, that he should satisfy the desire and the pleasure [*jouissance*] of the other. It is not sufficient for him to plead for mercy, he has to go to work. And when you work, there are rules, hours—we enter the domain of the symbolic. (Lacan, 1988a: 223)

Throughout Lacan's oeuvre, jouissance remains associated with work and production, or what Hegel calls the labor of the negative. The slave sacrifices or sublimates his or her jouissance for the jouissance of the master, who does not work. Work is of course not just the negation and transformation of nature, it is also the work of knowledge. In the enlightenment tradition, knowledge and enjoyment are often located in the same place, but never at the same time, the one always displacing the other. Kant located the origin of reason in the concealment of the sexual organs, the use of the fig leaf, while, for Hegel, the master enjoys the fruits of the slave's labor but is an unreflecting idiot. He enjoys, but knows nothing about it. This is how the imaginary degradation of the interhuman bond is played out in the dialectic. The master enjoys at the expense of the slave, but is a degraded figure, and subsequently all manifestations of enjoyment may be regarded as an excess, a degradation, an immoral libertinage or *plus de jouir*, a surplus taken at the expense of the subject of labor. In *Television* (1990), Lacan will find this structure at the heart of racism where the Other who does not work, or works too hard, or who has noisy parties, is seen to be enjoying at the expense of the subject (Lacan, 1999: 32; see also Miller, 1988: 129). Jouissance is located therefore as the end and meaning of work and thought, but it is always sacrificed to, or taken by, the Other that represents the law precisely in the form of enjoyment.

Ultimately, the mythical master is only the imaginary representative of the Other in the form of the law and the signifier of jouissance. That is, the law of the Other not just in the form of the symbolization that enables the differentiation between master and slave, or that lays down the hours of work, but the law of the signifier without a signified, death. Death is the stake, risked by the master, but not the slave, that differentiates and names the couple to begin with, and that designates the dialectic as an effect of "a rule of the game" (Lacan, 1988a: 223). Jouissance, therefore, is indelibly associated with a risking of death, playing the game to the limit, and giving oneself up to the destiny of the signifier.

So even though in Seminar I jouissance is a name for pleasure, it is not simply "the enjoyable sensation that accompanies the satisfaction of a biological need" (Evans, 1996: 91). All the coordinates that will take jouissance altogether beyond the principle of pleasure are there in the dialectic. Jouissance is associated with death; it infuses the law with an imperative to work, and since it is enjoyed at the expense of labor, reason, and (slave) morality, it is evil. Furthermore, the signifier of this jouissance has no signified other than death, which cannot be subjectively known, which can only be imagined and feared; the signifier of jouissance is therefore empty, but all the more powerful and directive for that.

These coordinates of the plane of jouissance are laid out explicity in 1960 in both Seminar VII (1959–60; Lacan, 1992) and in the paper "The subversion of the subject and the dialectic of desire in the Freudian unconscious." The latter was delivered at a conference in 1960 and also published as a chapter in Écrits (1966; Lacan, 1986). In Seminar VII in a reading of Sade, Freud's Beyond the Pleasure Principle and Civilization and Its Discontents, jouissance is firmly located beyond the pleasure principle in the domain of transgression, evil and suffering (1992: 184). Jouissance is precisely prohibited by the principle of pleasure and the good, and the rationalist, utilitarian, and liberal systems that seek to govern in the name of the good. God is dead, but "jouissance still remains forbidden" (184) in secular regimes—indeed its prohibition is redoubled. And therein, ironically, jouissance retains a spiritual dimension, albeit in a negative and paradoxical way appropriate to Sadean atheism. Or perhaps jouissance retains an aura of mysticism in an atheological Bataillean sense in which jouissance can be reconfigured as a moral summit beyond the polarities of good and evil. An inhuman jouissance that here would constitute a summit that "corresponds to excess, to an exuberance of forces [that] relates to measureless expenditures of energy and is a violation of the integrity of individual beings" (Bataille, 1992a: 42). For Bataille, Christ on the cross constitutes such a summit since it is "an extremely equivocal expression of evil," a simultaneously tragic and joyful signifier of death (42).

In the "Subversion of the subject" chapter from *Écrits*, the prohibition of jouissance is regarded as a domestication of its structural impossibility for speaking beings. Indeed, the idea of prohibition merely sustains the illusion concerning jouissance and its possibility. Jouissance is impossible because of the symbolic castration that results through gaining access to the social existence made possible by the signifier. The signifier of this castration, the phallus, consequently becomes the focus of the desire for jouissance, for completeness, totality, oneness. In the paper, Lacan argues that it must be called the phallus for cultural, anthropological, and historical reasons that inform the reality of analytic experience. It is called the phallus because the image of the penis is "negativity in its place in the specular image. It is what pre-destines the phallus to embody *jouissance* in the dialectic of desire" (Lacan, 1986: 319). But the erect penis comes to "symbolize the place of *jouissance*, not in itself, or even in the form of an image, but as a part that is lacking in the desired image" (320). Obscene and off stage, the erect penis is the image of the Other's desire that is lacking, that does not signify. The erect penis is substituted by the phallus, that is: a signifier of the Other's desire in socially acceptable form: truth, totality, woman.

In Seminar XX, Lacan returns to the distinction made in Seminar VII between jouissance and utility in order to reconfigure the law of jouissance as essentially an economy. "Jouissance is what serves no purpose (*ne sert à rien*)" (1999: 3). The essence of the law, meanwhile, is to put that purposelessness to use as a means that can have no end in itself, and "to divide up, distribute, or reattribute everything that counts as jouissance" (3). But what does it mean to put uselessness to use as a means of dividing up and distributing everything that counts as useless? Such a question becomes even more problematic when this economy of jouissance is considered in relation to postmodern capitalism where the distinction between utility and uselessness is extremely difficult to draw, where it can perhaps only be determined retrospectively in terms of the surplus (of useless jouissance) that it generates. As Jean-Joseph Goux writes, "is it useful or superfluous to manufacture microwave ovens, quartz watches, video games, or collectively, to travel to the moon and Mars, to photograph Saturn's rings etc.?" (Goux, 1998a: 198).

Even as the economic law of jouissance is supposed to divide up and distribute everything purposeless that counts as jouissance, Lacan goes on to argue that it is divided up between the sexes and distributed unequally. Indeed, this unequal distribution is both a determining factor and effect of the 'sexuation' of speaking beings. Jouissance is divided between a phallic jouissance available to those beings sexed male and female, and a jouissance of the Other available only to those beings sexed female, or at least available to males only on condition that they give up on phallic jouissance. This condition is not required of females, however. There is no need to go into Lacan's formulas of sexuation here (see Lacan, 1999).

However, some characteristics of the different modalities of jouissance could be noted. Phallic jouissance is essentially unsatisfactory, narcissistic, masturbatory, and idiotic—for male or female. "I designate Phi as the phallus insofar as I indicate that it is the signifier that has no signified, the one that is based, in the case of man, on phallic jouissance. What is the latter if not following, which importance of masturbation highlights sufficiently—the jouissance of the idiot" (1999: 81). It is a jouissance focused on and channeled through the sexual organs that renders one unable to enjoy the Other's body because what one "enjoys is the jouissance of the organ" (1999: 7). Unlike males, however, females are not wholly determined by the phallic function of jouissance.

Instead, the position of the woman (who does not exist) makes available "a jouissance that is hers about which she perhaps knows nothing if not that she experiences it—that much she knows. She knows it, of course, when it comes (*arrive*)" (1999: 74). 'The' woman, famously for Lacan, does not exist because she is not whole, but she marks out a place of 'ex-sistence' beyond the phallus available to anyone. This jouissance of the Other, that one experiences and yet knows nothing about, that is beyond the phallus and outside of knowledge, and therefore both deeply interior and exterior to the subject of self-reflection and self-knowledge, puts one on the path of ex-sistence (77), that is, the real. Since for speaking beings, existence necessarily implies speech, the path of ex-sistence leads to the reality that resists symbolization absolutely. It again suggests a mystical domain of jouissance since, historically, the jouissance that is beyond has been intimated by saints and mystics, and, Lacan suggests, the 'God face' of the Other could be considered to be "based on feminine jouissance" (1999: 77).[2]

These two modalities of jouissance are dignified, in the Lacanian lexicon, with their own algorithmic signs: JΦ (or Jφ) for phallic jouissance and JO for the jouissance of the Other. In Lacan's overall system of the structure of the Real, in which Imaginary, Symbolic, and the real are interlinked in the form of a Borromean knot, JΦ is located in the intersection between the Symbolic and the real, while JO is located between the real and the Imaginary. The question of Meaning is interposed in the relation between Imaginary and Symbolic (see Fig 1.1).

In my elaboration of the order of joy I wish to draw on elements of Lacan's concept in its different manifestations, to use it as a reference, but only to modify it for my own purposes. These modifications do not seek their justification in a revised form of psychoanalytic practice. This book has nothing to say or to contribute to the analytic experience. Rather, justification is sought in two main areas: first the theoretical work done by Lacan's contemporaries and peers in writing that relates to or connects with his, and that brings with it a different perspective outside the specifics of the analytic experience. Justification is also sought in the work of a younger generation of philosophers and thinkers who have engaged and contested the philosophical grounds of Lacan's thinking. But this is only done because of the second reason, which is not so much a reason as an intuition that certain fundamental cultural premises necessary to the formulation of the understanding of jouissance have changed. Transformations in both imaginary and symbolic registers have been caused and caused to alter the relation to the real, which has correspondingly caused a mutation in the structure of affect. These transformations have taken place in the twentieth century, and promise to accelerate in the twenty-first. They profoundly alter, I argue, the configuration of pleasure and unpleasure from both the inside and the outside. These changes, cultural, social, economic, scientific, and technological, do not simply

Fig. 1.1   The Structure of the Real

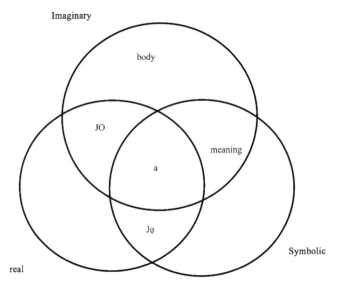

Fig. 1.2 The Order of Joy

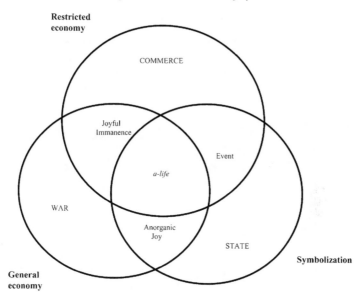

alter the contemporary field of existence, they also have effects retroactively as the understanding of speech and being alters accordingly.

The following questions, therefore, need to be posed to the concept
of jouissance in an era when the concepts of work, leisure, knowledge,
production, truth, meaning, the good, utility, sex, the body have become
problematized to such a degree that they barely seem operative. All of
these concepts are essential to the meaning of jouissance, essential to any
understanding of what 'enjoy' meant. In what follows in the succeeding
chapters, all these concepts will be examined, along with the jouissance
that they sublimate, promise, defer, distribute, or divide. In particular, the
following chapters look at where these concepts have been placed under
strain by transformations in three overlapping domains: commerce, war,
and the state. These three areas have all altered in different ways, both
subtle and profound. The way in which the world of commerce and finance operates in the global economy affects, and is affected by, the way
in which war is waged by the world's major power. In turn, revolutions
in military affairs and transnational corporations transform the role of the
state, and state functions, in different ways. Nevertheless, these three domains remain interlocked and interdependent. It is where they intersect,
however, that the new divisions of joy can be discerned, divisions that dis-
close the characteristic symptomatology or structure of feeling that characterizes supercapitalism. It is these three interlocking areas, and their
extimate core that structure the divisions of the order of joy (see Fig. 1.2).

THE MODALITIES OF JOY:
WAR, COMMERCE, THE STATE

The terms "restricted economy," "general economy," and "symboliza-tion" mark places through which flow the various formations of joy's ex-penditure. In the order of joy, there is no opposition between restricted and general economies, just as the presence of war does not mark the fail-ure of commerce, or vice versa, but simply denotes a different modality of joy. Symbolization marks the place where the question of command and control, of operativity, efficiency, and homeostasis persists, precisely as a question concerning the drive of the machine.

War

I MYSELF AM WAR

—Georges Bataille, "The Practice of Joy Before Death"

"What hit me?" The encounter with the real is always traumatic, and missed. This "essential encounter—an appointment to which we are al-ways called with a real that eludes us" is named by Lacan *tuché* in Semi-nar XI (1976: 53–55). In his analysis of the encounter with the real, Lacan notes that its function first presented itself to the history of psy-choanalysis in the form of trauma. This trauma was not just the effect of the disturbances of psychic reality disclosed in Freudian case studies, but also and perhaps preeminently revealed itself in the effects of war. If the real has a preferred modality in its encounters with speaking beings it is war, a war that is continuous, perpetual, unrelenting, and always missed. It is a war that provides the condition of the rhetoric, blood and thunder of historical action, a war that lies beyond the automata, the rapid re-sponse, the automatic weaponry, both psychic and prosthetic, of the ma-chineries of desire and combat.

Real war constitutes the field of battle, rather than takes place on one. As Deleuze writes, in his commentary on Nietzsche, "all reality is already quantity of force" (1983: 40). Immanent to the real is war be-tween different quantities and relations of force, both active and reac-tive. The real insists in the order of things precisely through this war in convulsions of violence, chance, catastrophe, and sudden changes in the relations of forces. "Every force is related to others and it either obeys or commands. What defines a body is this relation between dominant and dominated forces. Every relationship of forces constitutes a body—whether it is chemical, biological, social or political" (1983: 40). Fur-ther, any two forces, being unequal, constitute a body as soon as they enter into a relationship. This is why the body is always a fruit of chance (40). War is continually punctuated by chance encounters and alliances that introduce different possibilities and distributions of force, forming new bodies and assemblages.

Foucault's understanding of power is perfectly in line with this assumption about the perpetual war underlying politics and the history of struggle and contestation. "Power is war, the continuation of war by other means" (2003: 15). In his essay, "Nietzsche, Genealogy, History," Foucault, like Deleuze, outlines his own assumptions in terms of Nietzsche's philosophy:

> Humanity does not gradually progress from combat to combat until it arrives at universal reciprocity, where the rule of law finally replaces warfare; humanity installs each of its violences in a system of rules and thus proceeds from domination to domination. (Foucault, 1984: 151)

In the series of lectures given in 1976, but posthumously published in 2003, Foucault gives a much fuller expression to the war that has exerted its grip, sometimes noisily, sometimes silently, on western Europe for over a thousand years. It is a story of how state functions—institutions, economic inequalities, language, disciplinarity—have been deployed in order to maintain and reinscribe a particular relationship of force. "Politics is the continuation of war by other means," states Foucault, inverting Clausewitz's famous dictum, but so also is law, culture, economy. Ultimately, one force exerts its dominance through the offices of the state by seizing the monopoly of violence and the ability to make war, with violence the cutting edge of a tool of government.

In his argument, Foucault is keen to disassociate his theory of power with political economy, as if the role of power was secondary, to be understood in terms of its economic functionality. Foucault wishes to develop a different model to the Marxian one that sees the role of power as essentially the maintenance of the relations of production and the domination of one particular class over another on the basis of the appropriation of the forces of production (2003: 14). At the same time, he acknowledges that "power relations are deeply involved in and with economic relations, even if power relations and economic relations always constitute a sort of network or loop" (14). But precisely at the point where power and economy loop around one another and become each other's underside or support, they can both be seen as modalities of pure expenditure. This is precisely the logic if power and politics are simply war by other means. If not power and politics, what point does war have other than the joy of making war? Wealth and power are not the end of this war; wealth and power are simply the means to make more war, the chance for a body, an assemblage of forces, to dominate, subjugate and therefore "affirm itself with more joy" (Deleuze, 1983: 121).

On the plane of joyful immanence, war adopts increasingly commercial and economic methods, even as global war has become the modality of corporate capitalism. In this area where the state formation is suspended, there is no distinction between business and war, production and expenditure. War and business have become the same thing not just because the former supports the latter or because the latter capitalizes on the advantages offered by military and information technology. It is because of the way that the 'spirit' of bourgeois economy (for which war was traditionally the excess) has given way to a supercapitalism in which war is the modus operandi. The Protestant work ethic that was characterized by thrift, industriousness, petty calculation, and abstinence has disappeared, or become transformed, in a new intensity of aggressive competition and the work ethic "gone ballistic" (Goldman and Papson, 1998: 153; see also Wilson, 2008, for a fuller account of how commerce and war have conjoined in the form of supercapitalism).

Commerce

> The oldest and most primitive personal relationship is that between buyer and seller, creditor and debtor: it was here that one person first encountered another person, first *measured oneself* against another.
>
> —Nietzsche, *The Genealogy of Morals*

The exchange of objects, of signs and possessions, wealth, credit, and credence plays out the interhuman bond in an imaginary domain. It is above all an exchange of glances measuring oneself in the mirror of the other by looking him or her in the eye. Exchange is the modality of the romance of human rivalry, amorous, martial, and symbolic. Romance lies at the obscure origins of capitalism, according to Adam Smith, in the propitious event of a fall. The fall effects a division of "joysaunce," the archaic English word for jouissance.[3] In his famous account of the decline of feudalism in *The Wealth of Nations* (1976), Smith relates how joysaunce, in the form of the excessive expenditure on manufactured goods for personal use and vanity, brought the ruling class to their knees. In the *OED*, joysaunce is given two meanings:

1. The possession and use of something affording advantage.
2. Pleasure, delight, merriment, mirth, festivity.

For the ruling class of landed aristocrats there is no opposition between these two meanings. Advantage, in the form of social status and landed wealth, is already presupposed; advantage finds its meaning, rather, in pleasure, delight, mirth, and festive joy. The use of possessions is non-productive in that sense and joysaunce is a form of joyful expenditure. But, for Smith, modern economy begins with the splitting and opposition of these two meanings of joysaunce. In his account, Smith is critical of the economic inefficiency of the "antient method of expence" whereby lords kept large companies of retainers, tenants, and dependents, and shared and destroyed their surplus in great festivals of "rustick hospitality." Smith is even more severe on the "violence, rapine and disorder" that the lords permitted and produced in endless quarrels. And he is withering when it comes to the cause of their economic downfall at the hands of the middle rank of urban manufacturers, merchants, and traders in foreign commerce. The latter provided these great proprietors, the noble heirs of the German and Scythian nations that overwhelmed and overran the might of the Roman empire in western Europe, with "a method of con-suming the whole value of their rents" purely on themselves. This self-pleasuring vanity ultimately obliged them to let go of their retainers and dependents and therefore of their ability to disregard the laws of the growing metropolitan centres. And, most fatally, it rendered them unable to make war. Smith writes,

> For a pair of diamond buckles perhaps, or for something as frivolous and useless, they exchanged the maintenance, or what is the same thing, the price of the maintenance of a thou-sand men for a year, and with it the whole weight and author-ity which it could give them. The buckles, however, were to be all their own, and no other human creature was to have any share of them; whereas in the antient method of expence they must have shared with at least a thousand people . . . and thus, for the gratification of the most childish, the meanest and the most sordid of all vanities, they gradually bartered their whole power and authority. (Adam Smith, 1976: 418–419)

Strangely, for an economist so often invoked by those extolling the individualist virtues of private property and self-interest, the first class of people with the means of affirming that individualism through the accu-mulation of private property destroyed themselves. Rendered powerless against the creeping restrictions and confinements of the state, "a regular government was established in the country as well as the city" so that the ruling class found themselves "as insignificant as any substantial burgher or tradesman" and subject to the same rule of law (Smith, 1976: 421). The aristocrats were also vulnerable to the new wealth and economic efficiency introduced by those merchants "commonly ambitious of becoming country gentlemen" and accustomed to employing wealth in profitable pursuits, "whereas a mere country gentleman is accustomed to employ it chiefly in expence" (411). Eventually they were all but replaced by this new class of nouveaux riches. To the degree to which their descendants continued to simulate the luxurious vanities of the class they wished to emulate, this aspiring class also grew impoverished, some eventually having to sell off their own buckles and baubles, their family silver, portraits, suits of ceremonial armour, and so on.

Smith's account of the seduction, profligacy, and demise of the feudal ruling classes owes much to his opinion of contemporary eighteenth-century estates. Large estates in the hands of landed families, Smith observes, are clearly incompatible with the 'improvement' that comes with the profitable utilization of manageable resources. To a large extent, Smith is projecting back eighteenth-century landed lassitude onto the disorder and decadence of the feudal ruling classes, particularly the Plantagenets (386). The mythical fall of the feudal classes, or their mode of existence, is usually located sometime in the past on the basis of conditions in the present, but Smith's fall is at least located within rather than after feudalism. Shakespeare, in *Richard II*, seems to put the fall slightly later in the famous speech (brought out perennially to denote the decline of England's greatness) that he gives to John O'Gaunt. The speech, and indeed the play, heralds the collapse of the Plantagenet dynasty, the fall into the Wars of the Roses, and the redemptive rise of the Tudors—as a traditional reading of Shakespeare's History Plays would have it. For John O'-Gaunt, the youthful profligacy of Richard has meant that "this scepter'd isle," this "other Eden," that was England, is now "leased out . . . like to a tenement or pelting farm . . . bound in with shame / With inky blots, and rotten parchments" (II.i. 40, 42, 59, 60, 64). "England, that was wont to conquer others, / Hath made a shameful conquest of itself" (II.1.65–66). Which is to say that, through its excessive consumption—Gaunt speaks of Richard as "Light vanity, insatiate cormorant, / Consuming means" (38–39)—England has allowed itself to be conquered by its commercial and clerical classes. This late sixteenth-century representation of John O'Gaunt's demise in the late fourteenth century looks nostalgically back to the beginning of the Plantagenet dynasty in the late twelfth century. It looks back to the crusades where the nobility were "Renowned for their deeds as far from home / For Christian service and true chivalry" (53–54). From Adam Smith to Shakespeare and beyond lie six hundred years of nostalgia for a lost age of a nobility that glittered with the aid of diamond buckles. For it is possible to argue with Smith, and against Gaunt's misty nostalgia, that the consuming rot set in precisely with the first Plantagenet reign and the fashion for that amorous frivolity known as courtly love that he and his wife, Eleanor of Aquitaine, introduced in the twelfth century.

For what reason would a medieval warrior, used to the martial frenzy and manly austerity of chivalric *virtus*, ride into town to purchase a pair of diamond buckles? For what reason would these noble lords sell "their birth-right . . . in the wantonness of plenty, for trinkets and baubles, fitter to become the playthings of children than the serious pursuits of men"? (Smith, 1976: 418). Apart from war and hunting, courtly love and romance provided the main means of social entertainment and intrigue in medieval courts. Smith does not intimate whether his noble lord bought the buckles as a gift or for his own adornment; his point is merely that larger proportions of the surplus, which would have been destined for general distribution in public festivities, were being diverted into the private pursuit of (self-) love. Self-love always implies a gaze in the Other in relation to which one may appear loveable to oneself. Narcissism is always established in relation to an Other whose desire acts as the mirror in which one can recognize oneself as desirable. A whole art of love was inaugurated by the court of Eleanor of Aquitaine, and itemized by her clerk Andreas Capellanus. This pattern was maintained throughout the centuries by ambitious young clerks and courtiers through the writing of love poetry, romances, and narratives to such a degree that they now constitute the starred texts of the early canon of English literature.

As has been noted by commentators before, Smith demonstrates a certain ambivalence toward material progress, betraying a moral distaste for the objects and commodities that have commonly signified wealth. Smith seems to approve only of industriousness, of the processes of production, and the maximization rather than enjoyment of profit, while accepting that the prospect of such enjoyment is, regrettably, a necessary incentive. Similarly, while he argues that an efficient division of labor along rational or mechanistic lines is essential to the maximization of profit, he regrets some of the consequences, most notably "the loss of the martial spirit and virtues" (Hirschman, 1977: 105). Indeed, as Albert Hirschman notes, this was a regrettable effect of commerce in general. In the *Lectures*, Smith opines that "another bad effect of commerce is that it sinks the courage of mankind . . . By having their minds constantly employed on the arts of luxury, [men] grow effeminate and dastardly" (Smith, 1976: 42–43). Smith, then, is nostalgic for the manly martial virtues of the Germanic and Scythian barbarians and contemptuous of the effeminacy of luxurious consumption. Ideally, perhaps, Smith wants a chivalric industry or martial trade: a transformation of capitalism into a war machine in which the fruits of tireless industry are perpetually expended in the ascetic rigors of war.

Both Smith's political analysis of, and his famous ambivalence toward, the effects of commerce clearly demonstrate that in his modes of consumption man does not act in accordance with his own self-interest; indeed, he is barely aware of what his best interests might be. This is odd because insofar as economic theory is based on the classical and neoclassical eighteenth-century models of Smith, Ricardo, and so on, it relies on an abstract model of self-interest. But this notion of self-interest is the homogenized product of a variety of heterogeneous, historical forces, impulses, drives, passions, desires, vanities, and affects that have continually been identified, interpreted, and reinterpreted since the Renaissance. The famous passage from Smith, from which the abstraction of self-interest is derived, offers a variety of synonyms that give a highly complex meaning to self-interest. Smith writes that while man relies on the assistance of other men, he cannot expect this assistance to be given through benevolence only. Rather,

> he will be more likely to prevail if he can interest their self-love in his favour, and shew them that it is for their own advantage that to do for him what he requires of them . . . We address ourselves, not to their humanity but to their self-love, and never talk to them of our own necessities but of their advantages. (Smith, 1976: 26–27)

It is in the imaginary domain of self-love rather than in a purely economic or symbolic domain of self-interest that commerce takes place, in contradistinction to humanity. Self-love has rarely, if ever, been the same as self-interest (it cannot be in the interest of Narcissus to wither away in front of his own reflection, for example), and it is not at all in conflict with benevolence. One's egotism may be happily massaged by useful acts of altruism and benevolence. But at the limit man's self-love is incommensurable; it tends, precisely, toward the incalculable. Consequently, insofar as man spends in accordance with his self-love, he will always act against his best interests in restricted economic terms. He will, like Smith's feudal lords, go shopping for a pair of diamond buckles, perhaps, or something equally frivolous and useless. In this thing, he will measure himself and his self-love, not in accordance with the bargain—how much he makes in the exchange—but by how much it costs him, how much he loses.

Any hedonistic calculus that lies as the basis of commercial activity must take on a paradoxical character. Consumption, like joysaunce, is split into two parts, one part of which only concerns, in a preliminary way, the self-preservation of the individual and its productive or profitable activities. The other meaning of consumption, "represented by so-called unproductive expenditures" (Bataille, 1997: 167), concerns activities that have historically had no end beyond themselves and no value other than that determined by the loss that paradoxically results in the production of sacred things. The sacrifice of a fortune for jewelery, the memorials and medals for the death of sons and daughters in battle, the relics of religious sacrificial rituals, the intrinsically valueless signifiers of victory in games and combats for which considerable sums of money and energy are spent in quarters, animals, equipment, or men and women, where immense crowds may be present whose "passions most often burst forth beyond any restraint, and the loss of insane sums of money is set in motion in the form of wagers" (Bataille, 1997: 170). Smith approves of some of these activities (war, for example) and martial virtues that necessitate selfless acts of valor. What the fate of Smith's feudal lords shows, however, is that there is a plane of consistency in capitalism between the two modes of consumption. The question to address when considering the political implications of the rise of commerce is how a certain principle of loss and nonproductive or luxurious expenditure becomes deflected into, or by, a law of exchange, thereby setting off the delirium that became capitalism. A combination of a hunger for conquest, for mastery, for land, for novelty and for markets, for profit, for interests, exploded across the globe with the berserk rationality of a desiring machine (see Deleuze and Guattari, 1995: 53–73). In the conquest, by western European powers, of large parts of the globe, commerce played its part.[4] The merchants, manufacturers, and traders in foreign commerce replayed their little primal scene of seduction, encouraging the noble chieftains of North America and West Africa to give up land or slaves for buckles, baubles, and trinkets, thereby singularly failing to consume in their self-interest.

As Braudel and many others affirm, capitalism begins in Europe not because of the burgeoning nation-states of western Europe; the technical and economic conditions were the same, in different periods, in China and Japan. Following Braudel, Deleuze and Guattari speculate that "perhaps the merit of the West, confined as it was on the narrow Cape of Asia, was to have needed the world, to have needed to venture outside its own front door" (Deleuze and Guattari, 1984: 224). The conditions for global capitalism were laid down in the eighteenth century by a naval war machine immanent in the interstices of war and commerce.[5] Five centuries later, war and commerce are conjoined in a deterritorializing reformatting of the globe.

The State

> By *joy*, therefore, I shall understand in what follows that *passion by which the mind passes over to a greater perfection.*
>
> —Spinoza, *Ethics*

"There's no question we are all the more indebted to Lacan, once we've dropped notions like structure, the symbolic and the signifier" (Deleuze, 1995: 14). In an interview collected in the book *Negotiations* (1995), Deleuze pays tribute to the debt he and Guattari owe to Lacan, particularly in the two volumes on *Capitalism and Schizophrenia*. However, the tribute also takes the form of a decapitation of three of Lacan's most important concepts. Cutting off the governing notions of structure, the symbolic, and the signifier produces an acephalic Lacanianism in which unanchored flows of desiring production traverse the 'body without organs'. Desire in Deleuze and Guattari is not just preimaginary, a psychotic *hommelette*, it is also postsymbolic. Schizophrenic and joyful, desire walks out of the tragic theater of Oedipus and turns the unconscious into a factory, producing flows that bypass the signifier, and directly connect up part objects in multiple machinic assemblages that whir away in the ruins of the symbolic order. Fundamentally, desiring-production is primary and not dependent on its codification by the signifier in the symbolic.

In *Anti-Oedipus*, Deleuze and Guattari do not subordinate desiring-production to exchange, as an effect of the commerce of romance and rivalry. Rather they give a Nietzschean account of the formation of human memory, culture, and history that is consistent with Lacan's understanding of the role of the signifier and the symbolic order in his system. Drawing on the Nietzschean ethnology outlined in the second essay of *Genealogy of Morals*, tempered with a Bataillean reading of Marcel Mauss's work on the gift, Deleuze and Guattari characterize primary desiring-production as a form of joy-writing, or inscription as violent expenditure.

The first technical machine is not used as a tool or a weapon, as such, but as an instrument of torture: the means of violent cruelty and joy. The first machine is a branding iron that becomes the vehicle of a cruel joy that territorializes through marking and encoding a body, thereby producing it as a discrete, named, and branded item. Deleuze and Guattari write,

> The primitive territorial machine codes flows, invests organs, and marks bodies. To such a degree that circulating—exchanging—is a secondary activity in comparison with the task that sums up all the others: marking bodies: tattooing, excising, carving, scarifying, mutilating, encircling and initiating. (1984: 144)

The point to stress is that it is not a question of a primordial desire, or desiring-flow, that is simply redirected and divided up by forces of repression. The mark of repression (or territorialization) is the very mark or branding of desire and joy itself, a mark of and on the body. The brand enjoins the body to the realm of desire; desire is infused, incited, and excited by the desire of the body in the intensity of contact. Deleuze and Guattari refuse to ascribe to this continual infliction of pain an exchangist model of revenge and retribution ("no *ressentiment* will be invoked here"). The infliction of pain is an active and affirmative expression of life and joy. They quote Nietzsche, "in punishment there is so much that is festive!" Pain and torture are deployed in punishments not so much because it is unpleasant for the victim, but because it gives the torturer a feeling of joy (or joysaunce in an archaic, festive sense). Furthermore, such festive tortures are associated with sacrificial and initiatory practices, circumcisions, and other rites of passage that are bound up with a general economic process in which social bonds are forged through a continual process of expenditure. The economic dimension of the primitive territorial machine is not one of exchange so much as expenditure. Torture, sacrifice, scarification, and potlatch all have the same basic purpose of forging bonds of obligation and debt. The most important effect of these intense contacts is that they are replicated and establish a collective memory through establishing bonds of filiation through debt. It is debt that forms the basis of human history:

> open, mobile, and finite blocks of debt: this extraordinary composite of the speaking voice, the marked body, and the enjoying eye. All the stupidity and arbitrariness of the laws, all the pain of the initiations, the whole perverse apparatus of repression and education, the red-hot irons, and the atrocious procedures have only this meaning: to *breed* man, to mark him in his flesh, to render him capable of alliance, to form him within the debtor-creditor relation, which on both sides turns out to be a matter of memory—a memory straining toward the future. (Deleuze and Guattari, 1984: 190)

Deleuze and Guattari argue, after Nietzsche and Bataille but also looking toward Lacan, that man is bred through the intensity of a joy that is suffered and inflicted in the midst of the voice and gaze of the Other's joy. "The fact that innocent men suffer all the marks on their bodies derives from the respective autonomy of the voice, and also from the autonomous eye that extracts pleasure from the event" (1984: 191). In Lacan's framework, however, joy is recast as the jouissance of the Other in the dialectic of work and enjoyment that characterizes the interhuman bond for Hegel-Kojève. There is nothing festive about this jouissance, which is always located as the end of production, that is, from the point of view of the *ressentiment* of the joyless slave.

Nevertheless, for Deleuze and Guattari, like Lacan, the earliest territorial machine is not defined by exchange, but is rather articulated by a symbolic system of alliance and filiation. The system of branding is established in and for an Other that marks out the locus of law, signification, and memory (the unconscious), and opens out its field of visibility. It is the Other as an assemblage of voice-body-eye whose series of brands differentiate us from the earth as bodies, whose voice enables and enjoins us to speak or cry out for the joy of the eye that illuminates our being.

Deleuze and Guattari argue that the primitive system of pain-filiation-coding is transformed by a sudden violent incursion from the outside. An exterior, more powerful force arrives to replace the Other and recode its system of symbolization. Deleuze and Guattari cite Nietzsche's "blond beasts of prey, a conqueror and a master race" who reorder the interconnected bonds of alliance and filiation into one hierarchical structure. These are the "founders of the state" who introduce "a terror without precedent, in comparison with which the ancient system of cruelty, the forms of primitive regimentation and punishment, are nothing" (1984: 192). The state is "the product of an effective deterritorialization that substitutes abstract signs for the signs of the earth, and makes the earth itself into the object of state ownership and property, or an ownership held by the state's richest servants and officials" (1984: 196). The state overcodes the previous terrain, and in so doing binds its subjects in a hierarchical system of debt that reaches up to a central point that holds together a new bureaucratic symbolic order. The previous blocks of "mobile, open, finite debts finds itself taken into an immense machinery *that renders the debt infinite*" (1984: 192).

Here, Deleuze and Guattari's Lacanian analysis is at its most unequivocal as they incorporate a simplified version of the functioning of the master signifier as *point de capiton*, exemplified in Lacan's seminar on psychosis by the signifier of the fear of God. "To have replaced . . . numerous fears by the fear of a unique being who has no other means of manifesting his power than through what is feared behind these innumerable fears, is quite an accomplishment" (Lacan, 1993: 266–267). On the basis of all the old finite debts, the despot establishes an infinite debt that is justified by his singular relation with God; the despot functions in the name of this singular signifier, like that of the fear of God, to which all subjects now owe their existence. Whether or not the state in question is monotheistic, for Deleuze and Guattari, "there is always a monotheism on the horizon of despotism" because the debt has to become a *debt of existence*, a debt of the existence of the subjects themselves. While, in the primitive system, the desire of the Other exerted itself in the joy that was bound to it, the desire of the despotic body, veiled behind the signifier that represents it, can now only be raised in the form of a question: *Che vuoi?* What does the Other want? (1986: 312). As Deleuze and Guattari write, following Lacan, "with the debt of existence comes the question 'What does he—God, King, whatever—mean?' . . . Desire no longer dares to desire, having become a desire of desire, a desire of the despot's desire" (1984: 206). Joy becomes jouissance the moment it is abstracted in the form of the question of the knowledge of the Other's desire, rather than the raw experience of it.

The practical form through which the despotic state capitalizes on this infinite debt is money. "Money does not begin by serving the needs of commerce . . . money is fundamentally inseparable . . . from taxes as the maintenance of the apparatus of the State" (1985: 197). Again, Deleuze and Guattari render the question of the exchange-economy secondary and foreground the territoriality of a desire become abstract and subject to the regime of the signifier. The mark is replaced by the property that signifies wealth and mastery to an Other whose desire has withdrawn into the realm of the infinite. It is for this reason that Deleuze and Guattari do not believe that money, or the system of general equivalence, can detach itself from the imperial origins of the signifier, even when it is emptied of all signifying content and merely floats over an empty set.

> No water will ever cleanse the signifier of its imperial origin: the signifying master or "the master signifier." In vain will the signifier be immersed in the immanent system of language (*la langue*) . . . In vain will the comparison of language to exchange and money be pushed to its furthest point, subjecting language to the paradigms of an active capitalism, for one will never prevent the signifier from reintroducing its transcendence, and from bearing witness for a vanished despot who still functions in modern imperialism. (Deleuze and Guattari, 1984: 206–207)

While Deleuze and Guattari give Lacan himself the credit for this insight (1984: 209), in so doing their pessimism with regard to the imperial power of capital is the very mirror of those orthodox Lacanians for whom the institution of the father has been irrevocably damaged. A strange mutation has occurred whereby the paternalism of the signifier has evaporated even as its hollowing-out has facilitated the globalization of capital in the form of the system of finance. For Jean-Joseph Goux, the master signifier has become liquefied. Its transformation from the signifier of despotism to that of a general equivalent—money—that functions as a form of abstract mediation, becomes decisive when money detaches itself from any referent, like gold, whose material substantiality might arrest the fluctuations of value. It becomes instead a mobile unit of endless transferability (see Goux, 1997). For Goux, the master signifier has entered

> an as yet unheard of regime . . . detached from any natural anchoring (pure mediation, pure sign) just as [on the stock exchange, for example] the financial sign is nothing but the indefinite inscription and circulation of a debt by means of accounting, a writing game without any reference to real goods. (Goux, 1992: 72)

In the global system of finance, debt has been detached from the value inscribed in the infinite marked by the signifier. Instead, that value has itself been opened out to a space of pure mediation and infinite desiring, to become a game of writing, inscription upon a plane of intensity in relation to absolute otherness, a limitless joy without reference to a subject of need or desire. At the same time, the substance of this joy is composed of a mass of nonsubjective, yet febrile movements that constitute the volatility of the financial markets whose values fluctuate, on computer screens around the world, at an inhuman speed.

The system of finance which, as Alain Joxe notes, is not the same as the economy of commerce, is one of the three areas that constitutes true globality, the other two being the military sector and the sphere of electromagnetic communications (2002: 177). But these spheres operate without recourse to any global organizing principle or law. The role of the state has accordingly been diminished in the face of the rise of multinational corporations and the acceleration of transnational capitalism that has been made possible by the globalization of the system of finance and electromagnetic communications. The subsequent correlation between war and commerce, the revolution in military affairs and its relation to the business revolution, therefore pose a theoretical problem. For Joxe, this problem "lies in the fact that they establish direct contact between military criteria and business criteria, saying that it is not contradictory, except that it by-passes politicians. There is no derivation through politics. And politicians cannot restore a role for themselves even by intervening in trade legislation" (Joxe, 2002: 59). The correlation between war and commerce, and the globalization that enables and accelerates it through the financial and communications systems, place the state, along with other paternal, metasocial guarantees, in a perhaps terminal crisis.

Deprived of a master signifier, devoid of a global symbolic structure that could organize subjects into a shared system of belief, or of an other state that might provide the semblance of unity through opposition, governance has become acephalic, rhizomatic, immanent. An empire that is at once both military and economic, driven by the flows of the global finance system, dissolves and reconstitutes social ties according to the dictates of a depersonalized regulatory mechanism. But this regulatory mechanism is machinic in a wholly excessive way, and it is regulatory in a way that does not involve arborescent control and command structures (see Cebrowski and Gartska, 1998). Following corporate models, the military have, for example, shifted from platform-based warfare to network-centric warfare and one of the effects of this is to "enable forces to organize from the bottom-up—or to self-synchronize." The structure is rhizomatic in the sense that it operates in different directions and on different levels within interlinked information networks and feedback loops that enable maximum 'awareness' throughout the whole rhizomatic and acephalic body. The arborescent structure, where command and control always had to go through a central governing head or center of consciousness, has given way to a system of command and control that has become immanent to the network, moving at the speed of informational flows. In this respect, ironically, it is absolutely consistent with the (non)structure of the multitude and its affect that has been posited as the form of resistance immanent to empire:

> The multitude today . . . resides on the imperial surfaces where there is no God the Father and no transcendence. Instead there is our immanent labor. The teleology of the multitude is theurgical; it consists in the possibility of directing technologies and production towards its own joy and its own increase of power. (Hardt & Negri, 2000: 396)

But, as Alain Joxe suggests, the empire thrives on the disorder in which various multitudes assemble and disassemble in different divisions of joy. The immanent, machinic joy of the multitude supports the Godless yet theurgical surface of divine governance making it come, infusing and directing the increase of its power. The paternal, phallic signifier of excess, therefore, that was held in reserve in order to measure and guarantee the value of signifying circulation has become an imperial surface, an intensive skin or body without organs on which excess flows as its own principle. Paradoxically, excess becomes its major mode of control and efficiency: a super-efficiency released from any external form of limitation whatsoever, with no reference to any end other than its own inhuman acceleration directed by the Spinozist theurgical joy of "the passage to a greater perfection."

JOY'S DIVISIONS:
ANORGANICISM, IMMANENCE, EVENT

The work that follows is divided up into four sections that correspond to divisions internal to the diagram of the order of joy. These brief descriptions indicate the differences implied by the various intersections.

(*SÔr*) Anorganic Joy

Anorganic joy is experienced in the intersection between war and governance where modes of control overcode the real on a plane of intensity or body-without-organs. Anorganic joy is experienced in an intensive space evacuated by the phallic signifier that, for Lacan, provided the focus (in the organ) and the principle of organization of jouissance. Hollowed out as a space of pure mediation, phallic organization gives way to a form of excess control that destroys the organism in the name of anorganic life. Where the state intersects with war, state law either gives way to the raw power of the military, or governance itself becomes militarized, totalitarian, and control takes a combative and lethal form, particularly with regard to its own population. It is as if the principle of regulation folded in on itself in an implosive desire to regulate life out of existence. Where state law is exceeded by globalized communications systems, state and political governance wither as different modalities of electronic security and intrusion take over. A different form of symbolization, grounded in binary code, threatens to overwrite and abolish the real.

Information systems reduce the real to a closed set of pregiven alternatives linked to a potentially infinite series of finite combinations. Joy is expended in the exhaustion of the possible, an exhaustion that involves both the exhaustive and the exhausted.

This section looks at how information systems and digital media introduce a new order of affect that replaces the relation between knowledge and jouissance characterizing desire, work, and leisure in the West. Rather than the couple knowledge-jouissance that constitutes the structure of deferral proper to work and leisure, the new order of information is infused with a joy that arises as an effect of the exhaustion of the real. As such, anorganic joy correlates to the modality of excess control that animates what Deleuze calls the control society. The interdependent relationship between excess and control has superseded law and transgression as the governing modality of technobureaucratic, consumer culture. Control and excess emerge together, each directly implying one another. Beyond useful, rational, or moral purpose, control is itself excessive, distending and decomposing the vehicles of its compulsive, exhausting joy.

(I◊r) Joyful Immanence (There is No Other)

In the joy of immanence, where the domain of war intersects with the circle of commerce, an extreme activity meets and becomes indistinguishable from an extreme passivity, in a passionate hatred indistinguishable from love. The desire for imaginary plenitude, to be One with the Other, loses itself in the general economic play of forces, and commercial exchange is opened out by the pure expenditure of war and eroticism. As if Nietzsche's warrior, the solitary hero of single combats, were to be consumed by Madame Edwarda, Bataille's "GOD figured as a public whore and gone crazy" (1989: 155). The whore eats the warrior's head as he is carried away in his heroic fury. They constitute an assemblage of desiring-production where exchange is indistinguishable from expenditure. "The field of immanence is not internal to the self, but neither does it come from an external self or a nonself. Rather, it is like the absolute Outside that knows no Selves because interior and exterior are equally part of the immanence in which they have fused" (Deleuze and Guattari: 157). The joy that infuses the field of immanence is not defined by any opposite, by any sadness or horror. On the contrary, this joy is precisely the condition when "the fullness of horror and that of joy collide" (Bataille, 1989: 141). It is the immanent joy of the eater and the eaten where human transcendence from the animal world's order of intimacy can no longer be assumed. The inhumanity of incomprehensible horror and delirious submission takes its place in an intimate order of fractal conflicts in which sovereign forces are configured in the martial quiescence of the body, bacteria, the cell, the germ, the gene, and the genetic poetry of bioeconomic virtuality. This play of forces, which constitutes the plane of immanence, reassembles the bio-economic field, but also the social and cultural fields as the restricted economies of science, technology, and commerce become generalized.

On the general economic plane of scientific immanence, Albert Einstein experiences a 'religious' feeling of joy. Einstein speaks of a cosmic joy about which he knows nothing other than he experiences it as "a sort of intoxicated joy and amazement at the beauty and grandeur of the world . . . This joy is the feeling from which true scientific research draws its spiritual sustenance, but which also seems to find expression in the song of birds" (cited in Damasio, 2003: 280). But Einstein's world of beauty and grandeur is simultaneously a world congested by death and wealth, in which birdsong accompanies an enormous scream that pierces the clouds (Bataille, 2001: 221), a scream lifted by the shrieks and gasps of obese schoolchildren on billion-dollar roller coaster rides.

Here is an order of intimacy in which reproduction is no longer distinguishable from consumption and death, the three luxuries of nature being simple expressions of pure expenditure:

> In reproduction, in the violence of convulsions issued from
> reproduction, life is not only the accomplice of death: it is the
> unique and duplicate will of reproduction and of death, of
> death and of pain. Life only wanted itself in laceration; like
> floodwaters, the lost screams of horror sink into the river of
> joy. (Bataille, 2001: 234)

When commerce intersects with war, it is the joy of expenditure that retains the trace of general economy and sustains a principle of direction in
the midst of a generally unrestricted commercial economy. For there is a
paradox in the suggestion that all forms of heterogeneity (both sacred
and profane) have been restricted and utilized for profit. That would
mean that there is no point of sacred exteriority in relation to which an
economy can be restricted. Therefore there is no restricted economy either. In this zone there is, generally speaking, an unrestricted economy in
which hitherto sacred elements, relics, monuments, totems, objects of
beauty or abjection, waste, and so on are all subject to an unregulated
system of value. But one (absent) object sustains a principle of restriction
and therefore desire: life itself. Since, in the field of intimacy and immanence, life is unnameable and found only in laceration, it finds itself privileged as the fissure around which immanent, commercial desire pulsates
in genomic and bionomic creativity, while martial desire seeks out ever
more creative means to annihilation.

One of the specific but also ubiquitous sites for the play of war and
commerce is the screen. Drawing a comparison between the factory con-
veyor belt and the cinema that placed work and enjoyment on the same
technological plane of consistency for modernity, Lev Manovich notes
that for postmodernity, "the most direct equivalents are an arcade type
computer game and a military training simulator" (Manovich, 1996:
183). Commercial entertainment and military training not only share the
same technology but also the same research and development companies
and institutions.[6] (See also James Der Derian on the military-industrial-
media-entertainment complex or MIME, 1997.) It goes without saying
that the increasingly mobile screen provides the surface on which work,
leisure, and war take place, deterritorialized from the specific sites of the
workplace, the battle field, and the arcade.

But, further, the screen becomes a membrane, the boundary between a two-way movement between inside and outside, by which the
human-machine system is fused and facilitated in ever greater forms of in-
teraction and efficiency. Christopher Coker in *The Future of War* (2004)
discusses how the U.S. air force is investigating various ways of improving the communication between human and machine by growing neurons

in a silicon chip. This will allow chips to be activated by hormones and neural electrical stimulation:

> The Defense Advanced Research Projects Agency (DARPA) has a Brain-Machine Interface Program that, in its own words, aims to "create new technologies for augmenting human performance through the ability to access non-invasive codes in the brain in real time and integrate them into a peripheral device or systems operation." (Coker, 2004: 99)

The screen, therefore, quite literally becomes a brain, an extensive and intensive brain that is neither human nor machine but an anorganic assemblage. And there is of course nothing exclusively military in this since this technology is equally essential to the efficiencies of finance and ultracompetitive business. The question of the subject, therefore, concerns singularity and the event (the singular event) that takes place along the membrane of the brain-screen. The event irrupts to disturb or enhance the operativity of the assemblage in relation to its self-image in an experience of joy. The joy of pure functional perfection in the effortless killing of aliens, enemies, or of making a killing on the stock exchange.

(*I0S*) Event

Located in the conjunction between imaginary and symbolic registers, meaning is, for Lacan, a semblance, the metaphorical effect of a momentary pause in the passage of signification. Nevertheless, "analytic discourse aims at meaning" (Lacan, 1999: 78), at the sexual (phallic) limit of a meaning (*sens*) that can only indicate the direction toward which it fails (*échoue*). The failure of meaning is indelibly associated with a jouissance that is also always missed, an 'enjoy-meant'. Tragically, the life of speaking beings is afflicted with a lack of meaning, just as it is deprived of jouissance, but precisely as an effect of that lack, the meaning of jouissance and the jouissance of meaning are such a powerful unconscious force.

It is this correlation between signification and lack, in the determination of the absence of meaning that Deleuze and Guattari of course reject. Indeed, the question posed by meaning is a false one. It is not a question of meaning, but of function. "We're strict functionalists," claimed Deleuze and Guattari in an interview following the publication of *Anti-Oedipus*. "What we're interested in is how something works, functions—finding the machine. But the signifier's still stuck in the question 'What does it mean?'—indeed it's this very question in a blocked form" (Deleuze, 1995: 22). In their functionalist response to the question of the meaning of life, Deleuze

and Guattari are quite conventionally scientific. Most scientists respond to
questions of meaning by referring to function. Antonio Damasio, for example, in his book on neurobiology, *Looking for Spinoza* (2003), reflects on
the meaning of life and the deep yearning people have to answer the questions of existence by suggesting that this very yearning has itself an evolutionary origin and is an effect of natural selection. As such, it is a question
that contains its own answer within it. Along with evolutionary biology,
Damasio finds in Spinoza the inspiration to raise the idea of functionality
to a level equivalent to spiritual joy. In answer to a friend's questions on the
meaning of existence, and the life of the spirit, Damasio responds:

> First, I assimilate the notion of spiritual to an intense experi-
> ence of harmony, to the sense that the organism is functioning
> with the greatest possible perfection . . . Second, spiritual ex-
> periences are humanly nourishing. I believe that Spinoza was
> entirely on the mark in his view that joy and its variants lead
> to greater functional perfection. The current scientific knowl-
> edge regarding joy supports the notion that it should be
> actively sought. (Damasio, 2003: 284–285)

Pure scientific functionalism here reaches its apotheosis through looking in
the mirror of its own perfection, experiencing intense joy at the image of
its harmonious unity. The absence of meaning, of even a relation to meaning, is compensated by the passion of love and narcissism. While science is
traditionally a purely symbolic form, it requires an imaginary dimension
here in order to produce the sense of perfection and harmony that Damasio assimilates to the notion of the spiritual. Furthermore, Damasio con-
cedes that this dimension is not simply scientific. Along with secularity,
commercialism is also for Damasio an entirely appropriate means,
through the promotion of scientific reflection and aesthetic experience, of
promoting "effective emotionally competent stimuli behind the spiritual"
(285). Spiritual experience is in fact the experience of joy, which is for
Damasio the state of homeostatic perfection. Joy is the experience, the expression, and the form of efficient life regulation and governance. This
conception of joy is Spinozean since "Spinoza seems to have gleaned a relation between personal and collective happiness, on the one hand, and
human salvation and the structure of the state, on the other" (15). Functionality, therefore, rises to a spiritual level when the circle of commerce
(the concept of economic growth) intersects with the circle of governance
(the regulatory mechanism of operativity) in the event of joy.

   In the place of meaning—which was only ever a semblance covering
over the trauma of its lack—irrupts the event that requires event man-

agement. The event sustains the question of meaning not just in the sense of what happened? but by remaining virtual to anything that might happen. The event is "the part that eludes its own actualization in everything that happens" (Deleuze and Guattari, 1994: 156). Or, it could be added, in what does not happen and what could have happened but did not. By *What Is Philosophy* (1994), Deleuze and Guattari are no longer strictly functionalists in the sense that function has now become part of a triumvirate along with thought and feeling. Since the question of meaning, as Damasio shows, is always related back to function, thought can only circulate endlessly in the hollow of function. However, as Deleuze and Guattari note at the end of *What Is Philosophy*, each discipline has an essential relation with its negative, each discipline is only possible if it is "on its own behalf, in an essential relationship with the No that concerns it" (1994: 218). For science that is the force of feeling appropriate to art, or indeed the joy that is bound up with the very thing science wants to know nothing about, death. In Deleuzean terms this is the event of the concept or the concept-as-event. The event that must be affirmed is the death of meaning (or God or judgment), the event that irrupts precisely in the default of function.

a-Life

At the center of the Borromean knot sits Lacan's special symbol a, the lost object-in-desire. This symbol marks the place of the life of which the subject is deprived through gaining access to symbolized existence, and "which has assumed the value of that which binds him to the signifier" (Lacan, 1977: 28). The *objet petit a* is a purely virtual object but it can become actualized in any number of desired objects. However like the event, a denotes "the part that eludes its own actualization." Another term Deleuze uses for this power of virtuality is "*a* life." "*A* life is the immanence of immanence, absolute immanence: it is complete power, complete joy" (Deleuze, 2001: 27, translation modified). Although redolent of the simple humanity of *homo tantum*, *a* life is not the life of an individual endowed with character, subjectivity, qualities, or even identity. It is the "singular life immanent to a man who no longer has a name" (29). A kind of bare life, perhaps, stripped of all insignia, all forms of identity and personality, unexchangeable, unsacrificable, yet finding its illumination at the threshold of death.

This chapter looks at the proximity of the virtual life of the Lacanian object *a* and Deleuze's notion of the singularity of *a* life. But it also considers the relation both these ideas have to the concept of bare life introduced by Giorgio Agamben in *Homo Sacer* (1998). For Agamben, the determination of life becomes the political decision par excellence and defines the horizon of biopolitics for modernity.

Located at the extimate point of contemporary society, the life that is becoming barely virtual can be denoted in the following three ways depending on which two planes it articulates.

Immanence (I◊r − S)

As immanence of immanence, *a* marks the zone of indistinction between imaginary and real that is exposed in the withdrawal of the symbolic, or what Agamben calls the state of exception in which the bare life of *homo tantum* is exposed as both resource and potential.

Anorganicism (S◊r − I)

The point between symbolic and real denotes the subtraction of body image and the involution of the organ, particularly the phallic image of imaginary plenitude. Anorganic joy results from the points of intensity where different fluxes or machinic assemblages interconnect over the "body without organs." Alternatively, a similar relation in which symbolization, particularly digital symbolization, overwrites the real to take on a life of its own—a life of pure symbolization. Perhaps the evolution of previously unimaginable, computer-generated life forms is an interesting visualization of modes of becoming in the absence of the imaginary register.

Event (I◊S − r)

An event that is actualized in the corporatization of scientific functionality is the loss of the reality of death as a defining point for life. "Death does not authenticate human existence. It is an outmoded evolutionary strategy. The body no longer need be *repaired* but simply have parts *replaced*. Extending life no longer means 'existing' but rather of being 'operational'" (Stelarc, 1997). Instead of marking an end point, death becomes a purely functional, immanent principle of becoming that can evolve anorganic life to such a degree that it can survive the death of the sun. This absolute death is "the sole serious question to face humanity today" and, according to Lyotard, informs both scientific and imaginative work in the biotech, information technology, and new media industries (see Lyotard, 1988–1989). With the incorporation of death as a mechanism of becoming, new forms of anorganic life may survive in the inhospitable space of the cosmos.

Part Two

Toward
Anorganic Joy

CHAPTER TWO

Trainspotting with Deleuze

The locomotive is not an object, but an epic symbol, a great Phantasm . . . a pure death Instinct, blind and deaf. However clamorous the train may be, it is deaf—and in this way, silent.

—Deleuze, *The Logic of Sense*

What yis up to lads? Trainspotting, eh?

—Irvine Welsh, *Trainspotting*

CHOOSE LIFE

Choose life. Choose a job. Choose a career. Choose a family. Choose a fucking big television, choose washing machines, cars, compact disc players and electrical tin openers. Choose good health, low cholesterol, and dental insurance. Choose fixed interest mortgage repayments. Choose a starter home. Choose your friends. Choose leisurewear and matching luggage. Choose a three-piece suit on hire purchase in a range of fucking fabrics. Choose DIY and wondering who the fuck you are on a Sunday morning. Choose sitting on that couch watching mind-numbing, spirit-crushing game shows, stuffing fucking junk food into your mouth. Choose rotting away at the end of it all, pishing your last in a miserable home, nothing more than an embarrassment to the selfish, fucked up brats you spawned to replace yourself. Choose your future. Choose life. (Boyle, 1996: 3–4)

The soft Edinburgh accent of Ewan MacGregor intones over the opening sequence of *Trainspotting* (Boyle, 1996) to the purposeful backbeat of Iggy Pop's "Lust for Life": "Here comes Johnny Yen, again, / With his liquor and drugs / and a flesh machine / He's gonna do another striptease." Exuberant scenes of Renton and Spud tearing down Princes Street pursued by store detectives, stolen commodities tumbling from their pockets, a line of flight that is intercut with shots of energetic five-a-side football and Renton smoking and getting high. Renton continues his manic flight into Leith Street, by St. James's shopping mall, and crashes into a car emerging from Calton Hill. He bursts out laughing, apparently beyond the cares of life—and death. In contrast to these scenes, and their musical accompaniment, MacGregor's homily on the importance of choosing life scripted by John Hodge builds, with mounting irony and rage, into a sneering sales pitch. Life is brutally reduced to a series of commodities as work, friends, family, home, birth, and death enjoy an easy equivalence with electrical goods, leisure wear, and game shows, all available at a cheap rate from the shopping mall that is contemporary urban existence. The speech parades desire down a chain of objects and signifiers, on a road that, along every step of the way, signifies the death of the subject of choice. The very life of this subject that is promised continually, in every commodity, is deferred down a series of objects, in an effortless parody of Lacanian desire. "The subject cannot desire without itself dissolving, and without seeing, because of this very fact, the object escaping it, in a series of infinite displacements" (Lacan, 1988: 271). Because life is substituted for objects, its value is thus restricted, economized, and measured by the exchange value of commodities and technological obsolescence, a life defined by its culmination in and as a rotting, institutionalized death. Infused with an Adornoesque irony, the repetition of the imperative to choose life of course discloses only that such choice is forced by the iron hand of monopoly capitalism, the schema of mass culture by which a population is controlled, administered, and rendered docile from birth to death. No choice, then, or is there?

As the background track informs us, there is, it seems, another life on offer, a life to lust for. The opening sequence climaxes in an elision of two scenes: a football hits Renton square in the face just as his fix hits home and he falls back to the floor in Mother Superior's squalid tenement flat. Renton, MacGregor informs us, has chosen not to choose life, has chosen something else. As the juxtaposition of music, images, and words suggest, not choosing life does not necessarily mean choosing death. But it does mean laughing in the face of an oncoming car; it means a lust for life in the face of death. And it also means heroin. "Take the best orgasm you've ever had and multiply it by a thousand and you're still nowhere near it," purrs MacGregor. The myth of the thousand orgasms, or the beyond-the-thousand-orgasms, perhaps testifies not so much to the reality of the enjoyment offered by heroin, but to the desire to locate its joys in a different register to pleasure or enjoyment. The best orgasm ever times a thousand. And still nowhere near. The joy of heroin is not related to phallic enjoyment, despite the needle and the damage done. The mythic evocation of measureless excess places it beyond the locus of signification and measurement. Heroin is everything and then some. It lays bare the desire to go beyond the mundane pleasures and enjoyments of everyday life with a domain that lies beyond desire, a domain exterior to any limit that could define or provoke desire: a state of desirelessness and plenitude, an experience beyond standard or phallic measure. Its joys are beyond the orgasm and unrelated to the organ. Heroin "beats any meat injection, beats any fucking cock in the world," says Allison to Sick Boy, as her shot hits home, inducing her anorganic joy.

But addressing the apparent hyperbole seriously, what must an experience that can only begin to be evoked by a thousand simultaneous orgasms be like? Could a body possibly survive that—not just a hundred but a thousand, a million lacerating explosions of opium-induced ecstasy? It would surely be a joy impossible to survive, a total expenditure without reserve. The claim, or fantasy, is very reminiscent of Foucault's definition of real pleasure, recounted in an interview toward the end of his life, "the kind of pleasure I would consider as the real pleasure would be so deep, so intense, so overwhelming that I couldn't survive it. I would die" (Foucault, 1988: 12). Just as Renton's joy and laughter at being hit by the car in the opening sequence of the movie recall Foucault's example of the joy of a near-death experience (that also involved being hit by a car) (12).

"But I chose not to choose life. I chose something else." The something else chosen by Renton and Foucault in contradistinction to the life offered by what Theodor Adorno and the Frankfurt School calls mass culture lies not outside, or adjacent to, but in excess of that life in a singular and all-consuming relation to death. The commodities of mass culture fill up everyday life with the 'middle range pleasures' of consumer culture, but some commodities become associated with what Foucault calls real pleasure, pleasures related to death. These commodities commit the very life of those who take them on and represent a consumption that would culminate in the consummation of all pleasure. Such a mode of consumption can of course take the form of an addiction in which the relation to death is driven by a commitment formally expressed by repetition. As such, addictive commodities are, as William Burroughs said of heroin, the ultimate merchandise, since they articulate both senses of the term "consumption" in a continual being-for-death.

In their rejection of middle range pleasures, Renton and Foucault have things in common with the Frankfurt School, of course. In contrast to the reification and alienation of monopoly capitalism, which deflects an always already alienated desire down a chain of objects and brand names, Renton's desire is to move beyond desire into an area of sensuous immediacy. This order of intimacy would address not desire, but real bodily needs, "need like I've never known," as he affirms. Desire is replaced by real need, and all the vicissitudes of desire—work, status, amorous relationships, the accumulation of wealth—"really don't matter when you've got a sincere and truthful junk habit." As such, the inordinate sensual pleasure sought by Renton is perhaps close to that ideal of sensuous happiness and freedom, of the kind attributed to Adorno by Jay Bernstein as the position from which mass culture must be critiqued (see Bernstein in Adorno, 1991: 10). However, although the location of critique may be similar, its quality, truth, and authenticity are not the same (despite what Renton states, ironically or not). This is made clear in Adorno and Max Horkheimer's reference, in *The Dialectic of Enlightenment* (1979), to the illusion of happiness that narcotic drug addicts experience, an illusion to which they oppose "that which is like yet unlike: the realization of utopia through historical labour" (1979: 62–63). While it is perhaps no surprise that Adorno and Horkheimer would reject drug addiction, the *similarity*, the likeness that is yet unlike, between narcotic joy and social utopia, is interesting. The key difference concerns its authenticity and its relation to production, historical labor. The enjoyment of Utopia is thus posited as the end of production, the end of history or historical labor, and is therefore, as Jean Baudrillard and others have argued, the very mirror of capitalist production (see Baudrillard, 1975 and 1981). Alternatively, the ideal of sensuous happiness and freedom is yet another version of the pastoral domain that never fails to offer itself as a solution to civilization's discontents. In *Trainspotting*, the ascetic rigors of Scottish romanticism, another historical form of the pastoral, are briefly considered, in the shape of a mountainous landscape, only to be summarily dismissed along with Scottish nationalism and heritage. Renton and his friends may be stupid, as he says, but not that fucking stupid. Liberation from the state of things can only be found through things themselves, through the nonproductive utilization of things.

For Jacques Derrida, it is this distinction above all others that characterizes traditional or canonical objections to drug addiction: "The drug addict as such produces nothing, nothing true or real." "It is always nonwork that is disqualified. The authentic work, as its name seems to suggest, ought to be the result of an effort (the merit and rewards) and of a responsible effort, even up to the point where the effort effaces itself . . . And even if the work comes from an effortless labour, a work without work . . . we still require it to be authentic and not factitious . . . it is in the name of this authenticity that drug addiction is condemned or deplored" (Derrida,

1995: 241). But the drug addict is not always condemned, absolutely. Again, Derrida suggests that "he is legitimated, in certain cases, secretly and inadmissably, by certain portions of society, only in as much as he participates, at least indirectly, in the production and consumption of goods" (236). Even drug addiction, and indeed addiction generally, can be assimilated for the greater good if it facilitates the production and consumption of goods, though this facility must be explicitly disavowed.

It is this central opposition between work and nonwork, useful production and nonproductive expenditure, implied in the two contradictory uses of the word "consumption," that is of course essential to the distinction that Bataille draws between restricted and general economies. This distinction is nicely illustrated by the double meaning of the term "consumption." Its two common meanings are, first: to use up, expend, exhaust, destroy, or waste. Bataille gives this sense of consumption the name *dépense*, or nonproductive expenditure, an expenditure represented, among other things, by "luxury, mourning, war, cults, the construction of sumptuary monuments, games, spectacles, arts, perverse sexual activity (i.e., deflected from genital finality)—all these represent activities which, at least in primitive circumstances, have no end beyond themselves" (Bataille, 1997: 169). The second meaning of consumption concerns modes of expenditure that "serve as a means to the end of production" and is generally understood in relation to consumer society, being concerned with the exchange of goods and services, with what people choose to buy or purchase, consuming being to take up or take away something, a meaning that has its roots in the latin *con-sumere*. For Bataille, however, *dépense* must be distinguished from modes of useful consumption because with *dépense* "the accent is placed on a *loss* that must be as great as possible in order for that activity to take on its true meaning" (Bataille, 1997: 169).

For Bataille the deployment of excess resources in useful consumption is also inadequate because it reduces the human being, as a consumer, to the exigencies of things that are useful and necessary to a comfortable life. Human life is therefore defined by the threshold of utility, necessity, and comfort introduced by *things*: automobiles, washing machines, computers, and so on. Human beings themselves are therefore reduced to the level of things and are similarly valued according to their utility, or in other words their servitude to a system in which they must be useful and sell their labor. Bataille argues, however, that there remains within Western society a desire for sovereignty beyond the restricted world of useful things that can be achieved in forms of nonproductive or useless expenditure: eroticism, extravagance, chance, violence, intimacy, loss, and consumption in the form of the destruction of the utility associated with things. "Intimacy is not expressed by a *thing* except on one condition: that this *thing* be essentially the opposite of a *thing*, the opposite of a product, of a commodity—a consumption and a sacrifice" (Bataille, 1988: 132). Certain things, then, do not necessarily alienate or reify, but on the contrary can provide a means of opening out, through consumption, a sovereign, intimate space heterogeneous to the slavish world of useful activity. In *Trainspotting*, the ritual consumption of and by heroin, which binds the community of users together on the margins of Edinburgh society, involves the sacrifice of a useful and productive life. It substitutes need for desire, but the need is a paradoxical *needless* need: it is a willed sacrifice of will in a consumption of and for the body. It replaces the traditional festive mode of *dépense* embodied in the film by Begbie and his enthusiasm for the drunken violence and mayhem of a Scottish Saturday night.

CRACK

This joy of nonproductive expenditure, sacrifice, and death articulates the beyond of the pleasure principle and the beyond of phallic jouissance with the rejection of consumer society, phallocentrism, and the symbolic order. At the same time, heroin, as Burroughs suggests, provides an exemplary model of consumption in both senses insofar as the discourse of consumer culture resembles the discourse of addiction. How far is it possible to separate the two and extract from heroin, alcohol, or other forms of addiction, the alternative "life which it contains"? (Deleuze and Parnet, 2002: 53). Deleuze's concept of life traverses the life of the organism, and in his clinical ethics of literary evaluation he cites many writers who suffer the effects of the life that passes through them in the form of fragile health, alcoholism, drug addiction, or madness. But while Deleuze's creative conception of life is essentially destructive of the organic life that it runs through and dismantles, it is also infused with joy. Citing D. H. Lawrence, Deleuze argues that there is no art without joy, however ugly, terrifying, or repugnant (2003: 251). Further, this creative joy that animates life is directly related to the Spinozist conception of joy that multiplies "the affects which express or encompass a maximum of affirmation. [And that] make the body a power which is not reducible to the organism" (Deleuze and Parnet, 2002: 62). Perhaps one way of beginning to pose these questions concerning life, death, and the life that seems to traverse them both is to distinguish anorganic life from the death drive. This also entails separating Deleuze's account of the death drive (or death instinct) with Lacan's account and its pertinence to consumer culture.

Lacan derives the death drive from the symbolic order to the degree to which every drive remains "subjugated by the structure of the world of signs" (Lacan, 1992: 91). For Lacan, the problem of sublimation is situated in the field of the drives where the drives are invested in sign-objects that circulate *das ding*, the Thing of jouissance, but hold them back from directly encountering it. Jean Baudrillard in *Consumer Society* (1998) draws a very similar distinction between consumption and enjoyment. He considers that consumer capitalism "establishes itself on the basis of a denial of enjoyment" (Baudrillard, 1998: 78). This form of consumption is bound up with the purchase of signs ordered according to a social code of values rather than with the enjoyment of objects (78). This distinction is un-Lacanian, however, to the degree to which it seems to rely again on that pastoral domain where, once upon a time, before the emergence of signifiers and social codes, objects were consumed and enjoyed in all their sensuous immediacy. However, as Lacan dryly notes, "Great Pan is dead." Baudrillard is more Lacanian when he suggests that the system of production-consumption is predicated on the denial of enjoyment in the sense that such a denial thereby sustains the illusion that enjoyment exists somewhere, but is prohibited. But this is why Lacan situates the problem of sublimation at the level of the drive and, more particularly, the death drive since it is directed beyond the pleasure principle. That is, precisely beyond the level at which they could be satisfied by the pleasurable utility of socially approved objects (1992: 87–114). "That is *Das Ding* insofar as, if he is to follow the path of his pleasure, man must go around it . . . what governs us on the path of our pleasure is no Sovereign Good" (Lacan, 1992: 95). In the absence of a sovereign good, but in the midst of pleasurable, consumable objects, 'man' runs up against a fundamental problem, the problem of evil (97), that alone can promise to materialize, in negative form, a sovereign good. Since the death drive invests every path of pleasure, the death drive cannot simply be regarded as just another separate drive distinct from a 'life' drive. Or rather, "the distinction between the life drive and the death drive is true in as much as it manifests two aspects of the death drive" (Lacan, 1976: 257). Or further, "every drive is virtually a death drive" (1986: 848) for three main reasons, as Dylan Evans notes. First, every drive pursues its own extinction, second, every drive involves the subject in repetition, and, third, every drive seeks out that domain of excess jouissance, beyond the pleasure principle, that is experienced as pain and suffering (Evans, 1996: 33). Therefore death invests every drive.

For Deleuze also, in his discussion of alcoholism and the instincts in Emile Zola's *La Bête humaine*, the death instinct is central. As with his discussion of Scott Fitzgerald (in *The Crack Up*), the death instinct is designated as the 'crack' and distinguished from the other instincts:

> The crack designates . . . Death—the death Instinct. The in-
> stincts may speak loud, make noise, or swarm, but they are
> unable to cover up this more profound silence, or hide that
> from which they return: the death instinct, *not merely one in-
> stinct among others*, but the crack itself around which all the
> instincts congregate. (Deleuze, 1989a: 326)

The instincts and the big appetites, the appetite for drink, for money, for women, "gravitate around the death instinct" (1989a: 326), they "swarm through the crack which is the crack of the death instinct" (326). But while the instincts and their objects-syntheses bare the hereditary traces where historical and social conditions determine similar lifestyles and appetites, the crack betrays a profounder form of heredity that is neither social-historical nor biological. For Deleuze, like Lacan, the death drive is not related to biological processes. Rather, it is "the Idea of death beneath every fixed Idea, the grand heredity beneath the small" (327). Death can only be an idea in the mind of the living, the very image that articulates thought with the unthought, the impersonal with the personal. As an event, death is completely impersonal, ungraspable, unknowable, and without relation to the person who will fail to experience it since death removes the necessary consciousness of sensation. At the same time, one's death is intensely personal in the sense that it occurs only to oneself and can be actualized in a present whose "extreme horizon (is) the freedom to die and to risk oneself mortally" (Blanchot, cited in Deleuze 1989a: 156). Suicide and madness bring the two faces of death together, of course, but so do the use of drugs and alcohol. They bring death on the installment plan, which both enables and blocks an abstract thought at the limit. "When Fitzgerald or Lowry speak of this incorporeal metaphysical crack and find in it the locus as well as the obstacle of their thought, its source as well as its drying up, sense and nonsense, they speak with all the gallons of alcohol they have drunk which have actualized the crack in the body" (Deleuze, 1989a: 157). The crack at the surface introduces "a sort of schizophrenic depth" that inheres in the creativity of consumption, supporting and supplanting it (157).

A number of lusty big appetites are presented in *Trainspotting*, and their juxtaposition makes the opening so pleasurable for the movie viewer. The sense of flight, of movement beyond the law and the cares of life and death, is visible in the midst of a clashing double commentary. This clash is essential to the pleasure and success of the opening of the movie: Renton's Adornoesque rant versus Iggy Pop's "Lust for Life." But a rift or crack runs throughout the film holding together and apart the schizophrenic depths in which life and death face and reflect each other into infinity. Like the clashing commentary at the movie's opening, Iggy Pop's song is itself highly ambiguous. "Lust for Life" does much more than simply pitch one version of life against another. Its own cracked schizophrenic narrative actually prefigures the narrative of the forthcoming movie. From drug addiction to ironic rehabilitation, its chorus both contests and reaffirms the life defined by commodities, a "life worth a million prizes" that is both the pit and pinnacle of commodified life. It is in this way that Iggy Pop also bears the crack of 'grand heredity' in the context of *Trainspotting*'s narrative, not simply because he is the film's ambiguous hero, its patron saint. For sure, Iggy Pop haunts both the film and the novel as the spectre of a lost and unattainable sovereign life—that of an underground pop star of the 1970s. This was a time when pop mattered, or at least seemed to from the point of view of the 1980s, the period in which *Trainspotting* is set. Iggy Pop, as a metonymy for the New York jazz, rock, and pop art counterculture, functions as a kind of cultural Ego-Ideal, shot through with heroin, associated with Lou Reed, Andy Warhol's Factory, Charlie Parker, William Burroughs, and so on. For the Scottish characters in the film and novel, the sovereign lives of these American artists is purely conveyed in the glamor of the commodities that they consume. As such, these lives are inseparable from the commodities of consumer culture. However, the crack that scores through Iggy Pop and his lust for life spreads its network of fissures throughout the narrative. Later in the movie, Tommy, one of Renton's friends, is confronted with a choice: he can spend his dole money on a gift for his girlfriend or a ticket for an Iggy Pop concert. His fateful decision to buy the concert ticket leads to rejection by his girl, the compensation of heroin, addiction, HIV, and death. But "by means of the crack and at its edges thought occurs . . . in people ready to destroy themselves" (Deleuze, 1989a: 160). At the concert, in the novel, Tommy is arrested by the gaze of the great man: "Iggy Pop looks right at me as he sings the line 'America takes drugs in psychic defence'; only he changes 'America' for 'Scatlin', and defines us mair accurately in a single sentence than all the others have ever done" (Welsh, 1993: 75). "Better death than the health which we are given" (Deleuze, 1989a: 160). Iggy Pop, as fount of impossible joy, lies behind the investment in heroin as an unattainable point of sovereignty, always located in another time (1970s) and another place (New York, on stage). Pop-heroin opens up the space (difference) and the time (deferral) for a psychic investment in commodities (heroin, pop records, concerts, movies) that simultaneously provide a defense against the banality of the here-and-now that is an effect of its *differance*.

There are of course many differences between the movie and the novel; the former schematizes the latter's series of vignettes into more of an integrated narrative. The novel is an assemblage of mini-narratives that concern the four or five main characters, Renton, Sick Boy, Spud, Begbie, and Tommy. They are joined together by a variety of bonds, including drug co-dependency, but also the bonds of debt, violence, dark humor, and betrayal peculiar to British masculinity. The movie is less concerned with the social realism of the novel and the brutality of some of the characters than it is in heightening its black humor with some cinematic magic realism. The film replaces the minoritarian language of the novel with cinematic glamor. But both novel and film are split by the crack that marks the central ambivalence of both texts. This crack runs through heroin addiction just as it does commodified life, marking the boredom of literary novels and the tedium of commercial movies. The movie and the novel take the structure of a Möbius strip of the kind suggested by Burroughs in which heroin provides the underside and support of everyday life. It makes possible and indeed embodies the very structure of the life it denies: "I need junk to get out of bed in the morning, to shave and eat breakfast. I need it to stay alive" (Burroughs, 2002: 23). The crack renders everything junk; it is the death drive that invests every object of commodified life. Iggy Pop and *Trainspotting* itself are no different and are typical of all commodities in that they are products that are subject to a structure riven with the cracks of the commercial death drive that renders them junk almost as soon as they emerge. Novelty, the joy of the new, is in this sense an expression of the accumulation of junk. Renton's girlfriend helps him through his rehabilitation, and encourages him to leave Edinburgh and move on from heroin and Iggy Pop. In so doing, she discloses the death drive underlying the law of novelty, the primary law applying to consumer culture, as the means to his therapy: "You're not getting any younger, Mark. The world's changing, music's changing, even drugs are changing. You can't sit in here all day doing a bit of heroin and listening to Ziggy Pop (sic) . . . you've got to find something new."

This economic law appeals to need rather than desire or interests. It is the case that, in relation to American consumer capitalism from the 1920s, economists have begun to speak less about marketing goods in terms of interests or in supplying demands based on needs and utility, as creating desire. And it is clear that consumer capitalism evidently does not address itself to needs, at the level of subsistence, in any form whatsoever. Even the simplest foodstuffs are packaged as if they were appealing to a particular look or lifestyle (and therefore a desire), rather than a preexisting need. However, it could be suggested that hypermodern modes of production do indeed manufacture need rather than desire; it manufactures needless need, a concept very close to desire, but significantly different in that ultimately it collapses the spatial difference and temporal deferral necessary for desire, thereby precluding it. Consumer capitalism defaults directly to the drive, bypassing desire. If desire results from the subtraction of need from demand, then the return of a manufactured need forecloses desire from the equation. This is because there is no necessity for the consumer to articulate his or her demands in speech (thereby alienating demand in and as desire) because the demand is already presupposed, already prefigured in the manufacture of need. Few people ever express a demand for the next generation of technological equipment that they will soon need to possess and deploy in order to exist in the workplace, at home, at leisure, and so on. Junk manifests how commodities manufacture needs that did not previously exist, yet become in their deathly way essential to life, "need like I've never known": need for big televisions, washing machines, cars, computers, compact disc players, and electric can openers.

At the same time, junk is the locus of heterogeneity, of consumed and wasted bodies (elegant or not), that defines the parameters of homogeneous mass culture. Junk accumulates at the edges of the crack that, in Deleuzian terms, opens out beneath every line of flight, promising a plunge into its depths. For Deleuze, the line of flight involves treachery and betrayal, turning one's back on everything, as if that were possible, as if the crack did not always remain consistent. "There is always betrayal in a line of flight. Not trickery like that of an orderly man ordering his future, but betrayal like that of a simple man who no longer has any past or future" (Deleuze and Parnet, 2002: 40). Renton's friends trick and swindle each other all the time, though it is doubtful that in doing this they are ordering their future; each betrayal does not constitute a definitive turning away. On the contrary, it binds them further to each other. Only Renton, at the end of the film, attempts a definitive betrayal, assuming that after stealing Begbie's money scored from the drug deal, there can be no coming back. Renton betrays his friends and flees to Amsterdam and a new life—though the fact that he is heading to Amsterdam renders the precise nature of that new life highly equivocal. Nevertheless Renton's opening speech is revisited as the credits get ready to roll, but in an affirmative tone, apparently Renton is now finally content to join the rest of us in choosing life.

MYSTERY TRAIN

"Train I ride . . . sixteen coaches long / Train I ride . . . sixteen coaches long / Well that long black train got my baby and gone" (Parker and Philips, 1955). The train song articulates American folk, blues and country to the great juggernaut of rock and roll. Elvis Presley's "Mystery Train," recorded during Sam Philips's epochal Sun Sessions is exemplary. The mythical train whether it is headed to Memphis or Georgia, Heaven or the Promised Land is always ambivalent, always travels at midnight, is always long and black, a cannonball that hurtles through the night and never goes back. That is, from the journey over tracks laid by Irish and Chinese immigrant workers, freed blacks, tracks that opened up the West by displacing Indians from their homelands, on trains transforming the wilderness in a plume of black smoke, there was no going back. Along the tracks that score the journey of American progress, swarm innumerable personae, songs, and tales: the prospectors, whores, and gamblers rendered mobile and heading West, the outlaw train robbers, the robber barons, the hobos. Such a troupe of gun-slingers, guitarists, and minstrels provided the soundtrack to this epic national journey through its various transformations and wars from the American Civil War to World War Two.

"Train, train, coming round, round the bend. Well it took my baby, but it never will again (No, not again)." "Mystery Train" is a yearning and haunting record. Is his baby alive or dead? Is the fact that she will no longer travel evidence of her life and love, or death? By 1955, when the song was recorded by Presley, the railroad itself was beginning to die. As diesels replaced the steam locomotive, the train, as a mode of transportation, began to be superseded by cars and airplanes. As a mode of communication, the railroad was supplanted by the highway and the superhighway. And yet, even as it began to die after World War Two, its folk myth provided one of the major figures of American popular culture, particularly rock and roll, as it absorbed folk, country, and blues traditions. American rock and roll and pop culture generally has proved the most powerful solvent of traditional national cultures and effected their transformation in the face of what is now called global culture. Hollywood, pop music, soft drinks, junk food, and so on, have aggressively marketed themselves through evoking transgressive modes of identification and pleasure, appealing to generations of young consumers frustrated by the prospect of their parent's boring lives, yearning to get on that freedom train. Elvis blazed the trail, traveling on his own line of excess, his big appetites swarming into a crack that ran the length of the Mississippi, dead in Graceland at the age of forty-one.

Train, train. The locomotive, therefore, "is not an object, but an epic symbol, a great Phantasm" (330), a pure death drive insofar as it destroys the life that it over-rides, blind and deaf, amid its clamor, to anything but the silent becoming-machine of the West. In his analysis of the symbol of the train in Zola's *La Bête humaine*, Deleuze notes how the train bares the machinic 'logic of the instinct' that marks the line of the crack that runs through all the instincts and appetites. Before he embarks on his journey of murder and destruction, the character Jacques Lantier rejects one-by-one the legitimate objects of his appetite—women, wine, money—until he gives up on all the instincts except one. "He has given up the instincts; his sole object is the machine" (237)—the locomotive that he drives and that symbolizes the inexorability of his death drive. "Beyond the lost instinct, the machine is revealed more and more as the image of death or as the pure death instinct" (Deleuze, 1989a: 330).

In his analysis, Deleuze carefully distinguishes the train as an epic symbol rather than a tragic one. Revealing the "open space of the *epos*," rather than occupying "the closed space of tragedy," the train is not the vehicle of Oedipus (331); it is not a symbol of the phallus or the bearer of castration (sometimes a train is just a train). The train does not bear a chorus, but itinerant blues and country singers, rock and rollers who do not function as witnesses but as the very agents of movement along the tracks. Unlike the phallus, which instantiates the tragic law of the father in the closed domestic space of the family romance, the train opens up "a field of action . . . it traces an open space on the scale of a nation or civilization" (331). "So many men and rushing past in the thunder of trains . . . It was a fact that all the world went by . . . But they went by in a flash and she was never quite sure she had really seen them" (Zola, cited in Deleuze, 1989a: 331). Borne along at thunderous speed by the locomotive of modernity, the whole world goes by along the tracks that score open the crack left by the death drive of progress. But too fast for a witness, it was as if they were never there, as if they had never existed.

DERAILED

"Drive boy dog boy Dirty numb angel boy"

—"Born Slippy" by Underworld, *Trainspotting* soundtrack

Along with "Lust for Life" the biggest hit from the *Trainspotting* soundtrack, "Born Slippy," became a dance anthem, skillfully combining both the adrenaline rush of high-octane dance with the tripping ambiance of rave. Speed and intensive movement combined with ecstasy. The track begins with a single note from a keyboard that fade repeats with a melancholy echo amid a swirling sound that phases in and out like a strobe light. The plaintive vocal lays out, in a series, the boy assemblage that evokes the lives and characters of the novel or indeed in rave culture Britain generally in the 1990s. The track picks up, builds up speed, drum-machined hi-hat and drums doing eight to the bar, going like the clappers, like a steam train increasing its velocity in a rush, speech tumbling in a stammer of rage. "You're real boy Dog dirty dumb cracking boy You're getting wet boy Big big time boy Acid bears boy Babes and babes And babes and babes and babes And remembering nothing boy Do you like my tin horn boy It gets wet like at Angel derailed."

If Welsh's literary invention of Edinburgh-English creates a minoritarian language within the majoritarian one of metropolitan literary English, lyrically "Born Slippy" breaks language down to its essentials and exemplifies what for Deleuze is characteristic and superior about English. Unlike French with its intellectualized, redundant desire for purity, or German with its nostalgia for Being, English creates composite words whose only link is "an implied AND, relationship with the Outside, cult of the road which never plunges down, which has no foundations, which shoots on the surface, rhizome. Blue-eyed boy: a boy, some blue, and eyes—an assemblage. AND . . . AND . . . AND . . . stammering" (Deleuze and Parnet, 2002: 59). What Deleuze values about literature is the way in which great writers push their native languages to a point of disequilibrium and make them stammer or stutter (see Deleuze, 1998: 107–114). "He makes the language as such stutter: an affective and intensive language, and no longer an affectation of the one who speaks" (107). Deleuze's favorite writers (Kafka, Beckett, Melville) push speech into a form of precipitative movement, a stammer, stumble, or fall, so that it moves beyond speech into language itself, in a process analogous to the movement that "goes beyond the organism towards a body without organs" (1998: 111).

While it is not of course great literature, "Born Slippy" nevertheless treats song like an assemblage of aural samples conjoined together, words no less than musical citations, and synthesized variations. Precipitous, out of kilter, language is movement, sinuously pursuing the "continuous line of the and," dancing to a mechanical beat, a machined pulse building toward a joy indistinguishable from anger and melancholy.

Synthesized dance music composed of aural samples combining a potentially infinite continuous series of a finite combination of elements has been standard from the middle to late 1980s. From hip-hop to House to acid to nu-metal, tracks are assembled from samples of obsolete tracks increasingly rendered unrecognizable or forgotten. Musical history is replayed endlessly and tracks severed from any point of social or historical origin and emplacement. But it is not even a question of the composition of one particular track. Rather, each track is itself part of an assemblage of a combined series of tracks that constitute a mix according to the same principle. These assemblages operate together and constitute a plane of consistency that undulates in varying degrees of intensity that bypass desire. There is no narrative, no love song, no desire song, no train song. Rather it is the train itself: the machined beat and the drive spiraling exorbitantly in joy.

"Born Slippy" is not without negativity, but on the plane of intensity it is consistent in its ecstasy-fueled joy with the exhaustion and foreclosure of desire in the inexhaustible plus. The "continuous line of the and," the inexhaustible plus, which enables a majoritarian Anglo-Saxon multiculturalism to absorb and utilize all musical cultures, all its margins, its thresholds, its subterranean workings and dialects to the degree that they constitute the locus of junk that provides something new. Addition: the logic of the new and the same articulated by pure demand. "Shouting lager lager lager lager Shouting lager lager lager lager Mega mega white thing Mega mega white thing So many things to see and do in the tube hole" ("Born Slippy," Underworld, 1996). The white thing gets bigger the more it is filled out by the hole, around which the drive pulses attempting to satisfy its insatiable need for more and more of the same.

Confronted by what William Burroughs calls the algebra of need, from which it has been subtracted and prohibited, desire becomes spectral or retro. Foreclosed from the everyday life of the present, desire is split in two: the energy of desire devolves to the site of the drive, of a nonorganic hard-wired intensive body extimate (both interior and exterior) to the site of control and addiction. Its images and objects, those scenes that provide desire with its aim and direction, remain only as the ghostly past life of the subject. A numb Angel boy that remembers nothing, but is the figure of memory itself, is left wet with tears, derailed. The memory Angels haunt the present and become the retro site of support and resistance to the life of addiction in the midst of the mobile products of mass culture. As Deleuze argues with regard to the equivocal nature of addiction and its value, "It is once *object, loss of object, and the law governing this loss* within an orchestrated process of demolition." Desire and the objects of desire (love, money, national identity) are gradually demolished, but sustained nostalgically precisely through this interminable loss. The mode of existence of the addict is the *past perfect* of an "I have-loved, I have-done or I have-seen." "In drunkenness, the alcoholic puts together an imaginary past, as if the softness of the past participle came to be combined with the hardness of the present auxiliary . . . the present moment belongs to the verb '*to have*', whereas all being is 'past'" (Deleuze, 1990: 158). Desire is lost to the past, to another scene, "to triumph over this hardened and faded present which subsists and signifies death" (160). At the same time, in the midst of this death, and at the level of the drive, desire's energy burns in and as intensity. It is the lust for life that manifests itself in the consumption of excess and the excess consumption of addiction, providing the principle of disequilibrium that determines whether or not it is sustained as a principle of control.

The movie and the novel from which it is adapted have an enigmatic title. Train spotting is a peculiar, and a peculiarly British, activity. One of the most boring and uncomfortable activities imaginable is waiting on a cold, windswept, rain-lashed railway station for a train that has been interminably delayed. Train spotters do this simply for the pure joy of it. They sit in their anoraks with a little notebook and pen, and wait for trains. Then they make a little note, jot down the number, and the trains move off again. The train spotter never gets on the train, never leaves the station, involved in an activity most would consider a complete waste of time. A train spotter, like a heroin addict, is someone to whom one would say "get a life" in that odd phrase that came to prominence in the 1980s. Except that waiting for trains is an all-too common experience of those who commute to and from their productive, working lives. We spend much of our lives waiting for trains—the trains that, like desire itself, drive you, repetitively, back and forth, through each station of life.

The nostalgia for the locomotive of desire is of course evoked in the section of the book, "Trainspotting at Leith Station," that gives Irvine Welsh's novel and the movie its name. In the barren desolate hangar, soon to be demolished and replaced by a supermarket, Renton and Begie remark on the size and grandeur of the old station. "Git a train tae anywair fae here, at one time, or so they sais," comments Renton (Welsh, 1993: 308). "If it still hud fuckin trains, ah'd be oan one oot ay this fuckin dive," replies Begbie, as if nostalgic for another time, another place, another life he'll never have. Abruptly, an old drunkard lurches up to the pair and begins to taunt them. "What yis up to lads? Trainspotting, eh?" (309). The hopeless and homeless wino is recognized by Renton as Begbie's father. Leaving the son "strangely subdued and uncomfortable," the ghost of the paternal principle haunting the tracks laughs uncontrollably at the redundancy of desire, mocking the representatives of addictive and festive expenditures respectively for train spotting in a station derelict of trains.

CHAPTER THREE

Exhausting Joy

The greatest exactitude and the most extreme dissolution; the indefinite exchange of mathematical formulations and the pursuit of the formless or the unformulated. These are the two meanings of exhaustion, and both are necessary to abolish the real.

—Deleuze, *Essays Critical and Clinical*

THE PHALLUS

In the candy store, after paying for the *Times*, Sherman turned to go out the door and his eyes swept across a magazine rack. The salmon flesh jumped out at him . . . girls . . . boys . . . girls with girls . . . boys with boys . . . girls with boys . . . girls with bare breasts, girls with bare bottoms . . . girls with paraphernalia . . . a happy grinning riot of pornography, a rout, an orgy, a hog wallow . . . On the cover of one magazine is a girl wearing only a pair of high-heeled shoes and a loincloth. Except it isn't a loincloth, it's a snake . . . Somehow it's wedged in her groin and looking right at Sherman . . . She's looking right at him, too . . . On her face is the sunniest, most unaffected smile imaginable . . . It's the face of the girl who serves you a chocolate-chip ice cream cone at the Baskin-Robbins. (Wolfe, 1988: 64)

At the beginning of Tom Wolfe's satire on the 1980s, *Bonfire of the Vanities*, his young stockbroker hero Sherman McCoy styles himself a Master of the Universe. Poised to amass wealth to which "there was . . . no limit whatsoever!" (19), Sherman is already a "big swinging dick," in the then fashionable Social Darwinist parlance of the New York world of finance. But Sherman feels limited, feels constrained by his responsibilities to his wife and child, hog-tied and humiliated by social mores and their petty prohibitions. While he loves his lovely wife, his lovely daughter, and his lovely home, and doesn't want to change any of it, nevertheless, "I, a Master of the Universe, a young man still in the season of rising sap, deserve *more* from time to time" (Wolfe, 1988: 20). It is a predictable enough, age-old marital complaint, and totally unremarkable except for the pathos in the demand to some Other, responsible for the distribution of justice and pleasure, for the more that he feels he deserves. Sherman surely has everything; his wife and daughter love him, he has potentially unlimited wealth, but he feels he deserves *more*. The Other is holding out on him, withholding something. Sherman's demand enunciates a desire for more enjoyment, the enjoyment appropriate to a Master of the Universe. The irony is that this master cannot just take what he wants, he has, in a whining tone, to ask for it like he is asking his mommy for more candy like a good boy, placing the question of his value in the maternal Other.

For Lacan, as is well known, desire is always addressed to the desire of the Other and directed toward the signifier of that desire, the phallus. The fact that desire is alienated in speech, that it is directed toward a signifier, condemns it to proceed down an interminable signifying chain. This is why, for Lacan, even a Master of the Universe cannot get any satisfaction and, moreover, "his own desire for the phallus will make its signifier emerge in its persistent divergence" toward other women "who may signify this phallus in various ways, either as a virgin or as a prostitute" (Lacan, 1986: 290).

In the candy store, that American utopia of sweetly signifying consumables, the phallus is signified as impossibly both virgin and prostitute. The face of the magazine-girl who attracts Sherman's attention, the girl with the loincloth snake who glares at him like an image of his own desire, has "the sunniest, most unaffected smile imaginable." Her simplicity and spotless innocence sets her apart from the vanities and affectations of New York; she is an ice-cream girl. The candy store does not offer guilty shame and the enjoyment of transgression—it offers an Edenic paradise for the pleasure principle. For Lacan, the pleasure principle functions as a limit to jouissance, and the compensatory support for its prohibition. Appropriately here, the promise of jouissance is refigured as pleasure: sex as candy; and all kinds of sexual combinations and amorous play are promised in a setting that is imbued with virginal, preteen sweetness, maternal reward, and well-being. It's the Puritan pornography of a masturbatory hedonism.

The snake, of course, is integral to this scene as the threatening condition of erotic innocence. Desire hovers uneasily between the fantasy of maternal satisfaction, the imaginary stasis of the pleasure principle, and the reality of the dissatisfaction of the desire that seeks to go beyond it (see Lacan, 1977: 31). The snake introduces an element of difference, its gaze drawing Sherman's attention to his own gaze and the distance that separates him from the scene represented in the image, a scene from which he is seemingly forever cut off. Images of sexual pleasure that are fraudulent promissory notes; they are pieces of paper that deliver nothing but an empty promise, or rather they lead on to more promises, more images. They are tokens of the fall, and of death, small provocations that result in moments of solitary expenditure.

The image that arrests Sherman's gaze in the candy store is on one level a highly traditional, even biblical one, if the snake is taken symbolically as the Edenic serpent who tempts Eve to taste the forbidden fruit of the Tree of Knowledge. Genesis is one of the founding texts that relate knowledge to transgression, jouissance and its prohibition of course.

In Milton's vision of loveliness, the face of spotless innocence is that of Eve before the Fall, particularly the erotic Eve of Milton's *Paradise Lost* who, in her "wanton ringlets" yields to Adam "with coy submission, modest pride, / And sweet reluctant amorous delay" (Milton, 1983: IV. 306, 310–311). In terms of the narrative of Wolfe's novel, it is also an image of Sherman's own naivete before his fall from grace. Adam and Eve's initial uncorrupted innocence is absolutely necessary as the standard by which all the corruption, the pain and perils of the earth, may be measured and known, just as the value of gold must be pure and incorruptible for it to guarantee all possible pleasures. The phallus, then, must embody both purity and the possibility of its endless defloration: the purity of truth as innocence and the culmination of all possible knowledge; the purity of a total and complete joy.

But, on the other hand, Sherman McCoy, of all people, should know that the fantasy of a stable and incorruptible standard equivalent disappeared from the money markets (and indeed the global economy) many years ago. As a successful stockbroker on Wall Street, Sherman would know that value (and hence desire) is not measured in relation to a stable cache of intrinsic wealth held in reserve. It arises instead as an effect of speculation on a radically desubstantialized system of valuation based on the rapid fluctuation of share prices at any given time. The indeterminacy arises because the values of shares and securities are secured by the value of other securities in an interminable reflexivity, so that "speculation on share prices comes down to dealing in differences" (Goux, 1997: 172). Jean-Joseph Goux writes,

> What the dealer desires is not to own, but to "make a difference." The whole game unfolds in the difference between value at a time (t) and value at a time (t'). The appropriation

of value is only provisional, and must await the moment of
dis-appropriation, in order to profit from the difference. Here
again, it seems that an abstraction of content is in process, an
abstraction of the substance of the thing itself, in order to
profit from the difference. (Goux, 1997: 172)

So perhaps the image of the ice-cream-snake-girl-in-high heels captures the
dealer's attention not because it is a metaphor, a special signifier of jouissance for him, but simply because it functions as another minor variation or
fluctuation in the mass pornography market: girls . . . boys . . . girls with
girls . . . boys with boys . . . girls with boys . . . girls with bare breasts, girls
with bare bottoms . . . girls with paraphernalia . . . and so on. The image
that arrests the Wall Street stockbroker's attention perhaps hints, through
its incongruous presence in an upscale candy store, at an upturn in the hitherto highly specialized bestiality-fetishism niche market. The image of the
ice-cream-snake-girl-in-high-heels functions not as a metaphor but as a metonymy whose affect arises purely as an effect of the other links in a chain of
contiguous or *linked* images: girl with snake, boy with dog, two girls with
horse, two boys with pig, two bare-breasted girls with snake, bare-
bottomed girls with snake . . . girl with snake in high heels with ice cream
. . . and so on . . . that is in turn linked to a range of other possible special-
ist markets: BDSM, fetish, lesbian, gay, ebony, Latina, female dominance,
male dominance, pregnant. Just as wealth on the money markets has become a network of virtual streams of numbers fluctuating without apparent
order or regulation, so has jouissance on the Internet. As the indefinite inscription and circulation of investments (financial or libidinal), signifiers of
wealth or jouissance apparently become detached from any reference not
only to human needs or demands, but also desire. The wealth generated and
lost on the money markets outstrips any comprehensible index of human
wants. Indeed, the operativity of global corporations, industries, and the
commodities on which the markets are supposedly based are themselves
overwhelmingly automated in computerized networks linked to each other
and the Internet whose diffuse human ownership is largely anonymous and
increasingly virtual and nominal. In this context, the function of the phallus
as standard equivalent or signifier of jouissance becomes an empty mediating space in which metonymically linked images flow without anchor, reference, or relation to living beings. Indeed one might suggest that the
'human relation' takes over from the 'sexual relation' as the key question for
the destiny of human desire. A different order of desire is instanciated that
is desexualized and exhausted in the consumption of bandwidth.

Communication between computerized networks is not ordered
by a privileged signifier that orients desire, within a restricted field of sig-

nification, toward some notional end point, logos, or climax. All signifiers are combinatory; there is no special signifier that is an archetype of desire or of the One. Rather it becomes "an operand for indefinite substitutions: a generalized equivalence which deprives master signifiers of their function as ideal standards to retain only that mark, of token, of referral" (Goux, 1992: 73). The withdrawal of the phallus as standard equivalent leaves open a space of pure mediation and exchange. "Mediation imposes itself as an autonomous reality which pursues its game of references and substitutions in the absence of any *telos*" (72). The dissolution of the phallus that is the signifier of the desire of the Other in the form of a paternal prohibition (Eve and her apple) gives way to a machined Other that says "Yes!" But the machine does not offer a selection of goods ordered according to standards of taste or knowledge that could be assessed according to some external phallic measure. The machine makes everything virtually available, rendering choice infinite and therefore impossible. Desire short-circuits and devolves to the drives of a larval subject that is directly addressed and subjectified at the level of supplying demands before they have even been articulated and therefore alienated in and as desire.

The consumer of Amazon.com's services, for example, is confronted with a direct and personal address that promises everything in the world of books, videos, DVDs, and so on. That is, that nothing is forbidden so long as access is available, the purchasing data readable and creditable. While everything is available, the machine knows that everything is impossible, and that, moreover, this everything can be merely suggested on the basis of an unpresentable, unsignifiable (lost) object. This is the little machined object of demand on which excess supply is predicated and generated. Amazon.com is organized according to the assumption that every subject is unique in his or her requirements, but also that these unique requirements can be automatically predicted, anticipated, and supplied even before they have been requested. This is evident in the personal address and the personalized recommendations that are endlessly renewed on the basis of the information produced through the subject's previous purchasing data. Indeed, the 'subject' addressed by Amazon is simply a product of the data produced by the system. But no matter how much data is produced, it is predicated on the notional demand for another object. The program operates according to a built-in assumption of an endless and insatiable demand for more.

JOY'S NEW LABOR

The new order of temporality and affect that has been introduced by information systems based on digital media has replaced the relation between knowledge and jouissance that has characterized desire, work, and leisure in the West. Rather than the couple knowledge-jouissance that constituted the structure of deferral proper to work and leisure, the new order of information is infused with an anorganic joy that arises as an effect of the exhaustion of the real. In this chapter, sex is the example of the real that is exhausted.

It could be argued that deferral is not necessary in a world where any information is more or less instantly available. Joy could be said to have arisen at the prospect of unlimited information and instant access. Over the past four decades, different generations have heralded the freedom of the superhighway, the liberation of information, the ecstasy of the new economy and dot.com speculation, even the Extropian rapture of posthuman oblivion. The different waves of enthusiasm could all be taken as evidence of little ripples of cyber joy. But this is not the same as anorganic joy, which has been opposed throughout this section to the Lacanian concept of phallic jouissance. Anorganic joy refers to "a joy that implies no lack or impossibility and is not measured by pleasure since it is what distributes intensities of pleasure" (Deleuze and Guattari, 1988: 155). It is of a different order to pleasure, and distributes a different order of pleasures. Joy is here linked to a power of exhaustion, which involves the involution of the organism in the exhaustion of the possible, an exhaustion that involves both the exhaustive and the exhausted. In contrast to the orgasm, that organic spasm that discloses the inadequacies of phallic jouissance, an anorgasmic joy insists along a plane or plateau of intensity "that is not automatically dissipated in a climax" but persists for an extended period (see Massumi cited in Deleuze and Guattari, 1988: xiv). The joy consists in the functional fulfillment of the anorganic life that is established along that plane of intensity, a plane that exhausts and dismantles the organism through the exhaustive pursuit of an infinite series of finite possibilities and combinations.

Unlike jouissance, this anorganic joy has nothing to do with knowledge, work, or sublimation; there is no labor of thought or the body here. You don't have to work for information in the same way that knowledge was only once achievable through the labor of thought. And even then, absolute knowledge, in the form of a complete encyclopedia or absolute truth always proved elusive, necessarily so, even after a lifetime's scientific or philosophical labor. But it is not just a question of the absence of work that makes everyone with a networked computer a master of the universe without knowing it. As is generally accepted, the concept of information has nothing to do with knowledge or meaning. Information is not meaning, and meaning has evaporated as the main reference of information or communication theory. All meaning, which might be assessed in terms of rational or empirical verification, gives way to a purely functional and affective dynamic between signal and noise, attraction and distraction, dissonance and repetition, recombination and exhaustion.

The shift from jouissance to joy is evident in the changing language of Internet culture. Meaning and labor have been abolished. "Labor" was always a term that derived from an essentially moral nineteenth-century discourse infused with negativity and *ressentiment*. The term labor confers value on a particular operation purely through the effort put in to it. Physical effort, struggle, confers dignity to labor and the poor, in contrast to the undeserving poor who waste time evading work in laziness or immoral pursuits, pursuits that are precisely immoral because they involve the evasion of work. In *L'Envers de la psychanalyse* (1970), Lacan locates jouissance in production and notes that capitalism takes a *plus de jouir* along with its surplus value. The immorality of capitalism is thus that the value of the labor invested in production gets stolen in surplus value, the bosses enjoy at the expense of the labor of others.

But it is important to note that the notion of work and labor is indelibly bound up with a certain romantic humanism. Only human beings work, of course; machines don't work, they simply operate. But what if humans are regarded as always already bound up in machined assemblages? And, further, if it is supposed that humans are operated by machines, or are located in assemblages that for the sake of efficient functioning and profitability do not require them to labor but to have fun?

In the transvaluation of nineteenth-century terms and values, undertaken by network culture and the new economy, the term labor is now abject. Of course, in British politics the abjection of the term labor dates from the leadership of Tony Blair. New Labour is business-friendly and good for business. In contrast to the labor of the negative, joy's new labor in network culture is not work, it is fun. Joy's new labor is not really labor at all, even if it can be exhausting. Sometimes it is described as free labor, by neo-Marxists who are still concerned about the political morality of the term. Participating in chat rooms, building, contributing to, and modifying Web sites and software packages, participating in mailing lists, compiling lists and links, is all done for free because it is fun to do. The original ethos of the information highway was fun, but this ethos continued with Silicon Valley and all the other subsequent silicon valleys that have emerged since. Andrew Ross's ethnography of the New York company Razorfish, for example, illustrates this transvaluation precisely.

> Razorfish, with its open-plan offices and its enthusiastic labour force, who did not consider work as "labour," constituted an important moment of experimentation with alternative modes of organization able to capitalize on the productive capacities

of an educated and alienated GenX milieu. (Terranova,
2004: 116)

As Tiziana Terranova argues, the fun of free labor is exhausted
by capitalism:

> Free labour is a desire of labour immanent to late capitalism,
> and late capitalism is the field which both sustains free labour
> *and* exhausts it. It exhausts it by undermining the means
> through which that labour can sustain itself: from the burn-
> out syndromes of Internet start-ups to under-compensation
> exploitation in the cultural economy at large. Late capitalism
> does not appropriate anything: it nurtures, exploits and ex-
> hausts its labour force and its cultural affective production.
> (Terranova, 2004: 94)

"Late capitalism" here is presumably a phrase derived from Fredric Jame-
son, demonstrating admirable optimism of the will in its implication that
we are near its end. Her use of the term exhaustion is also more limited
than the argument being developed in this chapter which suggests that exhaustion is the mode of expenditure that is immanent to the architecture
of the Web. But her observation nevertheless raises interesting questions.
What is this desire of labor to be free, or to give itself for free, or to liber-
ate itself from the concept of labor? What constitutes the joy of this fun-
free new labor that exhausts itself?

Terranova also links the phenomenon of free labor with the so-
called potlatch of the network economy, celebrated by new economists
like Kevin Kelly and George Gilder. John Horvarth argues that the 'free
stuff' offered around the Net "is either a product that gets you hooked on
to another one or makes you just consume more time on the net. After all,
the goal of the access people and telecoms is to have users spend as much
time on the net as possible, regardless of what they are doing. The objective is to have you consume bandwidth" (cited in Terranova, 2004: 93).
Even as users are having fun consuming bandwidth, it is not often clear
whether they are not simply consuming, but producing, not simply at
leisure, but maybe at work, or maybe both, or neither. Apparently, "the
best way to keep your site visible and thriving on the web is to turn it into
a space that is not only accessed, but somehow built by its users" (Terranova, 2004: 91).

The economy and indeed profitability of what Terranova calls cultural affective production has also changed significantly. As is clearly evident, it is no longer the cultural product—its meaning or affect—that is

important and profitable, but possession of a list that would enable one to access it. The compilation of lists and the efficiency of search engines dominate the activity of culturally affective production and consumption.

ANORGASMIC JOY

11/29 *12 Lesbian*—Yummy Amateur Girls Share an Apartment

11/29 *12 Facial*—Hot Amateur Girls Sucking Cock

11/29 *12 Amateur*—Young Teen Amateurs on Cam for the Very First Time!

11/29 *10 Lesbian*—Her First Lesbian Sex Amateur Wives

11/29 *12 Big Tits*—Naturally Busty Amateur

11/29 *12 Fetish*—Monster Cock Hardcore Fuck & Suck

11/29 *XX Big Tits*—Babes with Massive Bouncing Boobs

11/29 *12 Bisexual*—Young Amateurs Explore Their Sexuality at College

11/29 *50 Teen*—Wicked Young Perky Amateur School Girls

11/29 *08 Movies*—Young Amateur Cream Pie Pussy Dripping Cum

11/29 *12 Blowjob*—Amateur Girls Giving Head in Public

11/29 *12 Hardcore*—Hot Party Girls Having Sex in Public

11/30 *15 Blow Jobs and Cum Shots*—My Black Cock Breakfast

11/30 *20 Fetish/Bizarre*—2 Dirty Girls Get Pee in the Mouth

11/30 *15 Big Tits*—Drunken Ladies Night Turned into Wild Orgies

11/30 *16 Bbw*—Phone Sex with 50 F Bbw

11/30 *18 Mature Ladies*—Mature Woman Laying on Her Sofa!

11/30 *15 Hardcore*—Chubby Brunette Rides Cock and Drinks

11/30 *15 Latina*—Amateur Babe Anjali Sucks Cock

11/30 *16 Bondage/Bdsm*—Trainee Humiliation in Freight Elevator

11/30 *15 Fetish/Bizarre*—Extreme Pussy Insertions

11/30 *15 Trans*—Transexual Babe Doing a Straight Guy

11/30 *15 Mature Ladies*—Lusty Brunette Milf Gets a Pussy Sucking

11/30 *15 Blow Jobs and Cum Shots*—Cum Dripping Babe

11/30 *20 Hardcore*—Real Oldies Hardcore from the 1970's

11/30 *16 Fetish/Bizarre*—Pee Drinking Blonde Beauty

11/30 *20 Blow Jobs and Cum Shots*—Ponytail Babe Enjoys a Messy Facial

11/30 *16 Bbw*—Plumper with Big Tits Big Ass Spreads

11/30 *20 Gay*—Twink Taking Heavy Assride Action

11/30 *20 Interracial*—Cris Get Crunked in the Ass
11/30 *15 Trans*—Shemale with a Huge Cock Posing
11/30 *18 Latina*—Sexy Latina Getting Screwed in Office
11/30 *16 Black*—Yummy Black Naked Booty and Boobies
11/30 *16 Fetish/Bizarre*—Hospital Gyno Rectal Exam
11/30 *15 Anal And Ass*—Stiff Cock Slamming Her Ass Hard
11/30 *15 Latina*—Hot Indian Amateur Gets Naked
11/30 *12 Asian*—Virgin Asian Pussy Gets First Pounding
11/30 *16 Fetish/Bizarre*—Fishnet Feet Jerk Off Hard Cock
11/30 *16 Bondage/Bdsm*—Needle Play
11/30 *20 Celebs*—Pamela Anderson Nude and Having Sex

There is a set of pregiven alternatives that on the one hand is closed, but on the other opens out on to a potentially infinite series. Each link is likely to lead on to another list of links, and then yet another, and then yet another. Apparently every possible variation is available before a demand has even been enunciated in a click. Desire, in the Lacanian sense, is thus foreclosed. The exhaustive promise of the list constitutes a kind of exhaustion of the virtuality of the real, sex, in the sense of exhausting the reservoir of fantasy that makes sex possible for speaking beings.

In some ways the listing is reminiscent of Sade, whose attempt to introduce the disorder of desire into a world dominated by order and classification resulted in an attempt to fit all the potentialities of desire "into an absolutely exhaustive combination of events" (Foucault, 1989: 81). Poised in the gap between Foucault's classical age and modernity, Sade sought to "insert into the combinations of representations the infinite power of desire" (82). But the possibilities introduced by information technology and network culture evoke a different "situation of force in which a finite number of components yields a practically unlimited diversity of combinations" (Deleuze, 1998: 131). Here, in the digital order of joy, it is precisely not a question of a quasitranscendent power of desire driving representation to breaking point, but of a different combinatorial that links what biology, economy, and language became in the second half of the twentieth century. Following the move of language into the pure space of literature, life broke free from the organ into molecular biology, and labor liberated itself into network culture with the aid of cybernetics and information technology (see Deleuze, 1988: 131). Like literature and life, labor becomes bound up in a process of an endless reflexivity and play (131). Rather than Foucault's Sade, therefore, the literary figure to be invoked in this specific instance is Deleuze's Samuel Beckett, who introduces the combinatorial as an "art or science of exhausting the possible through inclusive disjunctions" (Deleuze, 1998: 154).

To illustrate this, it is necessary to add another character to the series of exhausted beings named Murphy, Molloy, Malone, and the Unnameable. The following is the story of McCoy.

The space McCoy inhabits is not a remote Gothic castle or monastery, sealed off from all law and society, beyond hope of escape. McCoy simply sits in a room. It could be an office. It could be a study. It could be a bedroom. It could be a shed. It is any space whatever, so long at it is linked, wirelessly or not, to a universe of links. McCoy clicks on his mouse and a multitude of these links appear, each site being primarily another reservoir of lists. He begins to work through them, methodically, following certain chains of links, according to particular features. Each link is another hook in a chain of links, referring back and on to another without any governing principle other than exhaustion. Exhaustively, McCoy explores all the different combinations, as they continue to be promised and offered to him with each new list of links. Sometimes, when he lights upon a new and previously unnoticed combination, an intensity will build in McCoy, though nothing will be visible. McCoy does not appear to move. He sits immobile, looking at a screen. One finger twitching on his right hand is the only visible sign of movement.

McCoy turns back to previous lists, works through a new path, a new series of connections. Often this new path will return to a page of links that he has previously partially explored, and a new set of combinations can be worked through again. Like Molloy with his "sucking stones," McCoy likes to work through all the different permutations of the particular perversion he is exploring. Or like Murphy, and the five small biscuits that he would eat in a different order each day, McCoy long ago vanquished all order of preference, preferring the joy of seeking total permutability itself. An amnesiac witness, McCoy sits there for hour upon hour, usually eight hours, but sometimes more, exploring links and accumulating images. He long ago exceeded the library of 4,000 images that Gary Glitter had assembled during his six to twelve hour sessions searching the Web. Of course, Glitter was interested in one particular combinatory set related to child pornography. McCoy does not limit himself to that. That is just one combinatory that can be linked in a multitude of different ways to many other different series. Furthermore, McCoy barely looks at the images. As soon as they are accessed, he moves on. Many more images are accessed, yet ignored as unseen, as are downloaded. They may remain to be encountered again by some chance or they may simply disappear. Only the lists produce an affect in him, maintaining a level of intensity. Pauses, delays, variations in speed, pop ups all contribute to the modulation of affect, the plane of intensity. But surely, without any sense that this is his aim, McCoy is compiling an archive of many thousands of images and combinations to rival the great libraries of the world. But this is only a secondary effect of the joy produced by the network as it modulates McCoy's intensive space with its fluctuating, even unstable variations and temporary connections, immersing him in its multidimensional informational topologies.

Ostensibly, McCoy is accessing pornography, but it could be anything. McCoy's activity seems to bear little relation to jouissance, or not phallic jouissance. He's not coming toward something that culminates in a climax, an end or meaning. Indeed, he seems to have left the orbit of libidinal desire and its various forms of sublimation completely. Even though the information is pornography—and it is not clear that that category has any meaning anyway—it functions purely as information. And if information is a statistical measure of entropy, the drive that dissipates and exhausts itself, perhaps it is no doubt again the death drive rather than Eros that is operative.

There is a functional resemblance to the death drive insofar as a kind of larval subject is exhausted, dissipated, mortified by a symbol, or rather a symbolic system, that induces repetition, that mechanically drives it along a set of pregiven alternatives. But there is no resemblance to the way that the death drive, for Lacan, constitutes the negativity of a desire that is governed by a phallic signifier that marks the place of the *objet petit a*, around which the drive repeatedly circulates. Rather, the logic of the signifier is replaced by the domain of the list and the disjunctive series that are introduced by the multiple links in the network. Here, it is possible that, uncoupled from the phallus, a virtual object, or virtual objects, inhabit the automatism, as the principle of differentiation itself, and thus compel repetition as an integral effect of their operativity (see Deleuze, 1989: 105).

Again, this principle of differentiation is not one of opposition or oscillation between the here and there of boredom and novelty. McCoy is not bored and he never sees anything new. Indeed he barely sees anything at all, driven as he is to exhaustion in attempting to exhaust the apparent but never exhaustive list. For sure, boredom is coextensive with pornography. Indeed, the effect of the American pornography industry seems to have been to instigate a massive worldwide regime of 'boredom-therapy' (see Lotringer, 1988) that has sought to cure the world of sex, something that, in its Anglo-Saxon form, is consistent with its Puritan origins (see Hunt, 1993). But this pornography does not signify as such, does not operate as such, for McCoy. There is no sexual arousal, no penis (not) in sight.

Nor is it a death drive that supports the libidinal intensity of that doubled auto-affection and auto-negation that characterizes early video and computer games. Just as McCoy is not at work, although he could be, he's not at play either, although he could be. But just at the moment he is not suffering the overstimulation that also demands passivity bordering on inertia, which Virilio argues is manifested in the dual imperatives of the telerepetition and acceleration of so-called new media. It is perhaps closer to "the ebb and flow of anxiety and satisfaction" (Poole, 2004: 200) that characterize the tempo of video and computer games. But that tempo, that arrangement of acceleration and delay, while traversing the hollow of the larval subject, distributes joy and anxiety purely according to its own technological rhythm, and does not return it to a principle of pleasure. Rather, the principle of differentiation generates the beautitude, betrayed by McCoy, of the passive synthesis between the hollow of his subjective constitution and the rhythm of the network that makes any kind of pleasure principle operative and denotes the field of what lies beyond it. It establishes the plane of intensity in which affects and intensities are distributed.

Perhaps this structure of affect correlates to the modality of excess control that characterizes what Deleuze calls the control society. The interdependent relationship between excess and control has superseded law and transgression as the governing modality of technobureaucratic, consumer culture. Apparently affirming this and welcoming the possibilities of 'soft control,' Titziana Terranova concludes her book on network culture by advocating a politics that bypasses rational analysis and debate. Instead, it is essential to employ the modality of an informational politics that appeals directly to the masses through generating "affects—that is with intensities, variations of bodily powers that are expressed as fear and empathy, revulsion and attraction, sadness and joy" (Terranova, 2004: 156–157). The fact of fascism, of course, demonstrates what can be achieved from a timely recourse to reawakened affective forces. But that is not to suggest that forms of affect that differ from those could not be generated, and that an organized understanding of the movements in society, of attraction and repulsion, might present itself as a weapon. But it would seem important to question how effective such an understanding might be when these dualities, of fear and empathy, attraction and repulsion, take place within a field in which control and excess emerge together, each directly implying one another. Beyond useful, rational, or moral purpose, it is a field in which control is itself excessive, distending and decomposing the vehicles of its compulsive, exhausting joy. To discuss this field further requires addressing the intersection between war and commerce. This is the zone of joyful immanence that lies adjacent to the zone in which joy is distributed and controlled in the space of postphallic mediation.

Part Three

Joyful Immanence
(There is No Other)

CHAPTER FOUR

Order of Intimacy

To eat and be eaten—this is the operational model of bodies, the type of their mixture in depth, their action and passion, and the way in which they coexist with one another.

—Deleuze, *The Logic of Sense*

CINEMANTODEA

Birdsong.

The camera pans across a field of poppies and dissolves into an extreme close-up (CU) of a long green insect cleaning its jaws.

A male actor's voice narrates over the images.

> In the meadows of Southern France it's the female that is the deadlier of the species.

The camera continues to pan, in extreme close-up, among the poppies, and discovers two more specimens of Mantodea, coming in and out of focus, clinging on to the stalks of some long grass.

> The femme fatale in question is the European Praying Mantis.

CU a large female mantis. Below her, a smaller, male mantis approaches, gingerly climbing on to her large abdomen.

The narration continues.

The smaller male courts his partner carefully. She can literally make a meal out of any male.

Extreme CU of head and mouth of female mantis, her mandibula sharpening her jaws as if they were four steel tongues.

The birdsong is replaced by an electronic musical soundtrack of movie suspense.

Cut to smaller head of male mantis.

But he has to mate to pass on his genes.

Cut to CU of male abdomen attaching itself to the female abdomen. Medium shot of the mantises grappling on the single blade of grass. The female turns her head and gives the male her full attention.

In this gruesome embrace, her love bite is the last thing he knows.

Extreme CU of the female mantis biting into the large left compound eye of the male. Her jaws hollow out the eye, mouth parts burrowing further into his head.

But even this trauma doesn't seem to unnerve him. He continues to mate as though nothing has happened.

CU mating abdomens.

Losing his head over a female helps nourish his future offspring.

CU female mantis reducing the head of the male to a ruined stump.

Astonishingly, decapitation even improves his performance. A tiny brain in his rear keeps him active.

CU headless body of male mantis. CU head of female cleaning her jaws. CU the male abdomen finally de-coupling from the female and falling to the ground.

This bizarre coupling can last a day. Even then, the discarded carcass doesn't give up readily.

CU *decapitated corpse twitching in the dirt.*
(Downer, *Weird Nature*, 2002)

It is another nature program broadcast by the BBC, designed to educate and entertain the nature-loving British public. This time the program focuses on 'bizarre' sexual practices of animals that frequently involve the sacrifice of the organism in the transfer of genetic material. Male mice compelled to mate continually for days with as many female mice as possible before expiring exhausted, their deaths enabling more of their offspring to survive on the scarce resources, underwater 'sexual confusion and gender-bending' involving female fish who can apparently change sex at will. Curious, comical, often grotesque, the appeal of the examples lies not simply in their educational value, but in the way in which they pull at the edges of human fantasy.

Pride of place is a sequence that depicts the well-known practice of the European mantodea in which the female devours the head of the male during an act of amorous combat. While the sequence deploys the standard narrative technique of the nature documentary, there are also moments of cinematic excess drawn from the sex and horror genres. Close-ups of the ferocious face and devouring mouth of the female mantis are intercut with medium and close-up shots of contorted, mating bodies. The electronic musical soundtrack manages to evoke both the porn movie and the suspense film as it helps the sequence build to its grotesque climax. Further, the close-ups of the faces of the creatures are intercut in such a way as to encourage audience identification as the viewer is treated to the different points of view of the two protagonists. We see the female licking her lips as if she were about to bite into our head; we see the vulnerable, starstruck gaze of the male as if it were an image of our own cinematic wonder. In further close-ups we watch them in their deadly embrace, writhing in the long grass. The sequence ends with the comically abject spectacle of the abandoned torso twitching in the dirt, blindly trying to couple in its death throes with an imaginary mate.

Education, here, forgoes the neutrality proper to disinterested scientific inquiry and adopts the fully affective mode of cinematic sex-horror. We are treated to the televisual spectacle of a supreme example of the immanence of the animal world, its order of intimacy, in which the female mantis enjoys what Bataille calls the three luxuries of nature all at once: she fucks as she kills as she eats her prey. These luxuries are the pure modality of what Bataille, in *The Theory of Religion* (1992b), calls the order of intimacy. This order is a plane of immanence that is exemplified by the indistinction of 'the eater and the eaten'. There is no relation of difference or exteriority when one animal eats another because "there is no relation of *subordination* like that connecting an object, a thing, to man, who refuses to be viewed as a thing" (Bataille, 1992b: 18). The apprehension of this plane of immanence is an effect of its apparent alienation in 'man'. For Bataille, man supposes himself profoundly alienated from the intimate order because of the mastery and dependence established by language and technology. There is, however, Bataille surmises, a longing to reenter what is imagined as a state of unalienated animal immanence, a longing that is, he argues, the basis for all spirituality and religious feeling. This is to say that the violence of immanent animality provides a point of reference for the horror and ambivalence inspired by the truly divine. Both the autonomous world of immanence and the world of the spirit are effects of technology, however, in the form of tools, weapons, and symbols. The desire for, and fear of, the world of sacred intimacy is an effect of humanity's dependence on technological prostheses, a dependence that condemns humanity to "the absurdity of an endless deferral" and an abyssal subordination and alienation in the world of things. At the same time, precisely because technology is imagined to have taken away the world of nameless feeling, technology is therefore imbued with the memory of its loss, and perhaps the promise of its recovery.

One particular symptom of the desire for technology to deliver immanence, and its imagined joy, can be seen in some of the cultural fantasies that speculate on the ability of technology to simulate, or record and replay, the experience of an other life and death. For example, the technology that William Gibson calls, in his *Neuromancer* (1984) trilogy, simstim involves the technical means of simulating the stimulations experienced by an actual body sensorium. Simstim allows virtual access to the sensorium of another being, and the ability to experience another's existence in its own physical environment. In *Count Zero* (1987), Gibson writes about characters enjoying one of these simstim tapes that offers a new wildlife experience, a "jungle fuck tape [which] phased you in and out of these different kinds of animals, lotta crazed arboreal action up in the trees" (59). It is a movement forward from David Attenborough and *Weird Nature*, but a logical extension. In the novel, the jungle fuck tape is a hit, and it is clear that Gibson is suggesting that the development and enhancement of such experiences would follow the economic logic that currently drives film, fiction, and theme ride—the more thrilling, the more sensational, the better. But no doubt there could be niche markets: the chill-out zone that will enable one to become an albatross and glide across the ocean to the sound of Fleetwood Mac. Further, such simulations could have the benefit precisely of pitching self-consciousness to its impossible limit, breaking beyond self-consciousness into its prereflective animal substrate through the offices of a hyperreflexivity. The closest we ordinarily get to this, Bataille argues, is through the experiences of horror and eroticism excited by the apprehension of evil and in laughter and tears. These experiences break open the restricted economy of self-consciousness predicated on the distinction between subject and object, on to a general economy of convulsive continuity.

In a short essay entitled "Virtual Bataille," Michael Weinstein speculates, in a very similar way, on the "impetus to intimacy in contemporary technocorporate society" (Weinstein, 2001: 79). Weinstein imagines an intimacy machine to which one could attach oneself and

> be wrenched into pre-reflective consciousness by extreme sensations and perceptions; indeed, one might even be able to experience eating or being eaten by a live animal. All of this would be a riskless adventure, except (emotionally) for the duration of the experience, and it would be paid for as a service, firmly within the order of production. (Weinstein, 2001: 79)

Weinstein's point is that the order of intimacy could be simulated and accommodated within the order of things as a leisure activity. However, he argues that it "would have none of the disruptive effects on the reign of things that would follow from public orgies of consumption; everything in the productive order would be intact . . . [and] the provision of virtual intimacy would be yet another business" (79–80). Weinstein thus argues that technocorporate society sustains the restricted economy whereby a slavish population is rendered servile to the order of production through having their self-consciousness walled up in simulation—in teletechnologies, shopping malls, theme parks, gated communities, fantasy resorts, video games, and so on. Simulations of intimacy therefore support the restrictive order of production.

No doubt this is true, but more interesting than how the distinction between restricted and general is sustained by simulation is how it exacerbates the well-known paradoxes of this opposition. Even in Bataille, each economy seems to define and therefore support the other—and ultimately even dissolve it. What is interesting is how increasingly the order of production *itself* is being understood as if it were a virtual order of intimacy. As if, like Disneyland for Baudrillard, the main purpose of the intimacy machines, the malls, theme parks, and video games, were to hide the fact that the whole network economy is one big intimacy machine whose purpose is to simulate useless expenditure.

For Deleuze and Guattari, the construction of simulation machines and an 'intimacy business' would simply sustain the 'lack' of alienation that capitalism generates and exploits. An experience of immanence is merely promised in commodified form. But for Deleuze and Guattari, immanence is not hopelessly lost through alienation in language, or hypostatized in a signifier 'God', nor is it the phantasmatic effect of technology. Rather, immanence is a plane of consistency that is composed of interconnected machinic assemblages that are natural and artificial, organic and inorganic. "There is no biosphere or noosphere, but everywhere the same Mechanosphere," in which "all that consists is Real" (Deleuze and Guattari, 1988: 69). Moreover, the Mechanosphere is continually being created and recreated, the real produced anew.

Perhaps there is one particular machine that more than any other provides the interlocking assemblages with their consistency—a sound and vision machine. In the twentieth century, Deleuze contends, reality became cinematic. Cinema establishes new assemblages between moving images, the eye and the ear, the brain, perception and action that operate along the same plane of consistency. Cinema enters through the eye and invades the circuits of the brain, tracing them out and inventing new ones, producing different modes of perception. Deleuze insists that it is "the biology of the brain, microbiology" that provides a more appropriate discourse than psychoanalysis or linguistics for understanding how images interact with the brain since "cinema produces reality" (Deleuze, 1995: 58, 60). In its production of reality, cinema produces "a shock to thought, communicating vibrations to the cortex, touching the nervous and cerebral system directly" (Deleuze, 1989b: 170).

In particular, Deleuze regards the close-up as a primary means in which moving images impact on the brain and reorder perceptions through the affects it generates. In his taxonomy of cinema images in his book *The Movement-Image*, the close-up is regarded as the primary affection-image. Close-up images of the face take on a life of their own, affecting the brain of the viewer directly by means of the "feeling-thing," the entity (1986: 96). The entity, with its feelers, bores into the brain of the viewer, turning it into a 'center of indeterminacy' between perception and action, or action and reaction. It establishes a direct continuity between image and brain as it produces a new reality of pure affect (58). In his two books on the movement-image and the time-image, Deleuze argues that the reality created by the cinema is not experienced through language, and rendered sensible by a symbolic order, nor is it articulated along a chain of linguistic signifiers. Instead, cinematic vision machines construct an immanent plane of moving images, "an acentred set of variable elements which act and react on each other." What binds different centers of perception to particular series of movement-images, however, or to the Open totality to which any particular series is related, is that feeling-thing that occupies the gap between an action and a reaction. In the gap, the affection-image facilitates the movement (or not) between the perception-image and the action-image:

> There is an in-between. Affection is what occupies the interval, what occupies it without filling it in or filling it up. It surges in the centre of indetermination, that is to say in the subject, between a perception that is troubling and a hesitant action. It is a co-incidence of subject and object, or the way in which the subject perceives itself, or rather experiences itself or feels itself "from the inside." (Deleuze, 1986: 65)

The idea is not that through watching the images of two mantodea a horrified and fascinated audience identifies with and imaginarily becomes the creatures. Rather, a cinemantodea bores into our brains, into the center of indetermination that lies at the heart of our imaginary being, and establishes a direct continuity with it, reconstituting perception and action or reaction in a different order of experience that is continuous with the reality of the image. The cinemantodea, in the form of the entity, enters the gap that separates perception and action completely; perception and action become absorbed in the affection-image that results either in immobility (total absorption in the image) or pure violence (drawn from the affective power of the image) (Deleuze, 1986: 86).

The cinemantodea produces a 'spiritual automaton' and forces it to think. It acts on thought in two ways. First, "the shock has an effect on the spirit, it forces it to think and to think the Whole. This is the very definition of the sublime" (1989b: 158). The cinemantodea shocks as it enters the brain, forcing the automaton to think itself in relation to the totality that the image has established with it along a plane of consistency. The 'spirit' of the automaton is thereby produced as an effect of the momentary apprehension of thought thinking itself in relation to the immanent whole. Second, the cinemantodea gives rise to thought through advancing the powerlessness of thought, as the image bores into the brain through the eye. Citing Artaud, in contradistinction to Eisenstein, Deleuze suggests that "it is a matter, as Artaud puts it, 'of bringing cinema together with the innermost reality of the brain', but this innermost reality is not the Whole, but on the contrary a fissure, a crack" (1989b: 167). The cinemantodea hollows out the internal monologue that sustains a subjective consistency and replaces it with a "figure of nothingness," a "hole in appearances" (1989b: 167). The sensorimotor system is suspended, or disconnected with thought, as though the brain could see all the better for having the eye at the center of the action-perception image devoured. The action-image twitches blindly, automatically and pointlessly in the dirt, and thought is left to contemplate its powerlessness in relation to a monstrous, acentered, nonhuman perspective to which it is nothing more than a fissure and a sliver of thought.

For Deleuze and Guattari, a plane of immanence is established when two or more machinic assemblages conjoin together and establish a plane of consistency. It is the assumption of this section that supercapitalism has established a plane of consistency through the conjunction of war and commerce (for a discussion of supercapitalism, see Wilson, 2008). At the center of this correlation between war and commerce, the screen that provides its plane of technological consistency, is the cinema. As Paul Virilio and others have shown, the systematic use of cinema techniques from World War One laid the ground for a "logistics of military perception" that, after the second world war, gave rise to a "strategy of global vision" (Virilio, 1989: 1). If cinematic techniques provided the consistency in which perception and deception became the primary modality of war, the content of Hollywood cinema became a primary means of propaganda in which "a supply of images would become the equivalent of an ammunition supply" (Virilio, 1989: 1). The correlation between techniques of perception and projection, simulation, dissimulation, propaganda, and marketing has resulted in what James Der Derian calls the military-industrial-media-entertainment complex (1997: 212).

Just as Deleuze believes that microbiology lies at the heart of understanding the cinema, so the plane of consistency established by the conjoined assemblages of war and commercial machines is consistent with 'the biological turn' that seeks to understand social and economic processes through reference to microbiology and new theories of evolution. The joy or process of desire that articulates and supports this plane of consistency resides in the principle of inoperativity that connects martial, commercial, technological, and biological assemblages on a single plane of cinematic immanence. Supercapitalism has established a network ecosystem that is not a fragile and intricate harmony of interactive and interdependent forces, but a fierce bioeconomic battle order of shifting alliances, symbiotic coevolutionary strategies or synergies aimed at locking out and destroying other competitors. Corporate synergies or symbioses establish the relations favorable to a process of coevolution that is necessary for survival as part of a continuously adapting ecosystem. Different species of actors are produced in this environment whose form and function are determined by their conditions of competitive existence within the ecosystem established by the network. The primary modality of affect within the network is neither the pleasure of objects nor the enjoyment of the lack that they fail to fill. Rather, it is the asubjective joy of the cinemantodea that connects the brain to the network via the consumption of the image. The cinemantodea provides the image of joy that is the process of desire in pursuit of its principle. It establishes the plane of inoperative consistency that connects up the electronic ecosystem's plane of immanence. Cinemantodea: "to eat and be eaten—this is the operational model of bodies, the type of their mixture in depth, their action and passion, and the way in which they coexist with one another" (Deleuze, 1989a: 24).

ECO-NOMOS

When economists, political economists, and economic commentators have sought to ground their theories in the real they have turned since Hobbes to nature or more latterly to biology. In so doing, however, economic theory has itself informed ideas about nature, particularly evolutionary biology, which has adopted Hobbesian assumptions about human nature, as a war of all against all, as the basis of its understanding of a genetic predisposition toward selfishness and self-preservation. For sociobiologists, intellectual history starts with Hobbes and proceeds through Hume and Adam Smith to Malthus and Darwin: "the Hobbesian diagnosis still lies at the heart of both economics and modern evolutionary biology" (Ridley, 1997: 252). But the Hobbesian conception of the state of nature was always mythical. Hobbes himself did not think it necessary to regard it as an originary state. Rather, as Giorgio Agamben insists, the state of nature needs to be understood as "a principle internal to the State revealed in the moment in which the State is considered 'dissolved'" (Hobbes, De Cive: 79–78, cited in Agamben, 1998: 36). Further, this state of nature that is also a state of war bears no relation to actual war, as Foucault has persuasively argued. Indeed it is posited in an effort to foreclose war and deflect attention from the actual war and the real struggle that had gripped England since the Conquest in 1066. This actual war was reaching one of its crescendos, of course, in the English civil war during Hobbes's lifetime. Hobbes's political theory attempts to 'eliminate and render impossible' contemporary historical work that directly locates itself in the historical struggle informing the civil war. Hobbes wishes to prevent political use being made of this historical work, according to Foucault. "A certain historical knowledge pertaining to wars, invasions, pillage, dispossessions, confiscations, robbery, exaction, and the effects of all that, the effects of all these acts of war, all these feats of battle, and the real struggles that go on in the laws and institutions that apparently regulate power" (Foucault, 2003: 98),[1] was ignored by Hobbes and replaced by his mythical situation. Instead, if we are to consider a "state of bestial savagery in which living individuals devour one another" (Foucault, 2003: 92), then a totally different situation has to be considered of quantitative inequalities, different relations of force, domination, attraction, alliance, and control. For Agamben, however, this state is no longer mythical; it is the state that best describes the current 'state of exception.' Sovereign law has been suspended and replaced by a *nomos* in which law and violence become indistinguishable (Agamben, 1998: 31). Tracing the significance of these terms back to classical antiquity, Agamben locates a *nomos* before the law, before the *Dike* given to humanity by Zeus.

> To men Zeus gave this *nomos*: what is proper to the fish, the wild beasts, and the winged birds is to devour each other, since there is no *Dike* between them. But to men Zeus gave *Dike*, which is much better [*Dike* = justice]. (1998: 31)

This state of nature governed by a *nomos* in which living individuals devour each other describes the mode of existence of the state of exception where the *Dike* of state law has been suspended. The idea of man becoming animal again (or reduced to bare life) is a frequent figure in Agamben's work both in the sense of the *nomos* of pure violence and in the reduction of humanity to the *oikonomia* of consumption in the "society of the spectacle."[2] At the end of history, according to Alexandre Kojève, "Man remains alive as animal in *harmony* with Nature or Given Being" (cited in Agamben, 2004a: 6). However, Agamben regards Kojève's posthistorical contented resignation as wildly optimistic. Citing the Nazi concentration camps as his image of the *nomos* of contemporary biopolitics, Agamben recalls another voice from the 1930s College de Sociology in Paris, a nightmarish vision in which "men are transformed into a sort of 'conscious sheep resigned to the slaughterhouse'" (cited in Agamben, 2004a: 8). At the end of history, the state withers away to reveal not just the happy grazing lands of consumer society, but the fury of political violence unconstrained by the rule of international law. The *nomos* of the West, its means of securing and maintaining its economic domination, is leading "it towards the global civil war" (Agamben, 2004b). The state of nature that Hobbes evoked in order to 'eliminate and render impossible' historical work that located itself in the struggle that found violent expression in the English civil war, is here envisaged as the transitional state toward global civil war. Or to put it another way, in Hobbes, the state of nature provided the threat that justified and supported the sovereign's rule of law in the monopoly of violence as a way of occluding and precluding civil war. With Agamben, on the other hand, the state of exception provides the modality of global civil war in the preemptive strike.

Hobbes's state of nature has been traditionally used to justify and account for the *nomos* that articulates evolutionary biology and economy. However, the Hobbesian tradition in modern evolutionary biology places a narrow and, in Bataille's terms, highly restricted understanding of economic processes on evolutionary forces. Self-evidently sociopolitical and moral, this traditional understanding applies the principles, justification, and regulation of classical capitalism to an understanding of natural forces and 'man's' relationship to them in a move that attempts to confer natural and rational legitimacy to both. The way that questions of contemporary bioeconomic existence are posed and understood seems curiously stuck in a nineteenth-century (and before) understanding of economics as an instrument of rational and moral utility. Like a Dickensian housekeeper, evolution's profits are "thriftily husbanded" (Dennett, 1995: 20–21), and reinvested over and over. At the same time, however, this heroic husbandry occurs in the midst of prodigious waste, so that the latter provides the amoral backdrop to the virtuous (despite itself) struggle of genetic replication and survival.

But capitalism has changed and disengaged itself from the morality of utility and rational self-improvement, if it were ever informed by such an ethos. Capitalism has become both more warlike and extravagant. Its understanding has been transformed by the spectacle of the wanton consumption of an overproduced supply of goods whose utility can only be determined retrospectively, precisely according to their consumption. In this system, prodigious waste is the governing principle and (financial) survival is subject not to a process of adaptation that responds to change, but to constant, speculative innovation: to risk, chance, the preemptive strike, and unexpected move that creates a difference and therefore a profit. This economy is not predicated on a competition for scarce resources, but on superabundance. For George Gilder, who argues this case in *Wealth and Poverty* (1981), Adam Smith's vision of the invisible hand is deceptive and out of touch with economic reality. Indeed, he argues that Smith's idea of the primacy of "a rational calculation of personal gain" only leads to the tendency to avoid risk and seek security and ultimately an ever-largening welfare state, the "root of our crisis" (Gilder, 1981: 321), a crisis that will be met in the 1980s by the unregulated capitalism of Ronald Reagan and Margaret Thatcher.

The new biological turn taken by the new right economists in the 1990s privileges the chance mutation that produces a tiny but devastating advantage over other species, locking out the competition. Similarly, this economy is not predicated on a competition for scarce resources, but on a fecundity that both generates and is an effect of the 'superwinners' whose exponential growth (in population or wealth) creates and benefits from a "winner-takes-most environment" (Kelly, 1998: 27). As Jean-Joseph Goux argues in relation to Gilder, so Kelly reproduces the terms of Bataille's general economy in his celebration of the network economy driven by new technology. This economy is an effect of abundance rather than scarcity, risk rather than calculation, generosity rather than thriftiness, obsolescence rather than conservation, innovation rather than consolidation, turbulence rather than harmony. Above all, it is about waste rather than efficiency because waste is "the source of art, new models, new ideas, subcultures, and a lot more. In a network economy, innovations must first be seeded into the inefficiencies of gift economy to later sprout in efficiencies of the commerce" (Kelly, 1998: 151). As this last quote suggests, however, such innovative, wasteful generosity is speculative and supposed to serve the purpose of returning an efficient profit, but it is still a risk, and when it succeeds, the efficiencies gained by lockout can overrun any notion of efficiency understood on a human scale.

Growth that occurs on such a monumental scale is best understood in biological terms and in the study of populations. In his adumbration of the new laws of the new economy, Kelly invites us to "embrace the swarm" and become part of the hive mind that a networked economy produces. For Kelly, "the network economy is often described most accurately in biological terms" not just because economic actors are best viewed as insects, but because the economic growth generated by new technologies resembles biological growth. "Tamagotchis," Kelly writes, "could be actual breeding animals judging simply from their growth rate because their sales curve follows the population curve of reproducing animals: biology has taken root in technology" (1998: 32–33). Kelly's vivid and breathlessly enthusiastic style produces many criticisms, but the idea that biological and population models should replace economic models based on the rationally interested needs and desires of individual subjects is uncontroversial. "The science of multitudes has definitely given up on the individual, which it dismisses as an epiphenomenon that is simply too coarse and rigid to be more than a by-product of emergence" (Terranova, 2004: 123).

The restricted economy of evolutionary biology has become generalized in new economic theory, as it has in different ways in microbiology and the study of populations. The profusion and extravagance of nature, the billions of different species that have lived and died out is no longer seen as a process simply of rational calculation. The explosions of color in flowers and plumage, the endlessly varied patterns, the diversity and lushness of life are not regarded as a simple by-product of genetic 'selfishness'. As Gilder argues of Adam Smith, this sort of rational calculation ought logically to lead to a lack of genetic diversity, to stasis and ultimate sterility. Instead, perhaps life, its laws, evolution, and history is "the effect of a wild exuberance," as Bataille argues. Further, instead of an idea of growth or progression from simple or lower or more primitive life forms to more complex or higher or sophisticated forms, life is regarded as a general process of continual mutation and change. This mutation and change being the expression of expenditures of energy whose essential (though not sole) source is the prodigious gift of solar energy. As Bataille writes in "Consumption," the first volume of *The Accursed Share*:

> I insist on the fact that there is no growth but only a luxurious squandering of energy in every form! The history of life on earth is mainly the effect of a wild exuberance; the dominant event is the development of luxury, the production of increasingly burdensome forms of life. (Bataille, 1988: 33)

This is also the view of the zoologist Bruce Bagemihl who argues that "contrary to what we have all been taught in high school, reproduction is not the ultimate 'purpose' or inevitable outcome of biology. It is simply one consequence of a much larger pattern of energy 'expenditure', in which the overriding force is the need to use up excess" (Bagemihl, 1999: 255). Yet nonproductive amorous or erotic activity is ever present and a further expression of energy that produces bonds and alliances that cannot be the simple linear effect of the rational calculation of genetic reproduction. Bagemihl shows that reproductive sex is just one, almost marginal, activity compared with the range of nonreproductive sexual activity of animals (in human terms, homosexual, lesbian, masturbatory, and nonreproductive heterosexual activity).

The idea of the luxurious abundance of nature, this line of evolutionary thought that is more consistent with general rather than restricted economy actually accompanies the intellectual history of the West either at its margins or in negative form. It is not new. It informs the history marked by the names Hobbes, Smith, Malthus, and Darwin claimed by the sociobiologists, and provides the prodigiously wasteful, amoral backdrop against which the thrifty husbandry of nature is supposed to progress. Indeed, its imagining could also been seen as an effect of the historical struggle informing the English civil war. According to Darwin's *Autobiography*, the two books he always took with him on his travels around the Galapagos and elsewhere were Lyell's *Principles of Geology* and a collection of Milton's poems. As Gillian Beer writes, "Darwin walks the tropical forests with Milton." According to Beer, Milton's poetry supplied Darwin with an imaginative language in which to think about nature and the problems posed by its abundance that was understood as an effect of fecundity and reproductive excess. Thomas Malthus, famously, drew social analogies with the 'prodigal productivity of the earth' and warned of the perils of overpopulation, particularly among the poor. For Darwin, however, "fecundity was a liberating and creative principle" and, according to Beer, Darwin's reading of Milton, particularly the arguments of Milton's "voluptuary and bacchic villain" Comus, provided an important point of reference.

Among the tropical forests, Darwin's 'rich, even ecstatic' descriptions of natural profusion and diversity come "close to justifying Comus's earlier (and very anti-Malthusian) view of natural superabundance" (Beer, 1996: 34). Comus, son of Circe, is represented as a libertine aristocrat, drawn directly from the tradition of Jacobean drama, bent on the seduction of a virgin, the embodiment of Miltonic virtue and chastity. Like a good sociobiologist, he seeks his rationale in nature:

> Wherefore did Nature pour bounties forth
> With such a full and unwithdrawing hand,
> Covering the earth with odors, fruits and flocks,
> Thronging the seas with spawn innumerable,
> But all to please and sate the curious taste? (Milton, 1983:
>   Comus 710–714)

Just as his contemporary Hobbes sought to locate the state of nature in the aristocratic vices of pride and martial competition, so Milton also produces a negative, though much more seductive version of nature as a field filled with aristocratic vice and luxurious evil. Comus's arguments anticipate Bataille. Nature's abundance is not just spectacular, it is also burdensome and the problem posed by nature is not one of conservation but one of expenditure. Nature demands constant consumption she

> . . . would be quite surcharged with her own weight,
> And strangled with her waste fertility;
> Th'earth cumbered, and the winged air darkened with
>   plumes;
> The herds would over-multitude their lords. (728–731)

Aristocratic sovereignty is here defined purely in terms of the consumption of excess; similarly, for Bataille, it is in this respect that the lion can be located as one of nature's sovereigns: "its continual depredations of predators represent an immense squandering of energy" (1988: 34). Bataille argues that "life suffocates within limits that are too close" (30) and so consequently has to burst through those limits and spread as far as it can, occupying as much space as will sustain it. Life's energy expands and extends until it is expended in the three luxuries of nature: eating, death, and sex. None is strictly necessary if life is conceived purely in terms of utility and efficiency. Death is not necessary. The simplest life forms do not die, but persist, divide, or mutate. Indeed, Richard Dawkins's selfish gene argument depends on the long-term survival of genetic material in contradistinction to the individual animals, the 'great lumbering robots' that it squanders with such abandon as soon as it has replicated itself. But even here, Dawkins seems to acknowledge that the gene is in fact a function of death rather than life, suggesting that genetic selfishness tends to lead to species extinction rather than survival. "How ever many ways there may be of being alive, it is certain that there are vastly more ways of being dead" (Dawkins, 1986: 9), and "99% of all species that have ever lived are extinct" (*Observer* 21.5.00: 21). As Bruce Bagemihl suggests, life seems to elevate death to lavish proportions, reaching a profusion of its own. Life serves death, feeding its insatiable, all-consuming appetite. Bagemihl himself uses the example of "hundreds of baby turtles, after hours of struggling to break through their eggshells, finally reach the sea, only to be picked off by the waiting jaws and beaks of predators" (1999: 254).

Eating, the consumption of one organism by another is also not necessary. Biologists would acknowledge with Bataille that one of the most efficient ways for life to sustain itself is to manufacture its own food by way of photosynthesis. Vegetation more quickly occupies the available space through this method of sustenance than do flesh-eating or plant-eating animals. "Much more energy is 'squandered' when one animal consumes another or consumes plant material" (Bagemihl, 254). Similarly, sex is not necessary. Sex, even when dedicated to reproduction, is 'costly, draining, dangerous' and wasteful. Indeed, the development of sexual reproduction is considered "the queen of evolutionary problems" (Ridley, 1993: 27) because it is generally acknowledged to be more than twice as expensive as asexual reproduction. It should, therefore, according to standard Darwinian logic, have disappeared altogether. The paradox has led biologists to the surprising conclusion that "sex is not about reproduction" (Ridley, 1993: 27).

ECOSYSTEM

The text from the mantodea sequence of *Weird Nature* is taken almost word-for-word from the beginning of one of the most influential bioeconomic texts of the latter part of the twentieth century, Richard Dawkins's *The Selfish Gene* (1989). Here the field of genetics provides another phantasmatic plane of immanence, composed of the amorous combat of selfish genes programmed to replicate at any cost to their organic vehicles.

Dawkins's example of the mating mantises is entertaining not just because it repeats the literary-cultural trope of the vulnerability of males to the sexually voracious female, it also introduces another element that adds comic bathos. The 'dumber' the male mantis becomes, in his communication with the female, the more joy he gets—and gives. Through consuming his head, the female succeeds in "improving the male's sexual performance." It is unusual to hear of an insect—or indeed any animal—being concerned about sexual performance. No doubt by performance Dawkins means enhancing economic efficiency rather than pleasure, but it is an arresting idea that cannot but be invoked by the language that he chooses. The issue is complicated because Dawkins suggests that the enhanced sexual performance is an added benefit, the primary one being that the female mantis gets a good meal. However, from the point of view of the replicating genes, the primary concern is that she conceive, so perhaps Dawkins *is*, in speaking of an added benefit, referring to enhanced sexual pleasure. The consumption of the 'inhibitory nerve centers' in the head, there presumably to prevent the male mantises being eaten by a predator before he has the opportunity to mate, releases the body to do its work. The male mantis gives himself up utterly if not to his own pleasure, then at least to the female whom he provides with added nourishment, which Dawkins supposes has the further benefit of nourishing the potential child. In this way, the example is instructive: the male mantis performs his evolutionary function with admirable efficiency in a process that is one of pure expenditure. The instructive black comedy of this example works because it seems to replicate recognizable fantasy versions of male and female behavior in a macabre fashion even as it illustrates the disjunction between knowledge and ecstasy, consciousness and orgasm, or at least from the position of the male. The individual mantis gives up his existence as a discrete, discontinuous being for a state of violent, convulsive continuity with another being, if one can think of mantises as discontinuous beings. For Bataille, this state of discontinuity is marked in humans by self-consciousness and the knowledge of death that gives a stark intensity to an individual life that must inevitably perish. But, as we have seen, though we know ourselves only as discontinuous beings, Bataille suggests that we "yearn for our lost continuity" (Bataille, 1986: 15). Correlative to the 'tormenting desire' that an evanescent life should continue, there stands an underlying "obsession with a primal continuity linking us with everything that is" (15). The incomprehensible yet tangible nostalgia for lost continuity "is responsible for the three forms of eroticism in man." The three types of eroticism, physical, emotional, and religious, are all concerned "to substitute for the individual isolated discontinuity a feeling of profound continuity" (15). Eroticism is a psychological quest for an intense consummating joy in the face, and in the midst, of death, in ecstatic continuity with God or with another being. For the male reader of Dawkins's text, then, the male mantis acts out this fantasy very nicely. For Bataille, this primal continuity is characterized by the expenditure, violence, dissolution, destruction, and waste of the general economy. But, of course, the genetic code is still transmitted in so far as it has been a successful copulation; information is exchanged, and maintained, in the midst of the erotic luxury of consumption and death. With the example of the female mantis, however, this anecdote describes a different form of excessive consumption, one that occurs at both ends, as it were, evidence of an unrestricted appetite that knows no bounds or limitation, and that goes on and on absorbing and consuming. Enjoying all three luxuries of nature at once, she is encoded for the simultaneous production and consumption of more—more mantises in this case.

Dawkins's book was a best seller, as have been many of the others that followed it like *The Blind Watchmaker* and *River Out of Eden*. This economic success is as much an effect of literary style as it is of the information that it contains. Dawkins's literary success is an effect of "economimesis—where *mimesis* is not so much the representation of one thing by another, but the imitation of a mode of production, a practice" (see Derrida, 1998: 272). Dawkins's mimetic production (and its 'memetic' success) imitates the natural processes he describes insofar as genetic transfer takes place in the context of violent, poetic expenditure. In Dawkins's style, econopoietic efficiency requires that sense or meaning operates only insofar as it produces the friction of an erotic response that precipitates consumption. The figure of the female mantis embodies a principle of excessive expenditure that is nevertheless designed to facilitate the production and reproduction of more things, objects, images, commodities, popular science books, nature programs. In this way, the meme of the selfish gene reproduces itself through the production of fantasy that supports the anxiety of discontinuity represented by death and the human-animal divide. It erotically animates the spirit of the automata, confronting it with the horror of its own redundancy in the face of implacable genetic determination and death.

While the success of such popular science writing precisely depends on both the depiction and the operation of these kinds of bioeconomic laws, they conventionally carry a pious disavowal. Even as the so-called selfish, amoral, mindless, violent yet biologically determining nature of genetics is lovingly explicated, the would-be social biologist withdraws his or her approval. "I am not advocating a morality based on evolution" writes Dawkins, at the beginning of his book (1989: 2). Why not? It is tempting to echo Bataille's provocative statement, in relation to Sade, that "without a profound complicity with natural forces such as violent death, gushing blood, sudden catastrophes and horrible cries of pain" there could be no wealth of creation. Just as, "without a sadistic under-standing of an incontestably thundering and torrential nature," there could be no full understanding and celebration of life on earth. Why not affirm the laws of nature that you discover, why seek to negate them in the *ressentiment* of "a revolting utopian sentimentality" (Bataille, 1997: 157). Or indeed, why introduce and continually provoke a moral dimen-sion through the use of terms like "selfishness" and "altruism" if it is not relevant?

Tiziana Terranova rejects Dawkins's Protestant-capitalist moraliza-tion, and its left-liberal apology, and suggests that it belongs to a very dif-ferent plane of organization to that of genetic coding. Terranova works in the Italian Marxist tradition, but has similar enthusiasms to the new right bioeconomists. For her, the effect of the phrase "selfish gene" is to indi-viduate a unit of code that is nothing but a genetic algorithm and return it to a discourse of subjectification so that it can be attributed with 'self-ish' motives or 'altruistic' tendencies in its calculations to compete or col-laborate. "If the gene is a unit of code that makes evolution a computing machine, the selfish gene is the subjectifying function that turns a multi-tude into an assemblage of isolated individuals" (Terranova, 2004: 126). Terranova notes the importance of Dawkins's model of the gene as a unit endowed with the capacity to replicate and to mutate, particularly in computational simulations of biological processes and evolution. How-ever, she prefers to regard it as the principle of dynamic mobility imma-nent to "the polymorphous and yet nondeterministic mutations of a multitude" (2004: 124). Selfish or not, Dawkins's gene still operates as the immanent principle of social, economic, and political life in a "natu-ralisation of social relations" (129). It operates there as the means through which biological computing enables the emergence and control of network societies. Terranova argues that all forms of critical inquiry and conceptual engagement must accept that this "game of power is the only game in town in as much as it identifies and enacts an *indetermina-tion* of the social and the natural across a microphysical continuum that denies the human the ontological status of an exception" (129). As the immanent principle of this game of power, genetic econommimesis deter-mines which forms of life emerge and survive or die.

The big difference between the naturalist claims of the classical and new economists, then, is that for the latter biology does not just best describe the natural laws of economy, but actually *constitutes* the *nomos* of an information ecosystem and what it will become. The emergence of biological computation models, along with network culture, is producing a hybrid form of bioeconomics that is more speculative. This is bionomics that, in contradistinction to both classical economics and natural history, sees the economy as "a self-organizing 'chaotic' information ecosystem" (The Bionomics Institute. www.bionomics.org/text/insttute/sop.html cited in Terranova, 2004: 119). The term "bionomics" first appears in a book by Michael Rothschild (1995) where in his description of the economic ecosystem he draws a detailed analogy between biology and economics, though the biology he cites is actually a lot more traditional, in terms of classical utility, than the Web site blurb of the Bionomic Institute. Further, Rothschild clearly states that he is drawing an analogy between biological and economic processes, not a homology of the kind sociobiologists draw. Rothschild rejects the sociobiological model of Edward O. Wilson, for example, who regards human society and behavior as directly descended from, and determined by, prehuman ancestry and genetic precultural predispositions. On the contrary, Rothschild regards the 'biologic' success of the human species as a result of its definite break with instinctive behavior, being the effect of advances in technical knowledge. Human culture, if not the human phenotype itself, extends beyond the limits of its organic body; it is as much the creature of its technical prostheses as it is of its genes. As Rothschild writes,

> technical information—the distilled knowledge of all past generations—is recorded in documents and databases, not in DNA. Since our technical information is isolated physically from the genetic information in our cells, these two realms are best understood as entirely separate, parallel domains. Each realm of information is alive and evolves independently. (Rothschild, 1995: 348)

Human life, both organic and inorganic, is stretched over two different modalities of evolution that coevolve along the same plane of immanence. However, this process of coevolution still has far to go. Speculating on the future of network culture in the 1990s, Kevin Kelly argues that classical economy is stuck in a very early evolutionary stage that consists of discrete blobs of primitive cellular life. "Our industrial age has required each customer or company to physically touch one another. Our firms and organizations resemble blobs. Now, by the enabling invention of silicon and glass neurones, a million new forms are possible" (Kelly, 1998: 6). Now that these neurones enable individual cells to communicate with each other over a distance, Kelly argues, "we are about to witness an explosion of entities built on relationships and technology that will rival the early days of life on earth" (Kelly, 1998: 6).

In an essay on the metaphysics of the gene, Howard Caygill argues that the correlation between information and cellular life in the gene participates in a metaphysical opposition. Couched in the gene is an opposition between "an intelligible unit of 'information'—part of a digitalization of Platonism inaugurated by Leibniz—and a part of physical nature subject to chance and natural selection" (Caygill, 1996). This 'instability within the gene' contributes to the anxiety that the totality of the human genome, rendered intelligible in the form of digital information, will become subject to manipulation and the abolition of chance. Or indeed, generates the fear and fantasy of the revenge of chance and the unforeseen consequences of genetic interventions in some future test of natural selection. Popular science meets this metaphysical uncertainty with a faith in science that replaces belief in God. Following Nietzsche, Caygill argues that the ultimate consequence of this faith in science is not only a "hostility to life" but also a "concealed will to death" (1996). The piety of popular science, Caygill argues, is similar to that of a slave-revolt against "an Epicurean imperial aristocracy." Caygill argues that "faith in science looks to science not only for guidance as to who is to be saved and who is to be damned in the next world, but also this world" (1996). The popular science of Dawkins and Terranova is no less bound up in the same metaphysical opposition in its faith in the biological turn. "What gives the biological turn its mystical tone," she writes, is the existence of an 'abstract machine' that can "facilitate, contain and exploit the creative powers of a multitude (human and inhuman)" (Terranova, 2004: 118). The element of unpredictability associated with the multitude enables it to partly escape "the constraints of sequential programming, almost at the same time as it is recoded, brought back into the fold by selection in the form of fitness functions" (2004: 118).

What determines "fitness" in the context of the information ecosystem is profitability in the commercial bio-war of network survival. Commercial success is metaphysically affirmed as an effect of the 'creativity' of the life of the multitude, even as it is proved retrospectively by the economic performance that demonstrates its fitness functions. Unprofitability, or the failure of information to affect, generate feedback, and replicate in the network means that this form of life will be 'selected' out of existence.

The establishment of an information ecosystem that enfolds the globe as the atmosphere in which different forms of anorganic life emerge and disappear, raises the question and offers the fantasy of its domination and control. Unsurprisingly, the military promise of the network is not just global vision but total spectrum dominance. This state of ubiquity would enable the U.S. military to perceive what it likes and to command and control the totality of its field of operations through the ability to act and react in real time. Total digitalization destroys the necessity of mediation, difference, and deferral; the hyperspeed it enables opens up the prospect of the U.S. military becoming, like a bioeconomic corporation, a networked global organism acting and reacting in real time. "With few exceptions," writes Kelly, "nature reacts in real time. Swarms need real-time communication. If you are not in real time, you're dead" (Kelly, 1998: 21).

CHAPTER FIVE

Return to Zero

It is not that there is merely a desire for war . . . rather . . . war in its intensive state is desire itself, convulsive recurrence, unilateral zero.

—Nick Land, *Thirst for Annihilation*

THE SCREEN IS A BRAIN

A tracking shot. A micro-endoscope camera retracts at slo-mo hyperspeed from deep within a CGI simulation of the brain. The images unfold to high-octane synthesized rock, as if the head was pounding with blood at a super-rapid pulse rate. Between a labyrinthine network of neural fibers, the camera arcs through a cavernous cranium. Molecular objects fly past, eerily magnified in an inner space as capacious as the cosmos, as credits emerge and dissolve in a sequence familiar from Hollywood sci-fi movies. Past clusters of cells amassed along the brain's gray corridors, the camera plunges through the lining of the skull, emerging from a tiny aperture, a pore in the scalp, past hair follicles and sweat. It runs down the skin and up the rough metal grooves of a barrel of a gun. As the camera retreats back and comes to a halt at human scale we see a close-up of the wide-eyed, terrified gaze of a man, the owner of the brain we have just vacated. The gun is stuffed into his mouth. A finger is on the trigger and the hammer is cocked. The camera cuts to a side view of the hand holding the gun in the mouth. Off screen a voice: "This is it. Three minutes. Ground zero" (Fincher, 1999). The brain-screen is about to be blown to pieces, shattered in a cinematic schizo-suicide, at the very moment when the controlled demolition of a dozen high-rise corporate buildings, home of the major banks and credit card companies of America, is planned to occur. The multiple points of light from the office windows glitter in the night sky behind the condemned man.

Only retrospectively, after the microscopic camera has emerged through the scalp, is the credit sequence comprehensible as a journey through the interior of the skull. The camera's journey pierces the membrane that connects the inside with the outside, retreating from the "psychology of depths" through the "cosmology of galaxies, the future, evolution" (Deleuze, 1989b: 206). This hypermagnified environment could have been anywhere, the alien landscape of inner or outer space. Rapidly, the camera withdraws from the deep interior of the brain, as if an expedition to locate the mind, or the soul, had only encountered the horror of a measureless, fractal void. In a literal simulation of Deleuzian cinematic affect, the motorized lens and automatic image have sought to produce a "shock to thought, communicating vibrations to the cortex, touching the nervous and cerebral system directly" (Deleuze, 1989b: 156). But the mechanical eye of the camera has plunged into the brain, to pour its light into the heart of subjective being, only to recoil and flee from some obscure terror haunting the bony cavern. There is no interior secret, no nocturnal world of the psyche, there is nothing but a gap, an interval, a zero. The CGI simulation constructs the brain simply as a void in which a network of neurofibers and microfissures criss-cross. It is a quasiscientific modeling of the brain in which we discover not a subject, a homunculus or command and control center, but a "probabilistic or semi-fortuitous cerebral space," a system that is as uncertain as it is acentered (1989b: 211). The shock with which we belatedly discover that this alien landscape is in fact our brain illustrates how, as Deleuze suggests, "our lived relationship with the brain becomes increasingly fragile, less and less 'Euclidean' and goes through little cerebral deaths. The brain becomes our problem or our illness, our passion, rather than our mastery, our solution or decision" (1989b: 212).

As the camera emerges from this brain and refocuses on a human scale, the image resolves itself as the point of view of Brad Pitt, or Tyler Durden, the character who is eventually disclosed as the action-hero alter ego of the main character played by Ed Norton in David Fincher's movie *Fight Club* (1999). An emanation from a schizoid brain, the movement is cinematically nevertheless from the unfamiliar to the familiar. A simulation of the cinematic probing of the material image of thought embedding itself into the brain recedes to the promise of a Hollywood movie of commercialized 'sex and blood' in which shock is confused "with the figurative violence of the represented" (Deleuze, 1989b: 157). Yet, as becomes clear, Pitt's hero of the sensorimotor system is merely a schizophrenic effect of a sick cinematic brain, flickering into life from a series of subliminal images to a fully psychotic action-image. The nerve-wave flows of the brain do not connect up the motor-sensory system but flow out of the brain so that action images substitute for thoughts. These action-images clash with the internal monologue that strives to make sense of the action, but fails to keep up. The film does not take place in a realist Hollywood milieu, but in a noosphere in which inside and outside, past and future, activity and passivity, paranoia and schizophrenia, capitalism and anticapitalism, revolution and fascism, circulate in an uncertain and acentered cerebral space.

Fight Club (1999) is an adaptation of a novel by Chuck Palahniuk (1997), but it is also, in its analysis of the relationship between paranoia, schizophrenia, capitalism, and microfascism, a critical essay on Deleuze and Guattari's *Anti-Oedipus*. While the convergence of themes between *Fight Club* and the first volume of *Capitalism and Schizophrenia* has been noted before (see Diken and Lausten, 2002), it has not so far been noticed that the film is also a parody of Deleuze's two cinema books, although the chronology is reversed. In Deleuze's books 'classic' cinema is characterized by the dominance of the movement-image that gives way, after World War Two, to a modern cinema in which the time-image predominates. In *Fight Club*, on the other hand, the movement-image emerges as a fascistic figment of the time-image's alienation and psychosis. As such, the parody could be said to be postmodern, in these strictly localized terms, since Deleuze's hierarchy is reversed even as the classical and the modern become the destiny of each other. The nameless character played by Ed Norton betrays all the characteristics of Deleuze's numb and dislocated bearer of the time-image. Unable to act, sunk in a catatonic insomnia, Norton can only approximate affect through seeking out the unbearable in the presence of the terminally ill. He attempts to simulate and feel the despairing joy before death expressed by the members of various therapy groups in passionate hugs. He is a tourist, like his future girlfriend Marla Singer, and consequently someone who *sees* rather than feels or acts. He sees sickness, suffering, and death—his job as an insurance representative is to examine fatal crash sites—but all he sees is a world of simulacra Xeroxed into infinity. "Everything is a copy of a copy of a copy." As Deleuze writes of the exemplary characters, often mentally disturbed, of the new postwar cinema of the time-image: "a female tourist struck to the core by the simple unfolding of images or visual clichés in which she discovers something unbearable, beyond the limit of what she can personally bear. This is a cinema of the seer and no longer of the agent [*de voyant, non plus d'actant*]" (Deleuze 1989b: 2).

At the same time, the existential dislocation and despair of the main character are knowingly and ironically presented. Directly following the opening scene, the first flashback cuts to Norton's head wedged between the 'bitch tits' of big Bob, suffering from testicular cancer, and played by Meat Loaf. The juxtaposition between the banal and the unbearable, between Ikea catalogues and the sexuality of the walking dead, is played out as black comedy. Norton's interior monologue appears to hold the narration and the continuity of time together as a series of movement-images that sustain a sense of empirical reality. Further, his ironic commentary maintains the audience in a position of security with regard to the apparent self-knowledge of the narrative. However, this structure is seriously undermined. With the emergence of Tyler Durden, as parodic a bearer of the movement-image as Norton's character is of the time-image, the narration becomes more and more perplexed and disclosed as always unreliable. It fails hopelessly to keep up with the action driven by Durden who rapidly outstrips the limits of both knowledge and perception, disappearing from the movie altogether for large sections. Further, far from the movie being a faithful representation of empirical reality, it eventually becomes apparent that we have been presented with a purely interior world of schizophrenia. Although this is an interior world that is also fully exteriorized, in which imaginary and real worlds become indiscernible.

For Deleuze, it is only the imaginary and the real that is at stake in the cinema because cinematic affects and thought processes occur below the threshold of the symbolic order. Deleuze's cinema is radically nonlinguistic, even though it is a semiotics. This semiotic is, however, presymbolic in the sense that "narration is only a consequence of the visible [*apparent*] images themselves and their direct combinations—it is never a given" (1989b: 26). In classical cinema, narration is an effect of the combination of movement-images according to the laws of a sensory-motor schema. Narration is an effect of a cinematic vision machine that produces 'spiritual automata'. Modern forms of narration, meanwhile, are an effect of the time-image, which actually undermines classical narrative through the images' powers of virtuality. Never an evident given of images, narration "is a consequence of the visible [*apparent*] images themselves" (1989b: 27). Both thematically and cinematically *Fight Club* constructs a mental territory in which the signifier as an organizing principle is suspended or impeached. The absence of the paternal figure is of course a constant refrain in the movie, but crucially the movie has no central point of perception or narrative unity. There is no subject of the brain, or of thought and action, but a crystallization of actual and virtual images in which there is a perpetual exchange between real and imaginary to the point where they become indiscernible (1989b: 273–274) in a general schizophrenia of myriad reflections. Rather than a center that perceives time unfolding as a succession of presents, there are multiple divisions in which there is a "strict contemporaneity of the present with the past," that is of the present that is passing and the past that is preserved (274). The time-image is this crystallization of images that realizes "the powers of the false," that goes "beyond all psychology . . . and all physics of action," to subject all formal models of truth to the radical becoming of time (Deleuze, 1989b: 274; 1995: 66).

It is in the sense of the time-image as time-as-duration that the cinema signifies invention, the "continuous elaboration of the absolutely new," new forms in the context of a general chaos (Canning, 2000: 337). This is why the cinema is exemplary as a plane of immanence in which "the world 'becomes its own image,' becomes uncanny to itself, mechanically conscious of itself" in an image of its own thought (Canning, 2000: 337). The cinema provides a machinic image of thought, of thought operating within machinic assemblages that constitute the plane of immanence. Cinematic thought, as a plane of immanence, assembles "cosmos out of chaos" in a cinematic cosmology that is also a generalized uncanny or schizophrenia in which imaginary and real become each other's simulacra in the generation of the new.

EROS IS SICK

The obvious retrospective appeal of *Fight Club* precisely concerns the uncanny way in which the world appears to "become its own image." This image is that of a deranged self-enamoration. An American narcissism violently sick of itself vomits out its own image endlessly in the form of commodities, assembling a commercial universe of the same.

The action of the movie unfolds in flashback during the long duration of the three minutes that are supposed to elapse between Tyler's annunciation of the coming of ground zero and the final shot of Jack and Marla romantically holding hands as they watch the towers collapse. This scene, in which the schizo-romance between Jack and Tyler appears to resolve itself into the redemptive familiarity of the heterosexual couple, frames the beginning and end of the movie. But since the towers collapse to the dulcet tones of the Pixies singing "Where Is My Mind?," this necessarily raises questions about the reliability of the scenes that conclude the movie. The referential reliability of the movie has of course been put under severe strain throughout its length since it concerns the fractured subjectivity of a schizophrenic. Nevertheless, since the end concerns the spectacular collapse of high-rise office buildings as a result of action by a self-destructive terrorist organization waging war against capitalism, just two years before the attack on the World Trade Center, it makes claims for the reality of the movie's schizoid unconscious if not desire. But while there is a certain pleasure in the anticipation of the prophetic return of the cinematic double in the realm of unconscious reality, strangely there is little sense of shock. The uncanny does not produce a frisson of horror even though it certainly provided a harbinger of death.

The lack of shock perhaps points to the peculiarity of an order of generalized uncanny in which no one is at home, even as everything is familiar in a corporate world of globalized simulacra. The logic of the double has given over to the global multiplicity of the same. In its uncanny prescience of the collapse of the twin towers of the World Trade Center, *Fight Club* is banal. It is no different from a multitude of Hollywood disaster movies (*Independence Day, Deep Impact, Meteor*) that sought to elicit a frisson of horror-pleasure at the imminent prospect of the end of humanity and 'our' way of life. There are countless movies that profitably exploit the thrill of imaginary annihilation in a return to zero. As if feeding off the discontent that is, for Freud, the inherent condition of civilization, these movies all, to a greater or lesser extent, furnish an unavowed yet general desire for the destruction of the West with jubilant images of exploding totemic U.S. buildings and ruined American cities. This affirmation of destruction is a commercialization of the thirst for annihilation. Here, affirmation takes the form of a commercial exchange that will both avow, in the most thrilling terms, as it visualizes, with all its powers of technological realism, the "joy of annihilation," the "*affirmation* of annihilation and destruction" (Deleuze, 1983: 174).

In its account of the destruction of the twin towers, Baudrillard's essay, "The Spirit of Terrorism" (2002), simply describes and restates *Fight Club* insofar as the event is inexorably a movie event. This is the case even though Baudrillard studiously avoids reading the event as a movie, as a simulacrum. On the contrary, he suggests that it constitutes a real event, "the 'mother' of events," in fact, that rebirths the historical existence of the West in the form of a fourth world war (Baudrillard, 2002: 4). Mother of creation, historical life, and destruction all at the same time. And yet, by accident or design, the directors of the act, no doubt aware of the omniscient eye of the televisual gaze, timed the attacks perfectly as if it were the action of a long take, ready to be reedited for another disaster movie. Insofar as the action was undertaken for the cameras, it was unquestionably a movie event. And of course the action was captured on camera from every conceivable angle; the cinematic-machine of the American media clicked into gear and, immediately and automatically, maximized the levels of surprise, suspense, and climax so that they could be conveyed and endlessly replayed across the globe. There is no contradiction, here, between a real event and an imaginary movie event.

For Baudrillard, the disaster movies attempt to 'exorcise' and 'submerge', through the pyrotechnics of their special effects, the reality of the desire for annihilation. In fairly conventional psychoanalytic terms, these movies sublimate a death drive that exults the sublimity of the West's goodness in the form of a precious fragility that is established in its phantasmatic rape and destruction by an alien or inhuman power. But there is no alien or inhuman power. There is only the power of globalization itself, and the event of September 11, 2001, is simply evidence of "globalization fighting with itself" through the dual spectra of America and Islamic *jihad*. The double is the bulwark of an inexorable sameness that breaks up and reassembles itself on the foam of ground zero: the singularity of suicide-death that sustains both the power and the 'immense fragility' of the nihilistic system of 'zero death' (Baudrillard, 2002: 16).

At the same time, as every Western political and military analyst seems to insist, America's terroristic enemy cannot be destroyed, cannot be reduced to zero. There will always be a remainder that will generate even more, an excess virulent negativity that it will continually deploy in its drive to zero. For each terrorist who is killed, imprisoned, or cast away, even more will return, demanding further suspension of democratic laws and civil liberties. They lie at the end of invisible lines bound up in an indestructible network of interconnections disappearing and reappearing like a phantasmatic double multiplied exponentially into a rhizomatic swarm of incorporate terror. The lines proliferate, return to the United States, Britain, Europe, in innumerable threatening returns, an imaginary and real antagonism that is everywhere and in each of us. The relationship between ego and alter ego becomes impossible to maintain, even as the alter-ego takes on the glamorous face of an ascetic millionaire, media-friendly, with an animatronic indestructible life of its own. Networked terror: globalization's schizophrenic means of precluding, even as it ushers in, its disappearance and reappearance in and as the indeterminate mass of the multitude. It is of course a process dramatized by *Fight Club*, a process in which Lacan flows into Deleuze and Guattari.

For Lacan, the relationship between the subject and the signifier, ego and alter ego eternalizes desire in relation to death. It is the signifier that drives desire on a certain path toward death, not some inherent biological death instinct. When, in the main part of *Beyond the Pleasure Principle*, Freud speculates on the existence of the latter, Lacan argues that Freud substitutes a subject for nature and in so doing "evokes there his sublimation concerning the death instinct insofar as that sublimation is essentially creationist" (Lacan, 1992: 213). Which is to say that it evokes a desire to begin again—to cast away the world, nature, and all its works so that it can return again but this time differently, created anew from zero (1992: 212–213).

"This was the goal of Project Mayhem, Tyler said, the complete and right-away destruction of civilization" (Palahniuk, 1997: 125). "Only after disaster can we be resurrected," says the novel's narrator (Palahniuk, 1997: 70). *Fight Club*, of course, takes its bearings from the distinctions drawn out by *Beyond the Pleasure Principle*. The somatic pleasures of consumer society are rejected for the exhilarating joy of the fight and the destructive expenditure of continual loss. "It's only after you've lost everything . . . that you're free to do anything," repeats Tyler (70). The principle is extended to American society in general as Project Mayhem replaces the fight club as the means to reach the zero of redemption. "The plan is to blow up the Headquarters of credit card companies and the TWR building . . . If you erase the debt record then we all go back to zero. To create total chaos." But, as Lacan suggests, the desire to return to zero is a creationist sublimation. But this form of sublimation has become variously incorporated into the logic of capitalism, as another speculative leap, in an aestheticization of the death drive. But such an aestheticization is precisely not a representation, but a presentation on ground zero, a creation of the new predicated on the generation of heterogeneous chaos. Such an aestheticization implies a corporate fascism without nationalistic reserve. Paranoiac fascism mutates into schizophrenic fascism.

The lead character of *Fight Club* splits into Jack and Tyler on board a passenger airliner just at the point where the movie simulates its plunging crash and the destruction of all the passengers. Tyler suddenly appears as the glamorous, indestructible figure of destruction. Tyler's appearance follows a period in the narrator's life when he has only been able to affirm his existence through identifying with the pain and imminent death of others congregated at a series of support groups for people suffering terminal illnesses. Here, the other's pain underlines the simultaneously human and inhuman dimension of the subject's desire and empathy for the other. The pain of death affirms and conjoins with the pain of life that guarantees human relationship. A stumbling block, however, appears in the form of a woman, Marla Singer. The presence of the woman discloses that Jack's empathic pain is fake. The superego in the camp Gothic guise of a fatal signifier, "her chapped lips frosted with dead skin," Marla's demand for more jouissance is too much. "She wants it all. The cancers, the parasites . . . She never dreamed she could feel so 'smarvellous. She actually felt alive" (Palahniuk, 1997: 38). Marla makes it impossible for Jack to enjoy himself in the suffering of others.

THE NAME-OF-THE-BRAND

"What you see at fight club is a generation of men raised by women" (Palahniuk, 1997: 50), but the point of fight club is precisely *not* the reassertion of masculinity in the virile pursuit of pugilistic arts. On the contrary, fight club is a castrated virility beating up on itself because it got sold out by cheap television promises of future wealth and potency.

"We've all been raised to believe we'd all be millionaires and movie gods and rock stars. But we won't. We're slowly learning that fact, and we're all very, very pissed off." Fight club hacks at the bunkhole of masculinity. The point is not to win, or lose, but to get beaten to a pulp and bleed all over your assailant. The point is to sink to ground zero, to accept that "you are the all singing all dancing crap of the world," to joyously embrace a state of abjection. Furthermore, as the movie makes clear, the state of abjection is a literal rather than symbolic castration. From Bob with his bitch tits and the other guys with testicular cancer, to the Mayor and Tyler himself, everyone seems to be continually on the point of having their balls excised as if that, like Project Mayhem, would summon up the phallus.

As Tyler-Jack expound it, fight club and Project Mayhem are demands for love in the face of paternal abandonment. God, whose model is the abandoned or abandoning, inept father, is imagined hating the son (Palahniuk, 1997: 141). But that is not the worse thing that could happen. The worse thing is indifference. Project Mayhem is Tyler's means of getting God's attention. "Unless we get God's attention, we have no hope of love or redemption" (141). But God the father does not respond, nor does his Name cut any ice among the members of fight club. They are galvanized by the name of the brand, of the Project, that marks the place of his absence, a brand supported by the violent *ressentiment* of Tyler's rhetoric. Significantly, it is the unquestioning love and incessant demands of the members that eventually force Jack to confront the existence of his schizophrenic alter ego Tyler.

As Lacan argued in *Encore*, the demand for love is insatiable, and it demands more and more tokens, more and more objects to fill it. In the context of consumer capitalism the so-called paternal signifier is no longer "the name-of-the-father" in any simple sense. Rather, in the absence of any secure system of symbolic regulation, that function has been taken on by the brand name that acts as one principle of coordination or limitation to the generalized imperative to consume in accordance with the 'desire of the mother'. Where value is continually fluctuating according to the arbitrary tyranny of market forces, the desire of the Other seems to consist purely in the fluctuating drift of (maternal) demand that the subject must supply and satisfy. The name-of-the-brand, then, becomes the primary means to an attempt to stabilize value through a fetishism of the signifier. But in order to momentarily arrest the unanchored flow of desire, a brand needs to embody some thing of jouissance. An excellent example would be the fact that in the 1990s the Nike *swoosh* became the most popular item in North American tattoo parlors (Klein 2000: 56). Here, the body of the consumer of the brand name bears the burden, through pain, of the jouissance that it promises. For the members of the fight club and Project Mayhem, the brand is burned on to the back of their hands, the chemical lye scoring the vaginal shape of Tyler's wet lips in the shape of a kiss. Significantly, this scene is intercut with Tyler-Jack putting his hands between Marla's legs. Both the book and the movie insist that "all of this: the gun, the anarchy, the explosion is really about Marla Singer" (Palahniuk, 1997: 14). Marla's role is mainly iconic, and her mother is elided altogether in the movie. Marla's mother, whose fat provides the base substance to make the soap and the bombs, is generalized by the movie in the form of the red and black sacks of liposuctioned fat drained from "the richest thighs in America. The richest, fattest thighs in the world." The fat that is turned into luxury soap in order to fund the project. Woman is reduced to the excoriated bodily dejecta that becomes the base matter for purifying profit and explosions. Woman becomes the scene and substance by which the central antagonism of the phantasmatic double is generated as an effect of a general schizophrenia: the base substance of both profit and war.

In its staging of the antagonistic complicity of capitalism and war, *Fight Club* discloses that schizocapital is a battle order that not only rages around the globe, but is about to explode into space. "When deep-space exploitation ramps up, it will probably be the megatonic corporations that discover all the new planets and map them. The IBM Stellar Sphere. The Philip Morris Galaxy. Planet Denny's. Every planet will take the corporate identity of whoever rapes it first" (Palahniuk, 1997: 171). Contemporary corporate capitalism has become one big fight club. It is not about winning or losing, living or dying. It is a continuous battle involving warring camps that operate within the same order of business in which distinctions between work and leisure, work and play, and work, war, sport, and business have collapsed. Companies aim to mobilize consumers in that battle order, seek to gain access to their hearts and minds, forging a fierce brand loyalty, even to the point of shaping identities. Phil Knight, Nike's CEO, argued that while "nobody roots for a product," products can be "tethered to something more compelling and profound," something on which consumers can "concentrate their emotional energy" (cited in Goldman and Papson, 1998: 57). Schizocapital attempts to harness and utilize heterogeneous energies, the nonproductive expenditure of the fight that, in *Fight Club*, brings intimacy and salvation through loss/expenditure: blood in the case of fight club, cash in the case of capitalism. Supercapitalism is a form of capitalism that does not advocate a slavish dependence on things, as Tyler suggests in the movie, "the things you own end up owning you." But with supercapitalism the idea is to destroy and jettison bought products as soon as possible, even design them for destruction. Marla, in the novel, loves "all the things that people love intensely and then dump an hour or a day after" (Palahniuk, 1997: 67). Products, always already garbage, sustain the consumer in a continual state of consuming ardor and loss. Similarly, in Nike's athletic advertisements and Just Do It philosophy, consumption is enlisted only to be purged from the body (as the meat) as a process of streamlining, fitness, survival, and success—closing out and destroying opponents. "You see a guy come into fight club for the first time, and his ass is a loaf of bread. You see this same guy here six months later, and he looks carved out of wood" (51). Consumption is stimulated, accelerated, and maximized to machinic models of efficiency and performance that determine the general mode and measure of existence for consumers.

In supercapitalism, where war and commerce have become indistinct, war becomes subject to the deregulation of the market, the logic of exchange and technological hypermediation, the immediacy of death and destruction that has been incorporated into the logic of exchange. War is the form of nonproductive expenditure that grounds the marketing spectacle even as it is expended and evacuated from it. But the nonproductive expenditure represented by war is still essential to consumption. It is the trace of general economy that sustains a principle of restriction in the midst of a generally unrestricted market economy, to use the terms of Bataille.

Accordingly, the revolution in military affairs saw the military following corporate models, shifting from platform-based warfare to network-centric warfare. One of the effects of this is to enable forces to organize from the bottom up—or to self-synchronize. Like the cells of fighters prosecuting Project Mayhem, army units and business franchises "are capable of operating completely independent of central leadership." War and business have become the same thing not just because this is a necessary prerequisite and consequence of capitalizing on the advantages offered by information technology. It is also because of the radical uncertainty that is built into the speculative business of supercapitalism. Consequently, its entrepreneurs have to adopt the strategies of the artist or the gambler, or, supremely, the spirit that is infused with the celerity, untimeliness, and heterogeneity of the warrior. As Denis Hollier argues, drawing on the structural anthropology of Georges Dumèzil, the figure of the warrior has much in common with Bataille's notion of sovereignty.

> Bataille's concept of sovereignty (despite the name it carries) designates exactly that which is heterogeneous to the sovereign function [shared by Mitra-Varuna], and has but little to do with the sacralization of power (and of mastery) . . . It corresponds to something that is much nearer . . . to the noncontractual liberty

which is congenital with the warrior function. For the warrior
has nothing to do with what one understands as a soldier or that
Roman invention, "the military man." Even when he is not the
only one to be fighting, a warrior always fights alone: the solitary hero of single combats. And he fights for fighting's sake,
carried away by heroic fury. For the prestige of risk. Fundamentally undisciplined, he is the inspired warrior of the joust, the
vates of the field of battle who, like Plato's poet, can fight only
as one possessed, transported. (Hollier, 1988b: 39)

The warrior is literally a free-lance, a figure of pure desire, scornful of
human needs, and indifferent to the imaginary capture of recognition that
would lock the warrior into the master/slave dialectic of desire and recognition glossed by Kojève after Hegel. It is the kind of sovereignty claimed
by Tyler for fight club. "It's not about winning or losing fights . . . You
fight to fight" (Palahniuk, 1997: 51, 54). If the fight is about anything it
is "what Tyler says about being the crap and the slaves of history" (123).
In fact, the positions of master and slave are designated, in Hegel, precisely because the fight *does not take place*. One man backs down, and
in so doing becomes a slave. His 'fight', then, becomes purely bound up
with the dialectical labor of the negative that undertakes the production
of the universal homogeneous state. Project Mayhem is dedicated toward
freeing the slaves of history by getting them to fight, uselessly, purely for
the destructive joy of it. Dumèzil's warrior is a figure located both before
the Hegelian standoff inaugurates the history of desire, and beyond it.
For Deleuze and Guattari, the warrior, in contradistinction to the state
and its military and police apparati, becomes the metaphorical embodiment of a 'war machine' that operates outside the sovereignty of the state,
and prior to its law (see Deleuze and Guattari, 1988: 352). In contemporary society, the war machine is located, by Deleuze and Guattari, outside
the state formation in various manifestations in the form of worldwide
machines. For Deleuze and Guattari, the war machine is manifested in
multinational commercial organizations, religious formations like Islam,
and also in "the local mechanisms of bands, margins, minorities, which
continue to affirm the rights of segmentary societies in opposition to the
organs of state power" (1988: 360).

The relation between the so-called global, multinational commercial
organizations—they are more like transnational or intranational since
they occupy a space exterior to the state—and the local mechanisms of
bands is complex and dynamic. Often it is contestatory. Antistate packs
and bands are frequently, or ostensibly, anticapitalist, like Project Mayhem. But, just as often, the relationship is one of alliance or sympathy or

appropriation. Commercial organizations often locate their meaning, their transgressive value, and their authenticity in the mechanism of bands, margins, and minorities. They are also quite small since many of the brand-name multinationals have divested themselves of the means of production and instead exploit the efficiency of the network in order to consume and profit from a nomadic workforce—both in the West, but also in those areas of the globe where manufacturing takes place.

As corporations operate as if they were at war and national or supranational armies seek to be more like businesses, the question is clearly whether the military-machine and the state-machine have been overrun and superseded by the corporate-capital war machine, or rather what role the state has when its mode of governance has been incorporated into the overall mechanism of a war machine. Broadly speaking, it could be suggested that the role of the state is being reduced to a repository of waste expelled or rejected from the economic ecosystem that forms the conditions of possibility for social, political, and cultural life. The states and their nationalist ideologies are the location and locus of the ecosystem's foul-smelling residues, anticapitalist resistances, waste products, and excess energies—"the all singing, all dancing crap of the world." A locus that would include corporate burnouts and dropouts, beggars whose presence in the metropolitan cities does so much to encourage the working and consuming population, the human carcasses of exhausted and exploited labor, but also its fascistoid nationalists and racists. The nation-state, in terms both of its skeletal and variable welfare systems *and* its residual ethnic content provide the thin locus of heterogeneity and nonproductive expenditure in relation to which the war machine smooths out the space of its economic ecosystem.

SUBJECTILE

While, for some, American products might provide an imaginary conduit for energies compressed in an economically depressed society, for others it is consumer capitalism itself that represents homogeneity and ethnic rivalries and racial fantasies that generate the kind of negative energy precisely nauseated by overcommercialization and sentimentalization. One brand has become the master at generating and utilizing these sorts of heterogeneous energies. For Nike, the joy and suffering of African American experience in economically depressed areas of the United States has become the inspirational stuff of sports and leisurewear (see Goldman and Papson, 1999). In other commercials, even the Vietnam War represents a marketing opportunity precisely to the degree to which it can evoke the nostalgia for the alienation, disaffection, and anger felt by the baby boomers of America during the war, turning them into weapons against the state:

> I'm a street-walking cheater with a heart full of napalm
> I'm the runaway son of a nuclear A bomb
> I am the world's forgotten boy,
> the one who searches and destroys
> ("Search and Destroy," Iggy Pop and the Stooges, 1973)

Nike's 1996 Search and Destroy campaign and flagship advertisement redirects the imagery of the Stooge's Vietnam War song, and the rage of its nonproductive expenditure, into "a battlefield of track and field competitions" (Goldman and Papson, 1999: 156). Spliced into the music is the sound of a crowd's violent celebrations in the San Siro, home of the great AC Milan and their famous *rossoneri* ultras. As Goldman and Papson describe the ad, along with

> the culture of violence that sometimes surrounds sports in a scene of crowded stands at a European soccer match with flags waving and red smoke bombs going off. Spectacular shots convey moments of pain and intensity—hurdlers and runners fall down, blood spatters from a punch to a boxer's mouth, a runner vomits. A scene of an athlete being stretchered to a medivac helicopter testifies to the risks of competing in the arena before the crowds of frenzied fans. (Goldman and Papson, 1999: 156)

Nike assembles a series of affecting *Fight Club* images—of violence, joy, pain, intensity, blood, vomit, broken bodies—and sets them to the anguished, libidinal thrash of Iggy Pop and the Stooges in an attempt to produce and utilize heterogeneous energies. Goldman and Papson argue that with these kinds of advertisements Nike will "privilege a model of the self grounded in the intensity of aggressive competition and the work ethic gone ballistic" (153). This inverted Protestant work ethic "calls not for suffering in the work place, but a suffering of one's body in an activity pursued at no one's discretion, a suffering endured willingly . . . [thereby proving] itself worthy of recognition through suffering" (149). The expenditure of laboring bodies that is harnessed in production—say, the laboring bodies of young Asian women sewing and gluing Nike sneakers together in sweatshops—is supplanted by the nonproductive pain and suffering of boxers, athletes, and the violence of frenzied fans. The very scene of the fight club. The fantasy of the suffering body becomes, in its support of the image, the primary site of expenditure, and an unconscious equivalence is established between work and athletic achievement that is bound up and brought together in a signifier, a logo, and an imperative: Just Do It. Nike, as Goldman and Papson note, "constructs itself as a sign of performance" (52). But it is a performativity in which an expenditure that is immanent to a body suffering in joy or pain, at the extreme limit of endurance, becomes the affective model through which heterogeneous energies are harnessed by Nike's hypermodern modes of marketing and branded subjectile identity. Nike generates and expends (consumes) physical and mental resources—both productive and nonproductive—as the life-force that flows through the global all-consuming machine, the economic ecosystem.

Synergies establish the relations favorable to a process of coevolution that is necessary for survival. Different species of actors are therefore produced in this environment whose form and function are determined by their conditions of competitive existence within the ecosystem established by the network. A variety of life forms evolve in a symbiotic coexistence to form this firmament of interconnected and warring brands, functioning in different ways. Following the schizoanalysis offered by Deleuze and Guattari, it is possible to characterize different modes of individuation and dividuation. One particular mode of individuation operates within this battle-order as neither a thing nor a subject but rather as something that might be termed a subjectile. Within the ecosystem this mode of individuation has coevolved as a means of desiring and being-desired along with a mode of dividuation that has evolved as a means of coding it. Dividuation describes the means of assembling and coding desires as information, as part of a sample or market or as a particular strand of data that can be accessed, modulated, regulated, and maximized. The mode of individuation on the other hand deploys, as a kind of branded weapon or implement—a projectile or, rather, a subjectile. Subjectiles function within the network, but they don't work as such, they don't have jobs: they have careers, or career trajectories. These careers are best short-lived and intense, flaring up most effectively as a cobranded product within a synergetic environment. The Michael Jordan brand, for example, that has coevolved in a desiring assemblage with Nike, the Air Jordan, and the NBA, among others. But this does not just apply to famous sportspeople or celebrities. As Naomi Klein put it, "in order to be successful in this new economy, all of us must self-incorporate into our very own brand—a Brand Called You" (Klein, 2000: 252). Subjectiles need to retrofit themselves as consultants, service providers, and products, and particular nodes of information retrieval and exchange within the network. But, above all, like any other branded product, they need to generate desire above and beyond the threshold of any utility that might be supposed or imagined for them. The desirability of the Air Jordan has nothing to do with its efficiency and comfort as footwear, and Michael Jordan "long ago ceased to be a mere athlete" (Philip Martin, cited in Goldman and Papson, 1998: 50). To sustain their desirability, and maintain a successful career, the subjectile must continually subtract need from demand, heightening an image of sovereign indifference ('cool integrity') in relation to, and deep within, an assemblage of other brands. Indeed, a subjectile could be called a kind of subtraction machine, subtracting the utility from every manifestation of itself—whether it be a product, a service, or a link in a network—as an essential means of sustaining its desirability.

The subjectile, then, is the term for a mode of individuation that is constantly on the move within a desiring assemblage or brand canopy. Subjectiles are propelled by desire (they desire and are desired) and are directed by a *nomos* of consumption that informs the generalized and unrestricted *oikonomia* of the ecosphere. As we have seen, there is no distinction these days in the West between producers, workers, and consumers. Even so, there may seem a paradox in the idea that the subjectile subtracts need from demand and yet remains a mobile unit of consumption. As such, there is perhaps an analogy with anorexia nervosa in the sense that, according to Lacan, the anorexic does not starve him or self so much as consume (waste) his or her body through the consumption of 'nothing' in the name of desire. Just as, for Lacan, there is never an absence of desire—just a paradoxical and self-negating "desire not to desire"—so in consumer society there is never an absence of consumption, simply a consumption of consumption— a burning, wasting and suffering of the body, through the consumption of no-thing. Similarly, the subjectile works, but works for *nothing* in the sense that he or she produces nothing even as he or she consumes, wastes, and expends the body of labor. The anorexic or functioning addict is the perfect form of subjectile consumption. The propulsion of desire and the aim determined by the managerial *nomos* directs the subjectile from and toward nothing in an asymptotic relation to a consumption (or consummation) without reserve that would end all future consumption in zero. The subjectile is maintained in its desirable but, conventionally speaking, totally useless existence, and in its direction toward an impossible expenditure, ground zero, by the managerial principles of hyperefficiency.

If the *nomos* proper to the subjectile is established in relation to (nonproductive) expenditure, then so is desire, but in a slightly different way. Desire is propelled by and attracted, in horror and fascination, to the transgressive energy of expenditure. The destructive evil of expenditure provides the only possible point of imaginary certainty—precisely its

horrifying meaninglessness—in a world totally given over to the irregu-
larities of market forces. Therefore, expenditure has an inestimable value
in a world where all other values are contingent. This is the highly equivocal point at which the charisma of the brand draws its powers of attraction from the glamor of evil and alterity. Jay Doblin, for example,
acclaimed Hitler "the trademark designer of the century" (54). In ambivalent agreement, Virilio speaks of the swastika releasing such potent
affective associations that it could not be confused with any other symbol—"its stark simplicity still has an arresting power, as so much graffiti
continues to prove" (Virilio, 1998: 54). The affective potency of the
swastika and its survival in graffiti as a mark of fascistoid and unem-
ployed negativity also points to the relationship between the brand, the
tag, and the tattoo. The tag being associated with vandalism and latterly
art, while the tattoo of course being historically associated with criminal-
ity, malevolence, and deviancy.

If the U.S. government and military regard the globe as their own
terrain, U.S. companies and corporations already treat the world as a
global shopping mall. As Klein notes, "Increasingly, brand-name multinationals—Levi's, Nike, Champion, Wal-Mart, Reebok, the Gap, IBM
and General Motors—insist they are just like any one of us: bargain
hunters in search of the best deal in the global mall" (2000: 202). At the
same time, security is contracted out to private security firms by the Pen-
tagon. Areas unsafe for the consumption of American goods will be
closed down. Elements hostile to the economy will be eliminated. Just as,
in the malls themselves, 'undesirable elements' are ruthlessly excluded or
expelled by the security guards. The elimination of forms of heterogeneity from all walks of public and private life (not just drunkenness, va-
grancy, smoking, but any form of public assembly, demonstration, and so
on) is continuous with the excision of nonproductive expenditure generally and its replacement with the consumption of branded products.

Shopping malls are changing, of course, and as certain superbrands
become more successful and ubiquitous, the mall as an assemblage of
competing stores and brands is giving way to malls like Nike Town that
assemble a multiplicity of products under a single brand canopy. The logical extension of this colonizing of public space would be for a super-
brand company to build its own town and to fully take over a civic or
state function. And of course, it has already happened: Celebration, in
Florida, is owned by Disney. According to Klein, it is

> an homage, an idealized re-creation of liveable America that ex-
> isted before malls, big-box sprawl, freeways, amusement parks

and mass commercialization. Oddly enough, Celebration is not
even a sales vehicle for Mickey Mouse licensed products; it is,
in contemporary terms, an almost Disney-free town—no doubt
the only one in America. (Klein, 2000: 155)

Disney has eliminated all heterogeneity from its town, all traces of expenditure, even that represented by its own brand signature. Total brand
lockout produces a kind of brandlessness in which the brand has become
totally immanent to the community. In Celebration, there is a lot of
empty 'public' space, but there are no advertising hoardings because you
can't buy anything but Disney products and all so-called public space and
indeed all the people are owned or employed by Disney.

Jean Luc-Nancy is particularly severe on the dangers to any community when it attempts to embody the truth of an ideal, here of course
the fantasy ideal of an American utopia of 1950s family values signified
by Disney. In those circumstances, Disney immanence becomes the joy of
pure expenditure, and its community a work of death and annihilation:
"immanence, communal fusion, contains no other logic than that of the
suicide of the community that is governed by it" (Nancy, 1991: 12).
Everything and everyone is consumed (and will be consumed, wasted,
burned out, purged) from the purity of the brand. Since no one can satisfy it, we may all have to endure its purifying thirst for annihilation. And
return again to zero.

Part Four
Event

CHAPTER SIX

Surprised by Joy

Surprised by joy—impatient as the wind
I turned to share the transport—Oh! with whom
But Thee, deep buried in the silent tomb,
That spot which no vicissitude can find?
—William Wordsworth, 1812

THE EJECT

"Knowledge is neither a form nor a force but a *function*: 'I function'" (Deleuze and Guattari, 1994: 215). For Deleuze and Guattari, the question of knowledge does not concern meaning as such but function. It is not a question of who I am or what I am, but whether or not I am functioning. Self-reflexivity might further concern the question of how I know that I am functioning, or indeed malfunctioning. But self-knowledge poses a problem, however, to the degree to which it is strictly superfluous to the efficiency of operational knowledge. Pure functionality does not require a desire for meaning; indeed, the latter could itself be evidence of malfunctioning.

In their last book, *What Is Philosophy* (1994), it is precisely to the degree to which functionality is related to knowledge that Deleuze and Guattari regard it as an object of scientific discourse. This understanding of function, where scientific discourse takes its place alongside art and philosophy as one of the three planes 'cast over the chaos' (202), is slightly different than earlier in *Anti-Oedipus*. There, function is opposed to meaning, particularly in psychoanalysis. In an interview first published in 1972, Félix Guattari commented

> We're strict functionalists: what we're interested in is how something works, functions—finding the machine. But the signifier's still stuck in the question "What does it mean?"— indeed it's this very question in a blocked form. But for us, the

> unconscious doesn't *mean* anything, nor does language . . .
> The only question is how anything works, with its intensities,
> flows, processes, partial objects—none of which *mean* any-
> thing. (Deleuze, 1995: 22)

Meaning is irrelevant, or at best synonymous with use (Deleuze, 1995:
184), and the empirical subject has become a function of arrangements of
desire that are generated by machines, in the sense understood by Deleuze
and Guattari. Whatever meaning accrues for the empirical subject who
may appear as an effect of these arrangements is strictly subsumed to a
utility determined by the machine. By *What Is Philosophy* (1994), however, function has become purely the object of science, just as the concept
is limited to philosophy and affect or the 'percept' to art.

Psychoanalysis is not a science, nor does it claim to be one. Psychoanalysis can never be a science because of its adherence to the question
of meaning and its importance for the subject. Indeed, the question of
meaning for the subject is important precisely because it is there that demand, desire, discontent, and neurosis are located. Meaning is important
for psychoanalysis because it does indeed provide a locus of malfunction,
in scientific terms. The problem with science, for psychoanalysis, is precisely its ejection of a meaningful subject from its discourse. Although science is a 'knowledge of the real', its discourse continually departs from
the real to the degree to which it ignores death, which only has reality for
a subject. While science accumulates knowledge in relation to death in its
interest in everything that lives, or rather functions (and in this way is a
manifestation of the death drive for Lacan), it does not want to know
anything about it. Science turns death into an empty value that means
nothing. In *What Is Philosophy*, Deleuze and Guattari also acknowledge
that in scientific discourse the subject "appears as an 'eject'" (1994: 215).
In a double sense, the subject is ejected from discourse because it ejects
everything from that discourse that does not conform to "the terms of the
scientific proposition" (215). Or again, everything to do with the subject
is ejected apart from its functionality. The subject is a function; it *is* insofar as it functions.

But the plane of (scientific) knowledge is just one of the planes that
arc over chaos. There are two others: the planes of art and philosophy. The
place where these three planes intersect at one particular junction is the
brain. At this juncture, science, art, and philosophy do not emerge as mental objects from an objectified brain, but on the contrary are the three aspects "under which the brain becomes subject" (210). "It is the brain that
says *I*, but *I* is an other," three others in fact: along with the 'I function' of
science, there is the 'I feel' of art and the 'I conceive' of philosophy, none of

which are the brain of "connections and secondary integrations" (211). The latter is simply the brain considered as a determinate function in the discourse of science, whereas thought and feeling depend on relations with the world, the brain itself being drawn from these relations. Alongside, but heterogeneous to functionality, there is thought, and alongside, but heterogeneous to thought, there is feeling.[1]

Clearly by *What Is Philosophy*, Deleuze and Guattari are no longer strictly functionalists in the sense that function has now become part of a triumvirate along with thought and feeling. The trinity of art, philosophy, and science, force, form, and function assemble a structure similar to the one in Lacanian psychoanalysis (imaginary, symbolic, and real) as three planes that intertwine at the juncture of the brain/subject (see Fig. 6.1).

But does this also imply the return of meaning? Not in a positive sense, but precisely in the space hollowed out by its ejection. Where should the question of meaning be located? In the juncture between thought and function, perhaps. If, for science, the question of being is always referred to function, then a space should be opened for meaning in the fold created by function when it tries to think as an effect of its own operative requirements. For the neurobiologist Antonio Damasio, for example, the question of meaning is itself an effect of evolutionary adaptation, a function of "the powerful biological mechanism behind it" (Damasio, 2003: 268–269). But

Fig. 6.1   Deleuze and Guattari's Brain

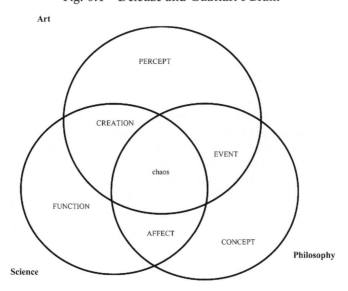

of course this simply negates meaning once again by referring it back to function. What stops thought endlessly circulating in the hollow of function, however, is the necessity that it pass through the plane that it negates. As Deleuze and Guattari note at the end of their book, each discipline has an essential relation with its negative, each discipline is only possible if it is, "on its own behalf, in an essential relationship with the No that concerns it" (1994: 218). For science, that is the force of feeling appropriate to art, or indeed the joy that is bound up with the very thing science wants to know nothing about, death. For Lacan, there was never a question concerning the ability of a machine to think; computing is a form of thought. But that a purely inorganic computer might know, that was another question, because the "foundation of knowledge is that the jouissance of its exercise is the same as that of its acquisition" (Lacan, 1999: 97). The question to ask of a machine, therefore, is not one concerning its thought or intelligence, but one of feeling: does the machine enjoy, does it suffer?

In order for thought to become more than just a function, endlessly turning in on itself in the circle of operative knowledge, it has to emerge from something other than itself. In order for thought to be conceived anew, it must break through the negation of feeling and experience the feeling of negation: joy before death. In Deleuzean terms, this is the event of the concept or the concept-as-event. This is precisely what defines the concept from thought-as-function, the excluded term that produces its consistency. "*States of affairs*, *objects* or *bodies*, and *lived states* form the function's references, whereas *events* are the concept's consistency" (1994: 151). Once the domain of meaning, politics and culture, 'states of affairs,' subjects, groups, and subjectivities, have devolved to the functionalism of science and quasisciences. The event, however, irrupts precisely in the absence of meaning and in the default of function. "This is what we call the Event, or the part that eludes its own actualization in everything that happens" (1994: 156). Perhaps it could be suggested that the Deleuzian event is an effect of the event of the erasure of meaning by function.

As has been argued in previous chapters, function overwrites meaning precisely through the withdrawal of the phallus that marks the limit of meaning "that can only indicate the direction towards which it fails" (Lacan, 1999: 78). As the phallus is deconstructed and digitalized as just another signifier or digit in an infinite series, it leaves a space of pure mediation and exchange. "Mediation imposes itself as an autonomous reality which pursues its game of references and substitutions in the absence of any *telos*" (Goux, 1992: 72). However, while the question of meaning is deprived of a limit and becomes a matter of the exchange of information, the technoscientific means of mediation, unencumbered with any interest in meaning, is nevertheless still characterized by a principle of operativity or functionality. This space of mediation and exchange, this principle of operativity, constitutes and governs the state of affairs. Without phallic limit, the event can only emerge at a point heterogeneous to this space of mediation in the accursed domain of the inoperative or dysfunctional. Or indeed, as Deleuze would argue, in the purely virtual. The event, however, is no event if it remains purely virtual. While "the event is not the state of affairs, it is actualized in a state of affairs, in a body, in a lived, but it has a shadowy and secret part that is continually subtracted from or added to its actualization . . . [this is] the infinite movement to which it gives consistency" (1994: 156). This is the virtual as distinct from the actual, and while it is "a virtual that is no longer chaotic, that has become consistent or real," it is a virtual real that is consistently ominous, a promise that is also a threat. "Why is every event a kind of plague, war, or death?" asks Deleuze (1993: 80). At the same time, since each genuine event is revolutionary, it is also necessarily joyful. The event is actualized in revolutionary joy, since there is no revolutionary act—conceptual, aesthetic or political—that is not joyful (2003: 251).

In his comments on the relation between the event and political action in a short interview on control societies, Deleuze draws a correlation between the event and the brain, in the process drawing a distinction between the notion of the subject and 'processes of subjectification'. Rather than 'going back to the subject' that is invested with duties, power, and knowledge, Deleuze prefers to 'speak of new kinds of events' (1995: 176). Momentary events that cannot be explained by their social or historical context, or even the situations to which they give rise. In this sense they have a similar structure to the Lacanian subject that also exceeds its symbolic emplacement. But for Deleuze (and Guattari) the subject of enunciation constitutes a 'black' hole' in the 'white wall' of signification (see Deleuze and Guattari, 1988). It is incapable of generating any event. Instead, Deleuze prefers to talk about the brain as "the boundary of a continuous two-way movement between an Inside and an Outside, this membrane between them" (1995: 176). Upon this membrane, events create "new cerebral pathways, new ways of thinking . . . I think subjectification, events and brains are more or less the same thing" (1995: 176).

Meaning has hitherto been central to subjectivity, a sense of self, and a sense of agency. Actors struggle to make sense of things as a precondition of acting, even though it is impossible to know everything, to judge correctly. At a certain moment, an action must take place, whose meaning cannot be predicted or assessed, and which will change forever the conditions of its reception and understanding.

Nevertheless, the nonmeaning of the act is driven by some force of desire or affect that has been actualized in an event that remains immanent to the act and its consequences. "The event is not what happens (an accident), it is rather inside what occurs, the purely expressed" (2003: 80). For Deleuze, it is essential that the event and its consequences in action be regarded without moral judgment or even historical analysis since it crushes the event and makes others less likely. In this view, Deleuze of course follows Nietzsche for whom the event was an expression of both desire and forgetting. Self-consciousness and historical analysis are not adequate to the event and fail to actualize it.

This chapter looks at the implications for action, and the subject of action, in the state of affairs where meaning has been displaced by the event. However is it possible, as Nietzsche seems to suggest, that the non-meaning of the event, purely expressed in action, is essential to the functionality of the state of affairs, essential to the nature of its efficiency? Does the action of the event, stripped of meaning, memory, and judgment, return a new and lethal efficiency to the principle of operativity? The joy of the event (the event-concept or concept-event) has a different temporal relation to the operative knowledge of the state of affairs to that of jouissance and knowledge. The temporal relation between knowledge and jouissance is measured according to the (lost) jouissance that gives the work of thought its meaning, as its end or goal, the *jouis-sens* or enjoy-meant, that it exercises in its attempt to acquire it. Unlike jouissance however, that is always lost, one can be 'surprised by joy'. As William Wordsworth's famous sonnet suggests, the joyful event occurs through forgetting yet accrues significance only in the nonmeaning of death. Death that is not subject to the vicissitudes of the states of affairs, and that is forgotten only to return again eternally in the event that must be affirmed in joy. And as Marcel Proust dedicated much of his life to showing, there is the possibility of 'the joy of time regained' that is the time of memory. Not the historical memory that unfolds in chronological time, but the time of duration, the memory that endures and that informs action or, in Proust's case, writing (see Ansell Pearson, 2001). Perhaps significantly, these examples of the event and its utility come not from the discourse of science, nor even of philosophy, but from literature.

LITERATURE-EVENT-CONCEPT

"Remember Me" (*Hamlet*, 1.5. 91). The last words of the ghost in his first encounter with Hamlet emphasize the importance of memory to action, in a play notorious for its depiction of rationalization, arrested desire, and deferral. Indeed, the sentiment is reiterated two acts later when the ghost reappears in his wife's bedchamber to remind his son not to forget to remember him, his visitation designed to "whet thy almost blunted purpose" (3.4. 100–101). In its recourse to meaning as a locus of civilization's discontents, psychoanalysis does not turn to science, of course, but to literature, and indeed myth. Hamlet's problems dealing with the state of affairs in Denmark, his hesitation, perhaps even his hysteria, manifested in long rages at himself and others, are disclosed by Freud to have their etiology in the myth dramatized in Sophocles's *Oedipus Rex*. Retrospectively, *Hamlet* validates Freud's ideas about unconscious desires of patricide and maternal incest.

Before he decided to place literature outside the concept, Deleuze also considered literature to have a very close, almost analogous relation to philosophy. Not only has Deleuze produced a number of monographs on literary figures such as Proust, Sacher Masoch, and, with Guattari, Kafka—works that are to a greater extent works of philosophy—he also has frequent recourse to literary examples in his purely philosophical works, most notably Lewis Carroll. Furthermore, these literary examples demonstrate concepts equivalent to philosophical concepts in the double sense that they constitute events as well as symbolizing ideas. For example, in *Difference and Repetition* (1997), it is Hölderlin rather than Fichte or Hegel who is the heir to Kant insofar as he sees that "the speculative death of God entails the fracture of the I . . . and the introduction of the form of time into thought" (1997: 87).[2] Whereas for Kant the form of time is necessary in order to determine the subject of the cogito, Hölderlin "saw in this form of time both the essence of tragedy and the adventure of Oedipus, as though these were complementary figures of the same death instinct" (87). In this way, Deleuze suggests that Kantian philosophy is the heir of Oedipus. Consequently, the northern philosopher, like the northern prince, declares time to be out of joint where the event breaks open the circular model of time. This model makes the past adequate to the present and the future so that beginning and end coincide, forming a circle. For Kant and Hölderlin, however, the event of the introduction of time into thought displaces the circular model of time with a model of time as an empty and pure form. Time becomes the most radical form of change that itself does not change.

Furthermore, the event that breaks the circularity of time is, for Hölderlin, a caesura, a figure from classical prosody that denotes a radical break in meter or rhythm. This break establishes time not just as an empty and formal order, but also establishes it as both a totality and a series. This is conceptualized well in literature, particularly tragedy, where the tragic caesura provides both an image of the totality of time and also enables the series. The symbolic image draws together the caesura that is the literary (or mythic) equivalent of the event: "to throw time out of

joint, to make the sun explode, to throw oneself into the volcano, to kill
God the father . . . the caesura, of whatever kind must be determined in
the image of a unique and tremendous event, an act which is adequate to
time as a whole" (89). All these symbolic images are literary in a profound sense that breaks open the boundaries of both literature and philosophy as determinate forms. In *Difference and Repetition* not only is
literature not located outside the concept, the symbolic image of the
caesura—this poetic figure from classical prosody—provides the exemplary model of the concept-event.

The event that is adequate to time as a whole separates time into a
series: a before in which the act is supposed "too big for me," the present,
which is the event itself, and a future that divides and disperses the self. In
the event there is a "becoming-equal to the act and a doubling of the self,
and the projection of an ideal self in the image of the act" (1997: 89).
This unleashes a future that

> signifies that the event and the act possess a secret coherence
> which excludes that of the self; that they turn back against the
> self which has become their equal and smash it to pieces, as
> though the bearer of the new world were carried away and
> dispersed by the shock of the multiplicity to which it gives
> birth. (Deleuze, 1997: 90)

In relation to the symbolic image of the event, "all is repetition in the
temporal series" (90). History repeats itself not by accident or because of
some empirical correspondence between the present and the past but because the past is itself determined by repetition in relation to the event.
"Repetition is never a historical fact, but rather the historical condition
under which something new is effectively produced" (90). Again, this is
not simply because historical actors act out political struggles in the garb
of previous actions. Although this fact is perfectly illustrated both by and
in *Julius Caesar*, when Cassius directly in the wake of the assassination of
Caesar exclaims: "How many ages hence / Shall this our lofty scene be
acted over, / In states unborn and accents yet unknown!" (*Julius Caesar*,
3.1: 111–113). In *Hamlet* this repetition is evoked again, with thick
irony, when Hamlet jests with Polonius who boasts that he "did enact
Julius Caesar. I was killed i'th' Capitol. Brutus killed me." In the presence
of the king, Hamlet acknowledges as if in anticipation that "it was a
brute part of him to kill so capital a calf there" (*Hamlet*, 3.2. 102–105).
Since in the Globe Theatre the actors playing Hamlet and Polonius would
most likely have been the same as those who had only just recently played
Brutus and Caesar, the repetition is highlighted, adding tension and

pathos to Hamlet's deliberations. The repetitions—historical, theatrical, textual—underscore Deleuze's contention that *"repetition is a condition of action before it is a concept of reflection"* (1997: 90).[3]

For Deleuze, then, in *Difference and Repetition*, literature (Greek tragedy and English Renaissance drama) provides the image of the event-concept long before it finds its philosophical conceptualization in Kant. Indeed, it is only when Hölderlin, writing in the tradition of German Romanticism, emphasizes the tragic caesura that he becomes the true heir of the revolutionary Kantian subordination of thought to time. In the cinema books, however, the relation between art and philosophy is reversed. Bergson's concepts of the movement-image and the time-image, discovered independently of cinema, nevertheless become the means through which the cinema 'thinks'. As such, the cinema is close if not analogous to philosophy. Perhaps it is closer to philosophy even than art. "The great directors of the cinema may be compared, in our view, not merely with painters, architects and musicians, but also with thinkers. They think with movement-images and time-images instead of concepts" (Deleuze, 1986: xiv). Since the movement-image and the time-image are concepts drawn by Deleuze from Bergson, it is difficult to see what distinguishes cinema from philosophy, at least in the thought of Deleuze. After all, in the first sentence of his Preface to the English edition of *The Movement-Image*, Deleuze states the intention of his book to "isolate certain cinematographic concepts," where these concepts are purely semiotic, thought-signs, or signs of thought (1986: ix).

Once the cinema starts producing these cinematographic concepts, these thought-signs, "they turn up elsewhere and the world 'starts turning cinematic'" (Deleuze, 1995: 65). Then, in a philosophical repetition after World War Two, the cinema experiences a Kantian revolution and "stops subordinating time to motion," instead making motion dependent on time. The world starts to become a Kantian cinema interested not in the content of thought, but its mechanisms. Cinema tries to construct an image 'of the mechanisms of thought' in which action is subordinate to time and repetition.

CONCEPT-EVENT-CINEMA

The film *Memento* (2000), directed by Christopher Nolan, brings together many of these themes. It seems a cinematic essay on the relation between thought, time, the event, repetition, and action. Based on an idea for a short story by his brother Jonathan (a story that was written at the same time the film was made), *Memento* locates these themes in a film noir treatment of the revenge genre. This old literary genre is of course presided over by *Hamlet*. Indeed, the title of the film and the short story ("Memento Mori") deliberately evoke the Renaissance iconography so memorably utilized in the play when Hamlet, in his inky cloak, holds up the jester's skull and reflects on the vanities of life, the passage of time, and death. The peculiarity of the film and the short story, however, is that the protagonist suffers from a form of amnesia, which means that he cannot learn new facts; indeed his short-term memory lasts as little as ten minutes. The condition, caused by an injury to the brain, occurred during an attack in which his wife was apparently raped and murdered. All memories prior to and including the attack remain intact, and inform his subsequent actions. His last memory, he claims, is that of his wife dying, all memories of subsequent events, however, vanish almost as soon as they occur.

The narrator of the short story is the protagonist writing to himself, externalizing in soliloquy an internal monologue that will otherwise be instantly lost. Echoing Hamlet, he writes to himself: "Your life is over. You're a dead man . . . So the question is not to be or not to be, because you aren't. The question is whether you want to do something about it, whether revenge matters to you" (Nolan, 2000). Revenge becomes the abiding principle of the protagonist's life—nothing else matters. While revenge gives the rest of his life a purpose, a goal, and therefore some form of meaning, a reason to externalize his memory in writing and Polaroid photographs, all meaning and purpose in a profound sense disappear with his wife's death. "She's gone and the present is trivia which I scribble down in notes." Ironically, given the self-conscious references to *Hamlet*, the play itself highlights the distinctions between different forms of memory and how the memory of one single event can and should blot out everything else for the avenger.

> "Remember thee?" Yea, from the table of my memory
> I'll wipe away all trivial fond records
> All saws of books, all forms, all pressures past,
> That youth and observation copied there,
> And thy commandment all alone shall live
> Within the book and volume of my brain. (*Hamlet*, 1.5:
> 97–103)

Hamlet, of course, fails to act decisively with regard to the murderer until he is himself wounded and thus, as Lacan suggests, enters a zone between two deaths, symbolic and real deaths. That is, he becomes fatally wounded, beyond the cares of "all narcissistic attachments," in a total identification with the implement and signifier of death (Lacan, 1977: 51). As Lacan notes, what is curious about *Hamlet*, particularly when compared to *Oedipus Rex* or other revenge tragedies, detective or noir thrillers, is that the drama is not structured by an enigma. There is no question of whodunnit, even if there may be a question mark over the status of the ghost, whether it is a "spirit of health or a goblin damned" who reveals the truth. Claudius's response to the mousetrap, however, dispels all doubts. Hamlet is a detective who knows. It is the fatality of that knowledge that determines that Hamlet must put on his antic disposition and feign madness, to render his knowledge the groundless discourse of a fool. The question concerning *Hamlet* is not the object of revenge, but its timing. "Hamlet is always at the hour of the Other," and that hour is the hour of his destruction in the repayment of all debts (Lacan, 1977: 24).

Memento changes the situation in various subtle ways. As Jonathan Nolan first suggested, according to the recollection of his director brother, unlike *Hamlet* the story is "about an investigator who doesn't know anything" (Nolan, 2000). Which is to say that everything he learns is more or less instantly forgotten, and that even if he succeeds in revenging his wife's rape and murder, he will not remember unless he records some kind of message to himself concluding "I've Done It." There is no hour of the Other for the protagonist of *Memento*. Leonard Selby has no idea how long ago his wife was attacked, how long he has been on the trail of her killer. The Other does not exist for Leonard in the sense that his absence of memory prevents the consistency of reference necessary to organize and externally guarantee the meaning of all his notes, tattoos, and photographs. Leonard's other is himself, the series of previous forgotten selves who have had themselves tattooed, who have taken the photographs, written the notes and instructions on which future Leonards will act. His archive is without memory, but is assembled according to an unshakeable imperative that bears no relation to external law.

But in the world of the movie there appears to be no law in any case. The representative of law, Teddy, is executed in the first scene of the film, and as it unfolds backwards in time, the audience discovers that this custodian is, by his own admission, 'a bad cop' who exploits and makes fun of Leonard. Throughout the movie, the audience is constantly referred to a photograph of Teddy with the caption, handwritten by Leonard, "Don't believe his lies." Ironically, by the time the movie reaches the chronological point where Leonard makes this judgment, it seems to do nothing but confirm the truth of Teddy's explication, no doubt rehearsed many times to Leonard but heard again as if for first time. In the derelict building, scene of another of Leonard's revenge-murders, Teddy informs him that he is the cop who helped him get his revenge over a year ago, but that he failed to remember. Subsequently, Leonard has been unwittingly helping Teddy execute various police suspects and rivals in his drug dealing, always under the delusion that he is getting his revenge. Further and even more devastatingly in terms of the reliability of Leonard's narration, Teddy discloses that his wife survived the assault, even though it caused his brain damage.

Here, the movie becomes less reminiscent of *Hamlet* as it does of *Oedipus*, becoming suitably Freudian in the process. It appears that Leonard has been protecting himself from the real cause of his wife's death through the construction of a screen memory. For Freud, a screen memory is one in which an apparent early memory is used as a screen for a later event. However, that early memory Freud regarded as a fiction, shaped and edited by the unconscious in order to protect the subject from the trauma or meaning of the later event. In Leonard's case, this memory concerns the parallel story that he tells at every opportunity concerning his earlier life as an insurance investigator assessing the claims of a man claiming to have the condition from which Leonard now suffers. The implication of Teddy's speech, and his affirmation that Sammy Jankis was rightly exposed by Leonard as a fake, is that Leonard's memory tells the story of his own unwitting murder of his wife. Determined to test the depth of his brain damage, or indeed through guilt at her frustration with his condition, Catherine Shelby arranges her death through deliberately mistiming the insulin injections that Leonard dispenses to her. She decides to trust, or not, that the depth of his love for her will supersede the short-term memory loss. The psychoanalytical account of Leonard's actions, therefore, would presumably be one of pure death drive, masquerading in the thinnest possible way as revenge in order to propel aggression outwards toward destruction in the form of the series of "John G's" who are no one but phantoms of himself. The self he is continually losing, the self to whom he continually writes notes, the self whom these notes are continually trying to discover and direct.

There are two events in *Memento* that become collapsed in the singularity of the drive. The murder/death of the wife is projected on to the rape/brain damage event. The rape and murder of the wife are sustained as a fantasy that drives out the knowledge of her survival and subsequent murder/suicide. The Sammy Jankis story screens the murder/suicide even as it repeats it as the act of someone else. The repetition not only establishing a fictional mastery over its meaning, but also Leonard's attempt, according to Teddy, of "conditioning himself through repetition" to remember Sammy Jankis until it becomes true. The phrase "Remember Sammy Jankis" is of course tattooed on his hand in order to be visible almost constantly.

Unlike Oedipus, Leonard discovers not that he has killed his father and married his mother but that he has killed his wife. He (re)discovers this whenever Teddy tells him, but fails to acknowledge or record the fact and hence forgets it all over again, instead reaffirming the memory of Jankis. There is no patricide and maternal incest, but a 'matricide' in the psychoanalytic sense of the wife as maternal substitute. For Lacan, the Oedipal patricide is a ritual reproduction of the 'originary' crime mythologized elsewhere by Freud in *Totem and Taboo*. It explains the mythical origin of the law in a primordial act of violence, retrospectively identified as a patricide, that instantiates symbolic castration. The law of the father, established in the act of his murder, determines that jouissance can only be sought via the "inverted ladder of desire." For Jean-Joseph Goux, this patricide and maternal incest constitute an event of a slightly different kind, one that symbolizes the birth of modernity in the form of a break with traditional masculine order. Traditional societies demand a symbolic matricide in the sense of a rejection of the mother as a part of the initiation into the austere order of manhood. The Oedipus myth, for Goux, marks a point of autodidactic resistance to traditional initiation. Through deploying independent reason to defeat the Sphinx and murdering his father, Oedipus retains possession of the mother. For Goux, the myth signifies the desire to master nature that is subsequently invested in both modern idealism and materialism in all its senses.

While, for Goux, symbolic matricide marks a traditional passage to a more austere order of manhood, this is not the case for Leonard in *Memento*, notwithstanding the sharp suit and macho sports car that initially denote him as a movie action hero. These we discover have in any case been appropriated from the man he murders in the final reel. Leonard's unwitting and traumatic 'matricide' does not lead on to entry into an order of masculinity because there is none. Teddy, whose name suggests a child's companion and comforter rather than paternal embodiment of the law, is a mischievous pal who plays games with him. As the short story emphasizes, paternal law can have no effect upon Leonard, since he is 'dead' already. It can do nothing to him. Paternal law, and indeed the law of desire, give way to a traumatized love and mourning driven by an insatiable demand for more. For more revenge, more death, more and more John Gs, until Leonard himself has been destroyed. Leonard's memory loss of course precipitates this, since all possible narcissistic attachments are completely trivial compared to his revenge, all forms of desire and recognition irrelevant, at best to be faked for strategic reasons. For Lacan, it was the oppressive presence of the mother, and the uncertainty as to her desire, that exacerbated Hamlet's anguish and his apparent endless deferral. In *Memento*, the death of Leonard's wife leaves a residual, ghostly demand for the jouissance of revenge. The obscene, superegoic dimension of this insatiable demand is nicely articulated by Teddy: "You wander around, you play detective. You're living a dream kid: a dead wife to pine for, a purpose to your life, a romantic quest that you wouldn't end even if I wasn't in the picture."

The impossibility of the end, the impossibility that precludes and propels jouissance, is presumably denoted in the final sequence of the film showing Leonard heading for the tattoo parlor with his own instruction to tattoo Teddy's license plate onto himself as another clue. Apparently having already forgotten the previous exchange with Teddy, Leonard resumes his internal monologue, urging himself to continue to believe in a world outside his own mind. "I have to believe that when my eyes are closed, the world's still there." When he shuts his eyes, the sequence cuts to a fantasy-image in which Leonard is in bed with his wife who is caressing his bare chest. The chest, however, is covered in the tattoos that he has had scored on his body after her rape and murder. Indeed, his wife runs her hands over his chest to reveal the last tattoo, the one that should give him the final instruction/reminder to stop his quest: "I've Done It." And indeed he has done it; the audience has just been told that it was actually Leonard who killed his wife. This is the fantasy-image of jouissance in the sense of total satisfaction toward which he imagines he is always coming, complete with resurrected wife in postcoital repose. This fantasy-image perhaps also denotes even as it protects him from the jouissance of killing his wife, which he acted out, but missed not least because he did not know he was doing it, and can no longer even remember it.

Coming at the end of the film (but chronologically toward the beginning of the narrative), the image also seems to exemplify Leonard's total delusion, or at least his complete absorption in a narcissistic image of his own pleasure. His final words, "We all need mirrors to remind ourselves who we are," seem to confirm this 'authorial' judgment—as does Nolan's commentary on the DVD. The director notes that Leonard is continually missing crucial clues and reactions if they do not fit into the picture that captivates him: "Leonard ignores things he can't process or deal with, he lets it go, lets it wash over him" (Nolan, 2000).

But there is one image of himself that Leonard finds disturbing, that doesn't wash over him. This is an image that when it is posted in an envelope under the door to his hotel room causes him intense anxiety. It is a picture of a joyful Leonard pointing to the space on his bare chest reserved for the "I've Done It" tattoo. Leonard of course can remember nothing of the image, but its meaning is disclosed to him in Teddy's explanatory speech. It was indeed taken after Teddy helped Leonard find and kill the real John G. Teddy's motive in posting the image to Leonard is obscure. It is ostensibly to get him to answer the phone in his hotel room, but thereafter its effects are unpredictable, since its meaning is clearly "I've Done It!" which, if understood, would preclude Leonard's use as a weapon in Teddy's drug-dealing scam. Teddy's justification of his use of the picture is somewhat obscurely explained after the murder of Jimmy—"Look how happy you are, I wanted to see that face again." This hints at an unconscious principle of joy at work in Leonard even as it discloses Teddy, yet again, as an obscene figure of enjoyment.

In the car, Leonard burns the image along with the photograph of Jimmy, his latest victim, and writes his warning to himself about Teddy. In burning the image of his joy, Leonard consecrates and sustains it as an immanent principle. But this principle is not one that is related to jouissance, since it has nothing to do with knowledge. Leonard knows nothing about his joy, even as he sustains it as the immanent principle and expression of his drive. While Jankis's failure to acknowledge the pain administered to him exposes him as a fake, because the body should be able to acquire a 'habit-memory', so Leonard's apparent failure to acknowledge the image of his joy exposes him as deliberately self-deluding. But since the failure to acknowledge is deliberate, the delusion is willed. "Can I let myself forget what you just made me do?" Burning the image, and thereby forgetting, simply means he can go on killing, the joy of which reinforces the impulse to do so through repetition. The pragmatism and paradox of this deliberate self-delusion sustain the meaning and purpose of his life. But this meaning and purpose are completely false. The jouissance of revenge is simply an alibi that Leonard at that moment recognizes as such. The important thing for Leonard is that his death drive is sustained and supported by an immanent principle of joy that enables him to function and act efficiently in the world. Indeed, it becomes an affirmation of his life and condition operating at the level of the mechanism (see Damasio, 2003: 284–285).

Teddy recognizes the efficiency that Leonard's singular passion for revenge gives him, and how it makes him so useful. "You're not a killer—that's why you are so good at it." But Leonard is already becoming something else as he decides that he can exploit himself as well as anyone else, and seals Teddy's fate by planting false evidence against him. This is perhaps the key event in the film—not so much the trauma of the rape or the injury that caused his amnesiac condition, or even the murder of his wife. "The event is not what happens (an accident), it is rather inside what occurs, the purely expressed" (Deleuze, 1993: 156). The event is actualized in the joy of killing that becomes the immanent expression of his life, both the totality of time and the series that it inaugurates. He becomes a superkiller, the pure instrument of his own joy, as a cinema audience has already witnessed in the first frame of the film.

MOVIE-IN-THE-BRAIN

The narrative of *Memento* when it is reconstructed in a number of view-
ings is straightforward. Indeed, it is very linear, just run backwards. According to the director, his main thematic interest in the film was not so
much the narrative, but the condition suffered by the protagonist and the
way in which the film uses it to exaggerate a normal condition. "The
script and Leonard's systems and the way the plot points come together
relating to memory are just extrapolations of the way I try and help my
own short term memory" (Nolan, 2000). The film therefore seeks to
highlight the unreliability of memory, its dependence on and role in interpretation, and the way memory and interpretation are bound up with
the emotional functionality of the mechanism. The film nicely illustrates
Deleuze's suggestion that the cinema is a Kantian machine that subordi-
nates subjectivity and action to time.

"What film helps us understand is how we think in and through
time in a situation where time passes in us and divides us from ourselves"
(Rodowick, 1997: 84). The technique here, however, does not involve a
distancing and alienation from the center of sensorimotor activity, but a
hyperidentification with it and its limitations that involve an utter dependence on time and prosthetic memory. *Memento* forces its audience into
the brain-damaged, decentered head of its protagonist. It does this
through a variety of means such as shooting much of the film through
Leonard's point of view, or of tracking close behind him, or through intense close-ups. Most notably, since the film runs backwards in time, the
audience has, like Leonard, no background knowledge with which to
contextualize his current actions. Like Leonard, they initially have no
memory of the verbal and visual clues and aids he is provided with. However, as the film unfolds, unlike Leonard, the audience has the opportunity to utilize its own short term memory and interpret and reinterpret
the scenes it has just seen in light of the chronologically anterior scenes it
is currently witnessing. This is quite difficult because the film is excessive
in its use of repetition, scene-cycles, visual and verbal echoes that confuse
the sequence of the narrative and its temporality. In itself, this puts pres-
sure on the short-term memory of an audience, demonstrating its fragility
in a very tangible way, and to a degree normalizes Leonard's condition.

The film's exposure of the dependence of subjectivity on time and a
memory that is both external, relational, and hence extremely fragile re-
iterates Deleuze's suggestion in *The Time-Image* that the relation to the
brain has changed since it has been disclosed as an acentered system.
Ironically, since for Deleuze the fragility of this relation to the brain becomes a feature of a cinema dominated by the time-image, neuroscience

has become more reliant on a metaphor of the cinema when accounting for the sense of self that is apparently produced in the brain. In neuro-biology, it is now improper to speak of a sense of self, because from the neurophysiological point of view, "the self simply does not exist." There is no homunculus in the brain operating the controls. Rather, a sense of self is produced as a necessary fiction generated by neurofirings and in-terconnections. "What we see as the self is really a construct, akin to the optical illusion that makes us believe that a series of photographic images projected onto a screen in rapid procession are people and objects in the real world" (Maté, 1999: 245; see also Lowe, 2002).

Perhaps surprisingly neurobiologists now appear to believe that the brain is no longer a command and control center, or a computer, but a cinema. Or at least it houses a cinema. The problem with this ex-planatory metaphor concerns how the brain makes its movies. How precisely do neurological units film, edit, and project the images that produce a sense of self that watches the movie. How does the brain make films, project them, and watch them all at the same time? Or as the neuroscientist Antonio Damasio puts it, "there is a major gap in our current understanding of how neural patterns become mental images" and indeed how those images "are synchronized and edited into what I have called the 'movie-in-the-brain'" (Damasio, 2003: 198). The term "image" here has to be understood as a mental pattern in any of the sensory modalities, "the movie has as many sensory tracks as our ner-vous system has sensory portals—sight, sound, taste, and olfaction, touch, inner sense and so on" (Damasio, 2000: 9). If the first problem concerns how neural patterns become mental images, then there is also a second problem of how

> the brain also generates the sense that there is an owner and observer for that movie. The two problems are so intimately related that the latter is nested within the former. In effect, the second problem is that of generating the *appearance* of an owner and observer for the movie *within the movie*; and the physiological mechanisms behind the second problem have an influence on the mechanisms behind the first. (Damasio, 2000: 11)

It is ironic, then, that just at the point where Deleuze argues that rather than linguistics or psychoanalysis the cinema should look to the micro-biology of the brain for principles to apply to cinema (Deleuze, 1995: 60), neuroscience is using the cinema as a means of understanding the images generated and edited by neural patterns.

Interestingly there are some similarities, perhaps superficial, between Deleuze's understanding of cinema and Damasio's understanding of the brain. For both, images predominate and are prior to language. Like Deleuze's cinema, Damasio's movie-in-the-brain cannot be subject to a Metzian semiological analysis. While language is the primary means of extending consciousness to allow the development of culture, it is not necessary for the construction of a self or to enable the articulation of that self with the external world. "Language—that is words and sentences—is a translation of something else, a conversion from nonlinguistic images which stand for entities, events, relationships, and inferences" (Damasio, 2000: 107). In Damasio's understanding of language the words "I" or "me" and the phrase "I know" are translations of a nonverbal self and a nonverbal knowing established in images (108). The understanding of language as simply words and sentences is quite narrow, of course, and semiology would include any image that signified in a way analogous to language—something that Damasio's images clearly do since they can be 'translated'. Damasio's movie-in-the-brain is evidently enormously *textual*, presumably generating significance and 'knowing' through a process of differentiation, in a way closer to Derrida perhaps than Saussure. But, as with Deleuze, the argument is that this textuality is not reducible to words and sentences, syntax and narrative, even though narrative must be readable from the text in order for extended consciousness to make sense of itself in its own movie. This 'core self' however is dependent on a neural textuality that always threatens to undermine it. The extended consciousness necessary for language is based on a core consciousness that does not require the sophisticated degree of self-consciousness enabled by language. Nevertheless, for Damasio, core consciousness requires a nonverbal commentary or narrative that is activated as an effect of the relation between the organism and the object world. An image of the organism (its body, its internal milieu, vestibular system, musculoskeletal frame) is generated by the brain as the organism interacts with external objects that are also mapped as images in the brain. This image of the organism becomes the basis for the "proto-self," and its image becomes a key component in the cinematic account of the relationship between the changing proto-self and the sensorimotor maps of the object that causes those changes (Damasio, 2000: 170). This account is a wordless narrative based on neural patterns that become images (movement-images) that are in 'the same fundamental currency' as the images of the objects that are generated. The image of the proto-self is generated in the very act of imaging the objects with which it interacts. "The images in the consciousness narrative flow like shadows along with the images of the object for which they are providing an unwitting, unsolicited comment . . . they are *within* the movie. There is no external spectator" (Damasio, 2000: 171).

Accompanying the generation of images there is also the generation of feeling and emotions. Again this is consistent with Deleuze for whom "feeling, affect [and] passion are the principle characters of the brain-world" (Deleuze, 1989b: 210). Emotion and feeling also preexist language and extended consciousness, but shape core consciousness. Indeed, Damasio suggests that the "basic mechanisms underlying emotion do not require consciousness, even if they eventually use it." In Damasio's understanding, there is a clear difference between feeling and emotion. Feelings are secondary to emotion, but at the same time more 'internal'. Feeling denotes the "private, mental experience of an emotion" (2000: 42). "Feelings are the primitives of consciousness" (2000: 314). But prior to feelings, which are individual, the term "emotion" denotes responses that are, or can be, automatic, collective and often publicly observable (42). Internal feelings are an individuated effect of external emotion, the inside that is a hollow of the fold of the outside.

Damasio's confidence in his contention that "the biological machinery underlying emotion is not dependent on consciousness" is based on his observation of a patient called David who suffers from exactly the same form of amnesia dramatized in the film *Memento*. He has, apparently, "one of the most severe defects in learning and memory ever recorded [and] cannot learn any new fact at all," not even "any new physical appearance or sound or place or word" (Damasio, 2000: 43). However, David did show evidence of emotional consistency toward persons and objects of which he had no memory. He would manifest certain preferences and avoidances that seemed to have no basis in knowledge or recognition. Damasio and his colleagues subjected David to a "'good-guy-bad-guy' experiment" (44) in which he experienced a week of consistently pleasant and relatively unpleasant experiences, respectively, with the two colleagues. Although each person and experience would be instantly forgotten, David nevertheless managed to identify with an overwhelming consistency the images of the two colleagues as persons he would be likely to avoid or go to for help without having any knowledge or memory of them. As Damasio writes,

> He did not know why he chose one or rejected the other; he just did. The nonconscious preference he manifested, however, is probably related to the emotions that were induced in him during the experiment, as well as to the nonconscious reinduction of some part of those emotions at the time he was being tested . . . David's brain could generate actions commensurate with the emotional value of the original encounters. (Damasio, 2000: 45–46)

Just in case a skeptical reader wonders about the quality of the physical attributes of the good and bad guys, Damasio reassures us that "the bad guy in our experiment was a young, pleasant, and beautiful woman neuropsychologist" whose contrary behavior successfully countervailed David's usual 'eye for the girls' (46).

The maker of *Memento*, Christopher Nolan, seems to have been aware of this scientific argument when he makes the observation in the DVD commentary that "Leonard is driven by an emotional memory he doesn't understand." As has been argued, this emotion is not primarily fear, horror, or guilt, but joy. Prior to the jouissance that is indelibly bound up with the signifier for Lacan, joy underlies Leonard's core consciousness generating the actions commensurate with the emotion. As Damasio affirms, joy and its variants "lead to greater functional perfection" (Damasio, 2003: 284); Leonard the investigator who knows nothing develops the emotional intelligence of a superkiller. To ventriloquize Deleuze in the style of Hamlet:

> And the Event all alone shall live
> Inside what occurs, purely expressed
> Within the screen, film stock and camera of my brain.

EVENT MANAGEMENT

I have been reading Deleuze and Guattari's *What Is Philosophy* backwards, from the concluding chapter, "From Chaos to the Brain" to the Introduction, "The Question then . . ." I have been reading backwards, through the clarification of the concept and the event, to the event that begins the book: the strange death of the philosophical concept. All the definitions of percept and function that give the concept its philosophical distinction unfold in the wake of the death of concept. In the introductory chapter to *What Is Philosophy* there is, as in *Memento*, the murder-event, or rather the murder of the event. Quietly announced, the philosophical concept has passed away to be reanimated in a different form in "the general movement that replaced Critique with sales promotion" (1994: 10). The concept moves to management where it meets an already managerialized science.

> Marketing has preserved the idea of a certain relationship between the concept and the event. But here the concept has become a set of product displays . . . the only events are exhibitions and the only concepts are products that can be sold . . . The simulacrum, the simulation of a packet of noodles has become the true concept. (Deleuze and Guattari, 1994: 10)

Philosophy's response to this appropriation of the concept is to get the giggles, to laugh at the commercial products and focus on the "singular point where concept and creation are related to each other" (11). When the concept is taken over by the functionality of a managerialized science, philosophy looks to its defining other on the plane of composition. In the next chapter, philosophy's 'giggles' are discovered creating a concept of joy's laughter immanent to the world of technoscientific bureaucracy. In the creation of a philosophy graduate, Ricky Gervais, and his colleague Stephen Merchant, *The Office* (2003) subjects sales promotion and management to the rigorous critique of laughter. It remains to be seen whether this laughter is not also integral, however, to the autodeconstructive power of management discourse.

As Antonio Damasio shows, scientific discourse has become managerialized along with philosophical discourse and culture (with its talk of vision, creativity, imagination). Managerial principles determine that the neurological cinema is organized to manage the 'self-component' that is required to both star in and watch itself in its own reality television show. The culture industry of the brain keeps postindustrial Britain going. The movie-in-the-brain is crucial for the efficient 'management of life'. Disruptions to the self-component of the movie is deleterious to "life management" (Damasio, 2003: 207), and in this way the subject is sustained as a neurological cinematic effect. The next chapter looks at how laughter operates as one of the primary emotions, interior to and exterior to the movie that functions both to regulate and manage the self-components, but also to open them up, infinitely.

CHAPTER SEVEN

Joy's Laughter

Singularity:
1. The quality or condition of being singular.
2. A trait marking one as distinct from others.
3. A point in space-time at which gravitational forces cause matter to have infinite density and infinitesimal volume, and space and time to become infinitely distorted.
4. $f(x) = 1/x$ (where $x = 0$, explodes to $\pm\infty$ and isn't defined).
5. *Singularity* helps its customers profit through process. Whether by deploying the award-winning *Singularity Process Platform*™ or by utilizing our services and solutions. *Singularity*'s customers build, execute, monitor, and optimize high-performing business processes that deliver tangible results.
6. *The Techno-Rapture*. A future time when societal, scientific, and economic change is so fast we cannot even imagine what will happen from our present perspective, and when humanity will become posthumanity.

THE FUNNINESS OF BEING

The deconstruction of the subject leaves a question that marks a place, "who or what 'answers' to the question 'who'?" (Derrida, 1995: 258). After every thing has been subtracted, every quality, every sign of self-identity, every 'what' or whatever is taken away, who is left? For Derrida, the 'who' that is both a question and the power to ask a question is overwhelmed and reinscribed in the experience of an affirmation (261). Even the "most primordial question implies . . . that 'yes, yes' that answers before even being able to formulate a question, that is responsible without autonomy, before and in view of all possible autonomy of the who-subject etc" (261). The 'relation to self' in this experience of affirmation "can only be difference, that is to say alterity, or trace . . . it is out of this dislocated *affirmation* that something like the subject, man, or whoever it might be can take shape" (261).

Writing about his affinity with the dominant theses in Deleuze's work, Derrida cites, as evidence of their close proximity and their friendship, above all his conception of difference, 'the joyously repeated affirmation ("yes, yes")' that lies at a level "'more profound' than contradiction" (Derrida, 2001: 486). This affirmative joy is prior to any program of desire, rivalry, love, or hate, and therefore outside of any jouissance related to negation. This presubjective affirmation of joy is necessary to the formulation of any question, necessary to the construction of any form of knowledge or intended enjoyment.

The term that Derrida uses to denote this proto-subject of joyful affirmation is "singularity." The 'who' has a singularity from which a question can arise posed both to itself and the other.

> The singularity of the "who" is not the individuality of a thing that would be identical to itself, it is not an atom. It is a singularity that discloses or divides itself in gathering itself together to answer to the other, whose call somehow precedes its own identification with itself, for to this call I can *only* answer, have already answered, even if I think I am answering 'no'. (Derrida, 1995: 261)

In conversation with Jean-Luc Nancy, Derrida links singularity's joyful affirmation to James Joyce's *Ulysses* and the words "yes, yes" that end (without ending) the novel, words that are spoken by Molly Bloom as she comes in masturbation (also see "Ulysses Gramophone: Hear Say Yes in Joyce," Derrida, 1992b). This joy has no opposite, no possibility of negativity or negation; it is a joy that is affirmative perhaps even despite itself, and determines the positivity of all possible exchanges. Yet this singular joy is nevertheless traced, in Derrida's text, in the outline of an other jouissance, a (fictional) woman coming to orgasm. It is the joy of a woman's jouissance that can't say no or whose "no" always means "yes." I think that's pretty funny; it is being funny despite oneself.

But laughter is indeed a force that divides the subject from itself in an involuntary utterance that derives from and proceeds toward the other. Like any utterance, for Derrida, laughter must be preceded by a joy of laughter that is the affirmative power to laugh, a laughter that precedes any negativity of laughter. Or as Georges Bataille affirms, "in laughter, ecstasy is freed, is immanent. The laughter of ecstasy doesn't *laugh*, instead it opens me up infinitely" (Bataille, 1988b: 103). In this chapter, I propose to look at the singularity of joy's laughter in relation to the subject, the subject of the state, and the bureaucratic state function. The term "singularity" has a number of contemporary meanings, so this chapter will, in the spirit of deconstruction, address the contemporary textuality of this term. This is necessary in order to trace the differance immanent to the signifier and its movement, in order to take account of its difference, its alterity, its trace, and open up to infinity the place marked by the addressee of the question "who?"

BEING FUNNY

1. The quality or condition of being singular.

In Europe, it is said that certain nations pride themselves on one characteristic above all others. That doesn't mean they don't value other qualities, but they overvalue one singular trait so that those who are perceived to lack it appear a little less than human. For the Germans it is respectability. For the French it is intelligence. For the Italians it is style. For the English, however, it is the possession of a sense of humor. It is through this quality that the English define their singularity, in the sense of it being a trait that marks them out as distinct from other nations.[1] And, as with so many other types of distinction, it is supposed to be something that other nations lack in quite the same way.

It may have been the case, some time ago, that the English would have regarded respectability as essential. For the Victorians, one imagines, respectability would have been much more important than a sense of humor. Queen Victoria herself is remembered for the catch phrase "We are not amused," which if it isn't to be regarded as a demand, suggests the Victorians lacked a sense of humor—although the example of Lewis Carroll and Edward Lear would qualify that somewhat. However, the English no longer regard respectability to be essential; indeed respectability is now regarded with a certain amount of suspicion. It is assumed that those who overvalue respectability have something to hide.

But surely it is important to be intelligent. What could possibly be wrong with the French valuing intelligence above all other things? Well, the English are very suspicious of intelligence, perhaps even more than respectability. The term "clever," for example, is more of an insult than a compliment in English. "He's a bit clever." Or "she's very clever" also means, she's superficial, or he's vain and foolish. "Common sense," which you simply possess through the virtue of being English, is much more important than cleverness or intelligence. As for style, well, like cleverness, it is also a sign of vanity and superficiality, and is slightly suspect.

The English regard these qualities as lacking in something that contributes to their overvaluation. And for the English that something is humor, especially irony. Where the English are keen to appear respectable, intelligent, or stylish, they will always be humorously self-deprecating about it. This ironic self-deprecation will suggest, to those who appreciate the irony, that the other quality is all the more genuine for being underplayed. The Americans of course lack irony, and are brash. The Germans have no sense of humor at all, and therefore can't see how hilarious goose-stepping looks.[2] This way of discussing national characteristics is highly unscientific, facile, and indeed itself a joke. But insofar as it is recognizable, it is instructive as an example of how each positive finds its definition in a negative. It is not enough that the English should value a sense of humor; other nations must be seen to lack it.

These special qualities are mythical in the sense that they appear natural, positive, and self-evident, but may actually cover up some negativity or conflict in society. Indeed I would argue that the myth concerning English humor and its continual reproduction on British television and social life is crippling. This is not because the negativity of laughter has not been perceived—quite the contrary. In fact, the past thirty years or so of English comedy, in theater and television, have been marked by a critique of humor as a modality of national and social superiority and social and racial abjection. An 'alternative comedy' movement arose in the early 1980s that both drew attention to, and rejected, the form of humor that drew its force from the ridicule and abjection of others. Jokes about women, other nationalities, and other races were the stock material of 'traditional' comedians in the 1970s. In the 1980s, these traditional comedians became the objects of scorn by a younger generation of comedians who combined youth and glamor with a left-wing political consciousness to drive out the old guard.

Consequently, humor became a modality of style, intelligence, and even respectability in the sense of a social conscience. Comedy became the 'new rock and roll' and also the new alternative politics. It was hip and it was concerned. In 1985, British pop music, lead by an Irishman, turned itself into an unlikely vehicle for famine relief in Africa. Eight million pounds were raised by a pop single, and 140 million pounds were raised in donations inspired by a huge concert held in London the following year. In the process, a number of rock stars prolonged their fading careers for a few years, but it is not my intention to be uncharitable. However, in the late 1980s, this charitable function was taken over by comedy stars. And every year since ordinary British people have been urged by celebrities to be funny at work and at school in order to raise money for charity. These days are known as Red Nose Days because the purchase and wearing of plastic red noses is the main device through which one can simultaneously give to charity and be funny. "Who says famine has to be depressing!," as David Brent will later exclaim in an episode of *The Office* that features this annual event. The penultimate episode of the second and last series is set on a Red Nose Day, a day in which the main character is also laid off from his job (Gervais & Merchant, 2002).

The Office (2003, 2004) was written and directed by Ricky Gervais and Stephen Merchant. The show is closely focused on ordinary people in a very ordinary, though stressful bureaucratic setting—the characters are working under the threat of redundancy. It is represented in a faux documentary style. *The Office* is a situation comedy that appears to be a documentary. In fact it could be argued that it introduced a new subgenre into the field of comedy. It is not just a situation comedy or sit-com but a situmentary or doc-com. It has the style of *cinema verité*, but far from ignoring the cameras, the main characters play up to them in the manner of reality television. Mainly in the shape of the major protagonist David Brent, played by Ricky Gervais, *The Office* relentlessly exposes and subjects to ridicule and cringing embarrassment the English overvaluation of humor. It subjects to a spectacular attack what Ben Thompson has called the comedification of the self in Britain (Thompson, 2004: 416). The question of whether that attack immediately transmogrifies into celebration is a mute point, however.

While, historically, professional humor may have been the province of clowns, fools, and people from the margins of society, in the 1980s and 1990s it became a sphere of glamor, celebrity, and aspiration. Everyday humor became a form of sophistication and mastery, a way of demonstrating your style, your wit, your intelligence, and popularity. In *The Office* it is made clear that Brent's identity is bound up with a continual mimicry of professional humorists, something that is enhanced and rendered self-conscious by the presence of the 'documentary' cameras. His office banter is continually accompanied by a series of asides to the camera in which he comments on his technique, and approves or disapproves of the ethical content of a joke or comic situation as it arises, usually with spectacular misjudgment.

Further, in the close-up talking-head shots, Brent takes the opportunity to give full rein to his comedy philosophy, and managerial expertise. This is in itself to partake imaginarily in the world of television celebrity since so many contemporary programs are nothing more than commentaries on other shows featuring actors and comedians who reflect on and celebrate their own brilliance and that of their costars. In this sense, Gervais's performance is clearly satirical and a critique on the absurdity of the world of media celebrity that has come to popularly define the value of a public identity in Britain in the late 1980s and 1990s.

The speculative, ironic gamble of *The Office*, therefore, was always that it would successfully participate in the process it satirizes. *The Office* is a sitcom about a boss trying to turn his workplace into a sitcom whose comic failure guarantees its success. The rise of the reality television show is of course the essential stake in this gamble. The phenomenal success of shows like Endemol's *Big Brother* is crucial. In these shows, ordinary people are turned into celebrities purely through being placed in an artificial domestic setting like that of a situation comedy. They are kept under total surveillance while being made to compete with their other housemates in popularity contests that may eventually result in their being evicted from the house. Like the characters in *The Office*, the Big Brother housemates are also working-performing in a stressful environment under the constant threat of layoff or eviction. Intermittently, they are called for interview and asked to reflect, in a close-up with the camera, on their thoughts, feelings, and views about the other housemates. The success of this show and others clearly shaped the conditions in which *The Office*'s realism proved effective. The actors very skillfully mimic the ways in which television cameras seem to produce a kind of gauche exhibitionism in English people. When it was first broadcast, *The Office* looked like a reality television show (later, there was a reality television show set in an office that naturally aspired to the condition of *The Office*).

The Office's main mode of humor, therefore, is ironic on various levels. As a comedy, its target is to produce an uncomfortable (if not hysterical) sense of recognition in the heart of 'middle England' where it is set: the predominantly middle-class, middle-aged, white Home Counties England that is at the center of power. Since the days of alternative comedy in the 1980s, when predominantly white, middle-class university-educated, southern Englishmen and women took over from working-class, northern, Irish, and Scottish men as the most successful professional comedians, this middle England has been the subject of humor in every sense. David Brent and *The Office* continue this trend, but they introduce the self-critical edge and negativity of alternative comedy into the form of the situation comedy where middle England has always had a more comfortable home. As subject and object of English humor, the irony that structures *The Office* exploits in its audience a shared anxiety about the importance of being funny in Britain. Since there is no being but that of being funny, our existence is anxiously dependent on the laughter of the Other.

ABJECTIVE IRONY

2. A trait marking one as distinct from others.

Of all the forms and figures of humor, a sense of irony is the quality with which the English, particularly the English middle classes, like to distinguish themselves. The English like to believe that it is their sense of irony, resplendent in their literature and natural wit that makes them distinct from others, no matter how humorous they may be. The Americans, for example, have a wonderful tradition of burlesque comedy and Jewish wit, but, for the English, they lack a sense of irony. As this form of imaginary exclusion would suggest, the structure of irony reproduces that of the crudest joke in that it establishes a bond between speaker and hearer at the expense of a third person or persons. Indeed, one of the main differences between the standard joke and irony is that the latter is so socially exclusive that the put-down should be subtly implied or hidden in such a way that it actually escapes the apprehension of the object of the joke. This is in contrast to sarcasm (which the Americans do very well) where the other person is supposed to understand very well that you are saying the opposite of what you mean when you say: "That's *sooooo* funny!" The success of an ironic statement in maintaining a sense of social exclusivity depends on the shared enjoyment of shared knowledge in relation to an ignorance it is keen to maintain.

There are many forms of irony and I am going to suggest that *The Office* introduces a new one. The main traditional forms are: (1) subjective irony, in which an utterance is marked by a deliberate contrast between apparent and intended meaning; and (2) objective irony in which an ironic statement alludes to a discrepancy between a false appearance and a shared or 'objective' knowledge of reality. While the first form is more common in literature, the second form is highly popular in drama— and is indeed sometimes known as dramatic irony in which a character's apparently truthful or self-evident statements are disclosed to be false by the context in which they are located. In contrast to the audience, and often the other characters, the character is blind to this objective reality or to a narrative fate of which the audience has a shared, prior knowledge. That is, they know what is going to happen. This occurs not just in comedy, of course, but in the most serious drama and tragedy. *Oedipus Rex* is the most famous instance of dramatic irony.

To give an example of how irony works in a national and political context, an article in *The Economist* discusses the persistent prevalence of an ironic tone among English diplomats (*The Economist*, 1999). The article recalls a (possibly apocryphal) story about Sir Oliver Franks, when he was Britain's ambassador in Washington after World War Two. A journalist asked leading ambassadors what they desired in the coming year. The Russian ambassador mentioned the liberation of colonial peoples; the French ambassador spoke of a new era of peace and international cooperation. Sir Oliver expressed a desire for a small box of crystallized fruit. Sir Oliver debunks the grandiosity of the French and Russian ambassadors' pious wishes by contrasting them with his own modest hope for a box of sweets, thereby alluding to, at best, their lack of realism or, at worst, their hypocrisy. Further, he does this through tacitly acknowledging the reality that Britain has no power in the world to bring about, or hope to bring about, such grandiose schemes (thereby obviating the need to try, one might also add). But if this kind of diplomatic irony functions as a vehicle of self-reflection and self-deprecation, *The Office* takes as its object the process of self-reflection itself, as if there is always something intrinsically funny about someone looking at themselves in a mirror. In *The Office*, an audience would be presented with Sir Oliver's direct-to-camera account of why he feels it's important to use his comedy in his role of ambassador.

The faux-documentary format of *The Office* allows the characters to talk directly to the camera, reflecting on their working lives and their relationships, thereby offering innumerable opportunities for objective irony in which their statements can be contrasted and contradicted by their actions. In quite a traditional way, Brent's claims about his management and 'people skills' are constantly belied by his ineptitude, vanity, and irresponsibility. Equally, Gareth's delusions about his military machismo, sexual charisma, and law-of-the-jungle social Darwisnism are belied by his gawky appearance, low status and sycophancy. The contrast between a character's self-knowledge and the audience's perception works in a similar way with Dawn and Tim, though in the opposite direction. In his addresses to the camera, Tim's modest but sincere statements about his lack of self-confidence and cowardice are set against his inventive, genuinely amusing play with Gareth and his charming flirtation with Dawn to suggest he is actually the most intelligent and attractive person in the office. The ironic construction of Dawn's character is similar to Tim's in that her lack of self-esteem, timidity and reticence obscures the fact that she is the moral center of the series. While the audience laughs at the routines and practical jokes that become the occasion of her romance with Tim, all attempts to make fun of Dawn fail. She is the first of the main characters to be introduced by Brent to the documentary-camera-audience in the first episode. Characteristically, he makes a joke to the camera—"I think every man in the office has at one time or another woken up at the crack of Dawn"—but rather than timid resignation, the joke is met with genuine outrage. More than any other character throughout the series, Brent's abjection is exposed in relation to Dawn's dignity.

The ironic presentation of these four main characters, then, the seductive gap opened up by the misrecognition of self-reflection, invites empathy and identification from the audience. This gap produces the documentary illusion of real people more than the two-dimensional representation of social types. Even so, comic villains like Chris Finch, grotesques like Keith in Accounts, the rude mechanicals in the warehouse, the female boss, the representatives of ethnic minorities and the disabled are all played as straight and as convincingly as possible. Their comic effect is generally produced through their potential to elicit something embarrassing from Brent.

In contrast to these two-dimensional characters, Brent's subversion lies in the combination of empathy and abjection that he elicits in an audience. The ironic construction of Brent's inept self-presentation ought to establish the bond of humor at his expense between the audience and the program makers (either Gervais and Merchant themselves or the fictional, silent documentary makers). The audience laughs at Brent's pretentiousness and self-delusion, laid bare by the 'objective' documentary form. Yet what happens is that the ironic gap disclosed by his mode of self-reflection actually draws an audience into a core of self-abjection. The 'objectivity' of the documentary realism combined with the intimacy of personal confession successfully constructs Brent as a mirror to middle Britain. Every male middle manager in England suddenly catches himself nervously tugging at his tie as his latest office joke falls flat. Consequently, every attempt at humor, every self-serving justification, every managerial cliché, each solicitation of support from his staff, just deepens the hole in which Brent and the audience sink in humiliated self-recognition. Objective irony gives way to an abjective irony in which abjection meets the uncanny in an implosion of subjectivity. Brent makes his audience cringe. We want to hide behind the sofa, crawl into a hole while dying of laughter.

Julia Kristeva argues that "there is nothing like the abjection of self to show that all abjection is in fact recognition of the *want* on which any being, meaning, language, or desire is founded" (Kristeva, 1982: 5). In its abjective irony, *The Office* discloses an abyss of want, hollowed out by the ontology of bureaucratic life. It is this area of 'darkness' that Gervais and Merchant consider essential to humor: a black hole of human subjectivity around which dreams, desires, and delusions circulate.

SUPEREGO

3. A point in space-time at which gravitational forces cause matter to have infinite density and infinitesimal volume, and space and time to become infinitely distorted.

While the English may not think much of the German sense of humor, the Germans do at least have a word for the English variety. The Germans recognize a *schwarzer humor* that they apparently regard as distinctively English. *Schwarzer* humor means dark or black humor, which is not easy for other nations to get or understand.

In an interview with journalist Ben Thompson, Ricky Gervais and Stephen Merchant reflect on their own version of *schwarzer humor*. Gervais gives the example that: "a clown running around in trifle is only so funny . . . But a man whose wife has just left him *falling over* in some trifle, that is absolutely hilarious . . . because that's where the darkness comes in" (cited in Thompson, 2004: 407). In complete agreement, Merchant adds, "Oh, his wife's left him, and he's covered in custard, and there she comes with her new boyfriend" (407).

Gervais is a philosophy graduate of University College London, and this account of humor is very reminiscent of Henri Bergson. In *Laughter* (1928), Bergson notes that "Doubtless a fall is always a fall, but it is one thing to tumble into a well because you were looking anywhere but in front of you, it is quite another thing to fall into it because you were intent on a star" (Bergson, 1928: 13).

In both cases, an inhuman agency appears to mock human tragedy or aspiration with the empirical bump of everyday reality. And while Bergson is of course French, this antiromantic empiricism is exactly the kind of comedy the English traditionally enjoy and like to claim as distinctively their own. Further, for Bergson, laughter is Benthamite, it "pursues a utilitarian aim of general improvement" through a process of correction, attempting to be rid of "a certain rigidity of body, mind and character" so that it can "obtain from its members the greatest possible degree of elasticity and sociability" (1928: 21). "This rigidity is the comic and laughter is its corrective" (21). As a purging of the comic, laughter is paradoxical in the sense that it would appear to want to extinguish the very source from which it draws its strength. Or to put it another way, the more laughter consumes and purges the comic, the more comic laughter itself becomes, turning in a vicious circle of endlessly generative self-negation.

As such, the structure and functionality of Bergson's laughter clearly resemble the superego in Freud. The superego is the "portion of the ego which sets itself over against the rest of the ego . . . and in the form of conscience, puts into action against the ego the same harsh aggressiveness that it would like to exert on others" (Freud, 1927). But further, Freud also notes that the superego is operative in many forms of humor, and that the superegoic function of humor is particularly operative when one laughs at oneself. Like Bergson, Freud considers that the deprecating negativity of humor can have beneficial effects.

In a short essay on "Humour" (1927), Freud gives the example of a condemned man who walks to the scaffold with the cheery phrase "Well, the week's beginning nicely . . ." For Freud this is an example of the humorous attitude bolstering the ego and the pleasure principle in the face of an unpleasant reality, imminent death. The superego is 'heir to the parental agency', but rather than being a prohibitive embodiment of the law, it is transgressive, rebellious, urging the ego to enjoy itself in defiance of reality. Hence the sense of elevation or liberation. Freud acknowledges that this is in fact an illusory repudiation of reality, but it is the superego's 'parental' attempt to console the ego and protect it from suffering. As if in the words of a parent, or a friend's banter, the insouciant superego dismisses the cares and tribulations of the world as "just worth making a joke about" (166). As comedy philosopher Simon Critchley put it, in a commentary on Freud's paper, the "super ego is your amigo" (Critchley, 2002: 93, 103).

As part amigo, part parent, and part chilled-out light entertainer, the superego would seem, in its repudiation of reality, to be doing precisely the opposite to Bergson's humorous agency that dumps a stargazer down a well. But the imminence of one's death is surely as profound an object of contemplation as the stars, and just as real. Do Bergson's humorous agency and Freud's superego amigo negate one another in their mutual rebellion, or does one enhance the other? What happens, who laughs and who consoles, when the superego falls down the hole?

Toward the end of the first episode of *The Office*, David Brent is concluding his induction of Ricky, the new temp. All day, Brent has been imparting his philosophy of laughter and its application to managerial practice to Ricky and the documentary team, in between emergency meetings with his CEO and dealing with rumors, rife among his staff, about branch mergers and staff layoffs. Relaxing in his office, Brent sums up for Ricky the main points of the day:

> You've seen the vibe. Chilled out. Oh dear. We work hard, I mean we play hard. Play hard when we should be working hard sometimes—partly down to me. I let them get away with murder and they let me. The girls love me. Not in that way. But I suppose I've created an atmosphere where I'm a friend first and a boss second. Probably an entertainer third. Hold on. Practical joke. (Gervais and Merchant, 2003)

Brent sees Dawn approaching his office with another fax and has an idea. Clearly drawing inspiration from the comic business we have just seen surrounding Tim's practical joke with Gareth (the latter discovers his stapler set in jelly), Brent proposes his own joke that will conclude the business of helping Ricky settle in. In the process he will cement the social bond his laughter has already established between Ricky and the office crew and, further, with the documentary camera that has been the constant focus of Brent's performance throughout the day. Brent decides to bond everyone together, including the camera-audience, with a 'parental' consoling joke about redundancy. Superficially, the joke will work at Dawn's expense, bonding Brent, Ricky, and the camera in relation to her. But everyone knows what a friend, benevolent boss and entertainer Brent is, so by acting 'superegoically' and making light of the fear of redundancy, Dawn should be liberated from the reality of the threat.

Brent motions Dawn to sit down and, with a straight face, summarily informs her that she's being dismissed for stealing Post-It notes. In the enthusiasm of his convincing masquerade, Brent refuses to accept any of Dawn's protestations of innocence, and she breaks down and weeps. There's a long pause. Ricky, excruciatingly embarrassed, twists in his chair as Brent's jaw finally drops at the effects of his humor. "That was a joke there," he whispers, head down, tugging at his shirtsleeve, his eyes furtively look up at the camera witnessing his catastrophe. The camera cuts to Dawn, recovering, in silence. "Good girl," Brent consoles, "that's a joke we were doing there. Good. Settling in. Practical jokes for the good." As Brent invokes Ricky's benefit and complicity, the camera mercilessly switches to record the latter's deep discomfort and shame. It returns to Dawn, close-up, in profile.

"You wanker."
"Come on."
"You're such a sad little man."

As he becomes smaller and smaller, disappearing into his profound well of wretchedness, Brent's abysmal and abyssal cataclysm sucks everything into its density. The bond between Brent, Ricky, the camera, and the audience gets sucked into the darkness, a black hole of cringing, prurient embarrassment. We can barely look, but can't resist, as the camera moves in closer to meet Brent's furtive glance looking up into the mirror of his humiliation.

With the character of David Brent, *The Office* presents a comical characterization of the superego being constantly tormented by the tyrannical superegoic imperative to transgress in order to be the occasion of the law's punishing enjoyment. Consistent with this, Brent's comedy is constantly accompanied by a spectacularly misjudged or hypocritical commentary on its political correctness. Indeed, in his exchanges with his female boss, black British and British Asian colleagues, and the staff member in a wheelchair, the commentary hysterically draws attention to his unconscious sexism, racism, and repulsion at disability. Superego and id converge on the 'dissatisfied fool' that is the ego and torture it into oblivion.[3]

In this black hole of abjective irony in which everything is consumed, time and space begin to get distorted as the distinctions between appearance and reality, upon which conventional irony depends, dissolve. Of course, *The Office* is not real. It would not have been real as a documentary; David Brent's behavior, like that of everyone else, is constantly bent toward, and distorted by, the presence of the camera that pursues the implosion at the center of his performative self-reflection. That is, a purely performative presentation of self-reflection that circulates the black hole created by the 'self's' infinite implosion. The laughter emerges as an effect of this singularity, the dense reality at the point of infinite distortion.

The superegoic illusion of bureaucratic abjection that would protect and console English white-collar workers and television viewers from the reality of office life and nightmare bosses, transmutes into reality. This is not because its realism successfully mirrors everyday life but because the seductive power of Brent's performance draws everyone into its infinite, ironic spiral of abject mimicry. It is not clear who is mimicking whom. Superego and id seem interchangeable, mirror images, laughing at each other into infinity over the abyss of the ego's infinite collapse.

THE FUNCTION OF LAUGHTER

4. $f(x) = 1/x$ (where $x = 0$, *explodes to* $\pm\infty$ *and isn't defined*).

What is the function of laughter? For Bergson, laughter is the means of the soul's resistance to the obstinacy of matter (1928: 28), vitality's deployment of automatism. The world of comic objects is that of matter and the body, whereas laughter derives from the soul even though it is of the body. Men and women are both animalistic and machinic, but as such they are funny. "The attitudes, gestures and movements of the human body," Bergson writes, "are laughable in exact proportion as that body reminds us of a mere machine" (29). Further, nowhere is that automatism more fully operative than in the modern world of technobureaucracy: "complete automatism is only reached in the official, for instance, who performs his duty like a mere machine, or again in the unconsciousness that marks an administrative regulation working with inexorable fatality" (46). Imitation, mimesis, repetition are all forms of automatism, in contrast to the life of a 'living personality' (32–33). Since it is precisely the absence of mechanism, what Bergson calls life that never imitates, "our gestures can only be imitated in their mechanical uniformity, and therefore exactly in what is alien to our living personality. The truth is that a really living life should never repeat itself" (43).

Laughter, therefore, comes from a sovereign impetus of pure vitality, inimitability, spontaneous and unrepeatable, a vivacity that is associated

with the animation of the mind. "Our mental state is ever changing, and if
our gestures faithfully followed these inner movements, if they were as fully
alive as we, they would never repeat themselves, and so would keep imitation at bay" (Bergson, 1928: 32–33). Laughter is the mind's way of chastis-
ing and correcting the body that is never as fully animated as it should be:

> the living body ought to be the perfection of suppleness, the
> ever-alert activity of a principle always at work. But this activ-
> ity would really belong to the soul rather than to the body. It
> would be the very flame of life, kindled within us by a higher
> principle . . . a vitality which we regard as derived from the very
> principle of intellectual and moral life. (Bergson, 1928: 49–50)

The sovereign impetus is strictly locatable nowhere and in no thing, not
even in the mind since it is the principle that causes mental states to
change. But it is associated with the ordering principle of knowledge and
moral life, and when it deploys humor it is in order to abject the base materiality and functionality of the body. As a humorist, writes Bergson, the
'higher principle' "is a moralist disguised as a scientist, something like an
anatomist who practices dissection with the sole object of filling us with
disgust" (128). The higher principle kindles the flame of life by abjecting
the body, and correcting the self through laughter.

For Bergson, laughter is itself abject in the sense that it is equally
mechanistic. "Laughter is simply the result of a mechanism set up in us by
nature". It is a mechanism that chastises itself, corrects the transgressive
embarrassments of bodily functionality in an equally automatic and similarly transgressive form: a fall, a fart, laughter. For Bergson, "there is
nothing very benevolent in laughter. It seems rather inclined to return evil
for evil" (194). Laughter derives from no place, is nothing and goes
nowhere, but it does have a function. The function of laughter can be
expressed mathematically:

$$f(x) = 1/x$$

This function has a singularity at $x = 0$, where it explodes to $\pm\infty$ and
isn't defined.

Exploding from a point of pure virtuality that is nothing other than
the absence of mechanism, materiality, and the body, laughter produces
variation through a process of division and difference. Which is to say
that laughter explodes from the 0 that marks the place of the vital impetus that animates the flame of life. In itself it is nothing—no thing—but
it animates everything through its negation of all that is mechanical,

repetitive, dead, and therefore disgusting. Such a formula necessitates that laughter is infinite, turning forever in a circle, automatically laughing at its own functionality, dividing the body into an infinity of living particles, hollowing out the 0 of pure bodiless vitality.

For Bergson, then, laughter automatically irrupts from nothing to divide the univocity of being into a multiplicity of becoming. Zero should not be understood here, as in other philosophies, in opposition with being as nothingness, the void over which being unfolds. Rather, zero is immanent to the One as its principle of infinite divisibility and becoming. Divisibility, not in the sense of a line divided up into a series of measurable points, but in the sense of the division of cells where zero marks the point of the vital impetus, the indefinable virtual point of infinite potential. "Life does not proceed by the association and addition of elements, but by dissociation and division" (Bergson, 1960: 94). The One continually divides from itself as laughter reverberates through the whole of creation, disassociating and driving each becoming to evolve, to adapt and readapt itself in relation to its changing milieu (Bergson, 1928:196). Virtual becoming is actualized in the singularity.

THE COMEDY OF EXCELLENCE

5. *Singularity* helps its customers profit through process. Whether by deploying the award-winning *Singularity Process Platform*™ or by utilizing our services and solutions. *Singularity*'s customers build, execute, monitor, and optimize high-performing business processes that deliver tangible results.

If laughter is evil for Bergson, the accursed expenditure of debased mechanism, it still has a social utility as a corrective. Irrupting from nothing, laughter may emerge from a position of radical evil in the sense of unfathomable alterity. But, in Bergson's scheme, this does not stop it from having a function. Laughter functions in a way that is consistent with another enlightenment conception of evil as the necessary, specifically human content of moral law. For Kant, in *Religion within the Limits of Reason*, for example, humanity is only conscious of moral law through its sense of transgression, through guilty conscience. The embarrassment caused by the laughter of others at some bodily failure or instance of mechanical inelasticity is further evidence of the consciousness of a higher principle. "A person embarrassed by his body" (51), suggests Bergson, is also keenly aware that this embarrassment is both a censure and a substitution of an essentially moral failure. "Any incident is comic that calls our attention to the physical in a person, when it is the moral side that is concerned" (1928: 50–51).

The Office not only draws attention to this particular function of laughter, it also deploys it to provide an ironic counterpoint to a similar structure in managerial discourse. It is in a form that is Kantian in this way that technobureaucracies also succeed in managing the human resources at their disposal. Of course, as capitalist enterprises, technobureaucracies have no governing principle other than profit, but this idea of profit is simply one aspect, a means, of operativity. Profit is not an end point, but occurs through process, and is related to an image of the corporation's singularity in the sense of optimum performance and functional perfection. It is quite wrong, therefore, to suggest that in corporations higher principles have been discarded in the face of a cynical drive for profit that disappears in the pockets of greedy executives and managers. That is an essential effect of profit, but not now its limit. Similarly, the idea of a higher principle does not govern the system from outside, as an end point or goal. The higher principle does not promise, as an effect of its achievement, the enjoyment of profit, the idea of knowledge, or the profit of jouissance. Rather, the higher principle is incorporated, immanent to the system, its governing process that corresponds to an image of joy. But here the term "image" needs to be understood in a way similar to Bergson and Antonio Damasio.

For Bergson, an image means "a certain existence" that is "more than a representation, but less than a thing" (1911: xi). In the technobureaucratic system, this existence consists in an aggregate of presentations that are related to, and modified by, a process of perception—appraisal, evaluation, audit—which is referred to the quality of one particular image of the corporate entity as a whole and its performance. As Damasio argues, images are also concrete (neural) constructions of an organism's interactivity with the world, inseparable from the affects that shape and infuse them. Where the organism has a capability for self-reflection, however, the aggregate of images and affects is related to one single image, the image of the organism itself in its relation with its own reality. An image of a "state of optimal functioning, subsumed by the concept of joy, results from the successful endeavour to endure and prevail" in that reality (Damasio, 2003: 170–171). For Damasio, emotions are part of the immanent (innate) and automated machinery of system governance (2003: 30), and joy is both the expression and experience of an image of a "greater perfection of function" (13).

Since the late 1980s, the term for optimal performance has been "excellence." Again, while it is an empty form designating a purely notional value of performance, its moral force is clearly manifest in the pervasive fear of personal failure it instills in every employee who may be deemed merely "satisfactory" or even "poor"—that is, inefficient or inoperative. The performance of employees is defined by two qualities above all else: their (self-) presentation and their efficient operativity.

That is, their ability to operate efficiently in relation to other operatives is inseparable from their mode of presentation and self-presentation. The two elements combined constitute them as 'images'. They are operative-images that operate with and affect other operative images in relation to the particular image of the joy of optimal functioning. In order to operate effectively, the images need constantly to be perceived, assessed, and monitored. In this way, the higher principle maintains the level of performance and operational affect through processes such as appraisal, peer evaluation, customer feedback. These processes correlate the affectivity and effectiveness of the operative-images in relation to the particular image of corporate joy. While the main affect is one of anxiety, the anxiety associated with inoperativity is necessary in that it keeps performance at optimal levels through a constant fear of failure. Failure itself is important because it enables renewal and therefore regularly allows and justifies the necessary degree of flexibility. This is crucial in a highly competitive and changing market environment. It enables organisms (or rather anorganisms) to adapt and change. A degree of maladaption is essential to evolutionary survival. The sustained operativity of an image depends on its virtuality: its ability to actualize virtual powers through innovation, flexibility, resizing, retraining, and reskilling.

The virtuality of operative-images enables the anorganic corporate assemblage to take advantage of the event that irrupts like laughter out of nowhere. As the previous chapter showed with reference to Deleuze and Guattari's *What Is Philosophy,* the event no longer produces effects that need to be understood, but rather managed. Just as the concept has migrated from philosophy into public relations, so the event that it constitutes has become the object of event management. This event gives Deleuze and Guattari the 'giggles', but, as this chapter has argued, such laughter is integral to management discourse and corporations. Hence the significance of joy's laughter and its difference from the superego. Certainly there is a functional resemblance to the superego, especially with regard to the subject-employee insofar as he or she regards herself as distinct from the machined assemblage of technobureaucracy. Just as the superego is cruelest to the most virtuous of us, so the better, the more efficient, the more hard working an employee, the more that employee feels she or he could do better. As such, the superego maintains the discipline of employees. But even as the higher principle is experienced by employees in anguish and anxiety, corporate efficiency, adaptation, and selectivity require that this anguish is related to an image of joy. Joy's laughter ironically affirms as it ridicules the necessity of human insufficiency and unhappiness.

Laughter is inherent to management discourse and provides a wordless commentary on process, particularly the process of managing employees' lives in radical absence of job security. Joy's laughter is absolutely integral to the experience of technobureaucratic life, and is avowed in complete negative inanity, which is why *The Office* had such a powerful reality effect. There is a beautiful scene in series two, episode two, in which Brent reviews the appraisal of Keith from Accounts. Brent looks through Keith's appraisal form and notices that he has left the Q&A section, concerning Keith's self-assessment, blank. "I thought you filled that in," states Keith neutrally. Brent assures his colleague that the Q&A is for his benefit, and runs through the questions. "To what extent do you believe that you have the skills to perform your job effectively?" Keith is required to tick one box from among four others labeled Not at All, To Some Extent, Very Much So and Don't Know. Keith opts, with supreme indifference, for the latter. Indeed, he answers Don't Know to all the questions, their reassuring concerns about adequate training, the accomplishment of goals, and flexibility failing to register anything but blankness. But Keith's incredulity registers that knowledge is not at issue here, only information. Indeed, Keith's indifference is simply continuous with the indifference of the form. All that matters is ticking one of the boxes. Under the heading "What are your strengths," Keith from Accounts puts "accounts." Under weaknesses, he puts "eczema."

Joy's laughter is generated, affirmed, and sustained by the creativity of new concepts like appraisal, team building, ethical orientation management, employee empowerment, impression management. Episode four of series one is set on a staff training day in which staff are treated to a seminar introduced by a video on customer care entitled "Who Cares Wins."[4] The film is narrated by the well-known British television presenter Peter Purves, but John Cleese used to make and star in these sorts of films for many years, pioneering the concept of comedy management. It goes without saying that a very lucrative opportunity would await Gervais himself in management-training DVDs if *The Office* did not itself already constitute the perfect example of the form.

The foregrounding of processes of managerial monitoring and technobureaucratic perception brings another significance to the fact that the world of *The Office* is continuous with the paradoxical *cinema verité* of Big Brother celebrity. This is an ironic comment on the world of technobureaucracy not because it is a world of total surveillance (from open-plan offices to e-mail monitoring), but because this surveillance provides the field of visibility that is the very condition of corporate existence. Without surveillance, there could be no performance. The successful naturalism of the world of *The Office* seems to confirm that everything is image, but not in a postmodern sense of the pure surface of a screen drained of affect. On the contrary, reality exists in images that are constantly modified according to their operativity and affect in relation to other images. In the case of *The Office*, the prevailing affect is laughter, which opens it on to the world of other images exterior to the fictional world of Wernham Hogg and Slough.

In this way, the presence of the faux documentary cameras fails to provide the barrier of a symbolic limit that would mediate and hold apart the 'real' world from television; inside and outside; self and other; work and leisure; serious from nonserious. The naturalism of *The Office* is not produced by the reality effect of the 'objectivity' of the documentary style in which the cameras are supposed to be hidden and behavior unfolds naturally as if they were not there. On the contrary, the naturalism is produced in the minimal technique of foregrounding the intrusive presence of cameras that provide the field of visibility and therefore existence itself.

That everyday life is defined by the intrusive, ubiquitous presence of vision machines and that existence is predicated on them is one of *The Office*'s main truth-effects. All the middle managers who felt themselves—to a lesser or greater degree—uncontrollably adopting Brent quirks, mannerisms, and gestures were simply becoming what they knew they already were, or rather had to be.[5]

THE RAPTURE

6. A future time when technological development, societal, scientific, and economic change is so fast we cannot even imagine what will happen from our present perspective, and when humanity will become posthumanity.

Punctuating many of the scenes throughout *The Office* is a single shot of a Xerox machine shuffling paper, making copy after copy after copy. The little machine provides an image of tireless work. As such, it serves as a nice metaphor for the nostalgia for office life in its archaic and very human version of mechanical work. Repetitive, boring, slow, the photocopier provides a link between the mechanical work of nineteenth-century clerks (the original computers) and their full automation and redundancy. Further, the Xerox machine recalls the threat, through its endless reproducibility, of a modern world of total homogeneity. In this way, the photocopier maintains a link to modernity; it still occupies a nineteenth- or twentieth-century bureaucratic world of ink and paper. It signals nostalgia for alienation, sustaining the difference, through analogy, of the worker and the machine, and the threat that the latter will render the former superfluous. This nostalgia is continuous with the phantasmatic threat or promise that humanity will be left behind in the wake of intelligent machines.

The involution of organic and inorganic life in the anorganic assemblages that make up networked transnational corporations promises a different form and speed of change, however. The computer, clerk, or Xerox machine is "no longer subject or object, no longer free or alienated—and no longer either one or the other: you are the *same*, and enraptured by the communication of that sameness . . . the ecstasy of the same" (Baudrillard, 1993: 58). The information and communications technology that constitutes the network in which all economic activity takes place (commercial or martial) threatens to precipitate a more advanced form of reproduction and evolution. This is joyfully anticipated by the techno-ecstatics, Transhumanists and Extropians, who communicate breathlessly on the Web. They anticipate the "imminent creation by technology of entities with greater than human intelligence." Given their greater scope of interconnection, these entities will rapidly transform the horizon of anorganic life. The mathematician and computer scientist Vernor Vinge has called this moment of technotranscendence the "singularity" (see www.ugcs.caltech.edu/~phoenix/vinge/vinge-sing.html). The term denotes "a time when change occurs at such blinding speed that mere humans will be rendered obsolescent." The event is also called the Rapture, a phrase that gives it a suitably quasireligious sense in abject anticipation of the joyful immersion or annihilation it promises. Wildly speculative, the ecstatic anticipation is nevertheless symptomatic in the way that it informs and infuses the apprehension of redundancy with joyful frivolity. Yet another joy before death, the imagined death of all humanity, that is a stake for the unimaginable rapture promised by technology. It is a rapture in which excitement at the possibility of technology is inextricably linked to the spectacle of catastrophe and global death, evident in countless Hollywood movies. It is the quintessence of the death drive that informs altruism for Lacan. Concern for the whole of humanity is expressed in the ecstatic fantasy of its destruction.

Much more modestly, in Wernham Hogg, the photocopier shuffles paper with particular insistence during the Red Nose Day episode, counting down the numberless days to the Rapture, the point that marks the horizon of human redundancy and salvation. The episode is the penultimate program of series two in which Brent is finally made redundant. In the face of the mounting dissatisfaction of his boss, Brent appeals to the morality of Red Nose Day to justify his continuing performance to camera:

> You've seen me entertain and raise money—use my humour and my profile to both help and amuse people. I'm exploring that avenue with my management training, but I'd like to do that on a global scale. And that's not saying: "Oh look at me. I'm entertaining whilst saving lives, aren't I brilliant?" It's saying, "if you think I'm brilliant then give generously and help save these guys who are starving, but are also brilliant." Not

as entertainers. A lot of them can't speak English. Don't give them their own game show, but save them from dying at least. (Gervais and Merchant, 2003)

In a satire on the obscene correlation between the spectacle of mass death and celebrity self-celebration, Gervais-Brent draws both together as abject images dependent for survival on the surface of televisibility. Celebrity and starvation become, in the Live Aid / Red Nose Day phenomenon, symbiotic, interdependent, and yet competitive, creatures of the same tele-environment. Bringing them together, Brent realizes he is in direct competition with the starving as a subject of reality television; they are equivalent and as such a threat as potential game show hosts.

By this point in the series, the Slough and Swindon branches of Wernham Hogg have merged and Brent's position as regional manager has been usurped by Neil, the head of the Swindon branch. Neil is the embodiment of English managerial desire. He is middle-class, good looking, self-confident, charming, authoritative, goal-oriented, and unruffled by any ripple of anxiety or self-reflection. He is the anti-Brent, or rather he represents everything Brent imagines he ought to be. True to form, Brent constantly acknowledges and draws attention to his envy and inferiority by attempting to stage scenes of rivalry and mimicry, like copying his leather jacket, in ways that continually humiliate him.

In the episode, Neil has already prepared and scrupulously rehearsed his own turn for Red Nose Day, performing with a female colleague an accomplished impression of a dance scene from *Saturday Night Fever*. Naturally, Neil fills the Cuban heels of John Travolta with ease. Genuinely impressed, his staff warmly applaud. Not to be outdone, however, Brent insists on upstaging this routine with his own dance. He improvises a "nightmarish assemblage of acid-house and break-dance moves." As Ben Thompson puts it, "as Brent flails around—haplessly but with absolute conviction— daring anyone to break the spell, he becomes a kind of human Catherine Wheel, illuminating the Slough of despond." In the process, his "self-consciousness is so extreme that it pushes on through to the other side and becomes a crazy kind of freedom" (Thompson, 2004: 416). It pushes on through to the other side of self-consciousness. What is on the other side of self-consciousness? Apparently, the freedom of a lack or beyond of self-consciousness. Usually, unselfconsciousness is opposed to self-consciousness, as naturalness is to artifice. Even when hard work and practice lead to the appearance of a natural facility or ability (as with Neil's Travolta routine), this opposition is still maintained. However, Brent breaks through the self-consciousness that is defined in opposition to unselfconscious naturalness to somewhere else, "a crazy kind of freedom" that is the ecstasy of a hyperself-consciousness. It also breaks through the parameters of celebrity abjection that define it.

The episode concludes with Brent in a red nose, dressed as a chicken, being made redundant by his new boss and CEO. But the laughter generated by Gervais-Brent as the human Catherine Wheel has nothing to do with the superegoic laughter that provides Freudian consolation, or indeed that urges us, in guilty humiliation and rage, to give to charity. It arises as two absolutely heterogeneous images meet at the same point of televisual humiliation and human anguish. Bataille makes a strangely similar connection, relating "this anguish of mine to the rights of the poor, to their anger, to their rage. How could I not ascribe all powers to poverty? Even though poverty could not crush the dancing in my heart, the laughter rising from the depths of despair" (Bataille, 1992: 80). In the context in which he is situated, as a desperate, desperately deluded would-be celebrity ineptly and nonsensically seeking to exploit, in front of documentary cameras, the miserable starvation and death of millions, Brent moves "from nameless horror to mindless laughter" (Bataille, 1992: 58). The laughter that is Gervais's own, which is itself continuous with the laughter that takes hold of everyone who watches.

In his short chapter on humor in *The Logic of Sense*, Deleuze conventionally notes that irony is integral to tragic theater, but continues that "what all the figures of irony have in common is that they confine the singularity within the limits of the individual or person" (1989a: 139). At the same time however, he argues, all the figures of irony are threatened by "an intimate enemy who works on them from within: the undifferentiated ground, the groundless abyss . . . that represents tragic thought and the tragic tone with which irony maintains the most ambivalent relations" (1989a: 139). For Deleuze this intimate enemy is Dionysus, the "demon who holds up to God and to his creatures the mirror wherein universal individuality dissolves" (139–140). As I have suggested, the abjective irony of Brent spirals down to a point of singular density, a groundless abyss, only to burst out at a point of sovereign self-consciousness in a joy that connects him, through the teletechnological network, with all the other Brents in the technobureaucratic assemblage. The day after this episode was first broadcast, Brent's little dance appeared as an MPeg on every office worker's computer around Britain. The impasse into which Brent and every worker is sunk becomes the immensity of laughter in which they are all dissolved (Bataille, 1988b: 117). In rapturous abjection, office workers across the country became continuous with Brent in a sovereign dance of corporate redundancy.

Part Five
a-Life

CHAPTER EIGHT

Becoming Barely Virtual

A life is the immanence of immanence, absolute immanence: it is complete power, complete joy.

—Deleuze, *Pure Immanance* (translation modified)

BAD MAN IN A COMA

A life and the life of *a*. In Deleuze's conception of life, the indefinite article is crucial. It denotes the singularity that defines an immanent life as a modality of "pure power and even joy" (2001a: 30). Singularity rather than individuality because the indefinite article marks the "determination of the singular" and the "indetermination of the person" (30). A life is also *autre*, then, other to the idea of the life of an individual as it is commonly understood. A life is distinct from the life of an individual that is inseparable from its empirical determinations. A life is asubjective, aneconomic, anorganic, immanent to life and death, or rather immanent to a zone that is neither life nor death. Deleuze's conception of a life (*a*-life) is not the life of a subject or a self with a career, interests, pleasures, and personal history. Nor is *a*-life to be understood as an object, a possession or thing that can be exchanged or sacrificed, that is something that can only be defined or understood in an economic relation with death. Further, *a*-life does not refer to the organism, the body, the conspicuous presence of animal or vegetable flora and fauna that so far marks Earth out from the other planets. A-life transcends the interior and exterior world of the subject and object because it is pure immanence of and in itself. Neither interior nor exterior, transcendent in its immanence, *a*-life could perhaps be said to be extimate to life and death. A-life is an extimate joy before death, an extimacy "playing with death" (Deleuze, 2001a: 26).

In his last book, *Pure Immanence: A Life* (2001a), the example Deleuze gives of his concept of *a*-life comes from fiction, Charles Dickens's novel *Our Mutual Friend* (1983). He describes Mr Riderhood, "a rogue,

157

held in contempt by everyone" who is found lying close to death. Though generally despised, his neighbors attempt to save him, led by his daughter and a doctor. After a period of artificial respiration, they eventually see a small "token of life" (Dickens, 1983: 504). "The four rough fellows, seeing, shed tears. Neither Riderhood in this world, nor Riderhood in the other, could draw tears from them; but a striving human soul between the two can do it easily" (504). In Dickens's description, the spark of life does indeed occupy an indeterminate zone between life and death. This spark of life is also distinct from Riderhood himself, although Deleuze emphasizes the moment when it becomes apparent to him, "in his deepest coma, this wicked man himself senses something soft and sweet penetrating him" (28). The man recovers, but as soon as he does, he returns to the life of empirical subjects and objects and the mutual animosity between himself and his saviors returns. Deleuze, therefore, focuses simply on that moment when the wicked man is in his deepest coma, a moment "that is only that of *a* life playing with death" (28, emphasis in the original). A-life is impersonal and yet singular, singularity being the point of the empirical transcendence of *a*-life's immanence. It could also be noted, although Deleuze does not, that this life is 'artificially' revived and sustained through technical intervention by the doctor. It is neither natural nor unnatural then, but immanent to a machinic assemblage. To use the language of Deleuze and Guattari, *a*-life is both an effect of, and immanent to, a desiring machine or machinic assemblage composed of the people in the room, its milieu, and the medical techniques and disciplinarity of the doctor. Or at least in the fictional world described by Dickens. Since it exists only on the page, this example of *a*-life is strictly immanent to a writing-machine and the assemblage it constructs. Immanent to anorganic assemblages, *a*-life is also distinctively human. Deleuze likens it to a *homo tantum* (only human), the simple humanity with which everyone empathizes and which attains a sort of beatitude (28–29). But again, though redolent of simple humanity, *a*-life is not the life of an individual endowed with character, subjectivity, qualities, or even identity. It is the "singular life immanent to a man who no longer has a name" (29). A kind of bare life, perhaps, stripped of all insignia, all forms of identity and personality, unexchangeable, unsacrificable, yet finding its illumination at the threshold of death.

The choice of example from Dickens, in which the immanence of *a*-life is sustained as an effect of artificial respiration, penetrating a man in deep coma, raises the question of its conceptual proximity, if any, to the bare life that constitutes the preeminent object of biopolitics for Giorgio Agamben. Bare life is life that cannot be exchanged or sacrificed precisely because it has been excluded or separated from all forms of symbolic nomination or recognition. For Agamben, the distinction between this bare life and political existence constitutes the fundamental opposition characterizing Western politics. One of his examples from the book *Homo Sacer* (1998) in which this thesis is outlined, concerns the comatose patient whose life is, or can be, sustained artificially and yet has been diagnosed brain dead. The conjunction of life support and transplantation technology means that a body may be allowed to live through prosthetic means, or harvested for vital organs for purposes of transplantation. The meaning of the terms "life" and "death" in such circumstances becomes highly problematic. For science, as we have seen, these terms have no significance, meaning itself being restricted to the question of function. Agamben comments, "life and death are not properly scientific concepts but rather political concepts, which as such acquire a political meaning precisely only through a decision" (1998: 164). It is essentially a political decision that defines the political for Agamben, that determines that a life in all its singularity can be killed without the commission of homicide in the name of life in abstract, the life that politics determines is worth living.

These two definitions of life Agamben discovers have their origin in Aristotle, where there is apparently a clear distinction between *bios* that defines political life, and *zoē* that is defined as simple natural life. The latter is characterized by Aristotle "as if it were a kind of serenity . . . and a natural sweetness" (1998: 2). Agamben argues that the politicization of *zoē* into the sphere of the *polis* constitutes the "decisive event of modernity" and the beginning of the biopolitical era whose defining image is the concentration camp. Bare life is neither *bios* nor *zoē*, but is the new product of the biopoliticization of *zoē*.

It seems to me that there are problems with Agamben's argument historically and philosophically, problems that essentially derive from his attempt to ground the argument in classical antiquity. Perhaps unsurprisingly, Derrida is skeptical about Agamben's reading of Aristotle. "The distinction between *bios* and *zoē*—or *zen*—is more than tricky and precarious," he writes, "in no way does it correspond to the strict opposition on which Agamben places the quasi totality of his argument about sovereignty and the biopolitical in *Homo Sacer*" (Derrida, 2005: 24). Notwithstanding the instability of the Aristotelian opposition, there is also considerable slippage in claiming that the production of bare life is an event defining biopolitical modernity even as it is located as the originary condition of sovereignty. It also finds its anthropological reference as the exclusion that defines the sacred across a range of different cultures ancient and modern, Western and non-Western in the form of *homo sacer*, the 'excommunicated' criminal who may be killed with impunity.

Agamben's purpose is to restore to the analysis of biopolitics the theoretical privilege traditionally given to sovereignty, something excluded by

Foucault in his analysis of biopower. Foucault memorably opposed the positivity of pastoral power to the negativity of law in his account of sexuality and the disciplines of modernity. For Agamben, however, Foucault fails to perceive the essential paradox of sovereignty that inaugurates itself through the exception that establishes its rule. He underestimates the significance of the exception marked by sovereignty and overlooks the zone of indistinction it establishes. This zone is precisely the area occupied by the body, the area in which the life of the body is politicized, and where individualization intersects with larger totalizing procedures. Agamben claims to be interested precisely in an account of the correlation between "subjective technologies and political techniques" (1998: 6). But he fails to acknowledge that a return to the problematic of sovereignty and the paradox of the law reintroduces psychoanalysis's contribution to this area. Instead, while this contribution is dismissed in reservations about "psychological explanations," his model is clearly compatible with Freudian and particularly Lacanian and neo-Lacanian accounts of the relationship between subjectivity, discourse and the law. Agamben's model of sovereignty that is erected on the basis of the exclusion of bare life closely resembles Lacan's account of the master signifier. In his discussion of the Aristotelian distinction between political and natural life, Agamben emphasizes that the separation of *zoē* from *bios* occurs through the introduction of language that constitutes humans as speaking beings. Speech opens the domain of political life, but excludes natural life even as it remains central to the being of the speaker. Bare life has the same extimate relation to biopolitical discourse. For Agamben the question of how man, as a speaking being, relates to the language that signifies that being corresponds exactly to the question: "In what way does bare life dwell in the *polis*?" He continues,

> There is politics because man is the living being who, in language, separates and opposes himself to his own bare life and, at the same time, maintains himself in relation to that bare life in an inclusive exclusion (Agamben, 1998: 8).

The sovereign operation is an effect of language that splits the subject that it brings into (social) being only to place it under erasure. Life becomes a lost object that is nevertheless central as the object-in-desire sought in every object of desire. As Lacan states:

> This is our starting point: through his relationship to the signifier the subject is deprived of something of himself, of his very life, which has assumed the value of that which binds him to the signifier. The phallus is our term for his alienation

in signification. When the subject is deprived of this signifier, a particular object becomes for him an object of desire, this is the meaning of $\$\Diamond a$. (Lacan, 1977: 28)

The *objet petit a* is Lacan's technical term for the life ("his very life") that is excluded in order that the speaking being may accede to the position of subject in relation to a signifier that represents him or her for all the other signifiers. This is essentially the same as the sovereign operation for Agamben and connects subjectivity to totalizing social structures. In relation to social structures organized according to the libidinal structure of phallic jouissance, male society is bound together in relation to a sovereign exception. That is, in relation to a sovereign (*pére jouissance*) who instantiates the law through embodying the jouissance-without-sanction that is generally prohibited (see Lacan, 1999). In *Homo Sacer*, Agamben's various examples show how bare life is the object in desire for biopolitics.

However, for the purposes of this book, it is not interesting to return Agamben's model to that of psychoanalysis or Lacan. Rather, what I want to do is emphasize Agamben's contention that the *nomos* of biopolitics depends not on the sovereign authority of the law, but its suspension. And further, this suspension is both indefinite and supported by a general impeachment of sovereign authority. As Agamben argues, sovereign power seems to be permanently in a state of exception. But what happens when the exception becomes the rule, rather than the deviation that proves it? When power itself becomes visibly naked or bare then something different occurs in its relation to the bare life that it desires. Power becomes continuous with its object.

The success of Agamben's concept of bare life has been precipitated in the early years of the twenty-first century by its pertinence to the war on terror prosecuted by the U.S. government. States are usually in a state of emergency during wartime and the indefinite war on terror justifies an indefinite state of exception. Similarly, the disposal of captured bodies at Guantanamo Bay and the treatment of captives in places such as Abu Ghraib clearly seem to illustrate the reduction of prisoners of war to the state of bare life. But the curious presentation of bare life in the digital photographs that have been circulated by the U.S. soldiers and camp guards suggested that there was no conventional depiction of sovereign despotism on view.

In an article on the photographs from Abu Ghraib, Susan Sontag notes that even though it is quite common for soldiers to take photographs as souvenirs or trophies, it is exceedingly rare for torturers and executioners to appear in their own snapshots. A comparable case she cites is the example between the 1880s and 1930s of lynching parties photographing themselves in front of their black victims. This seems, however, Sontag suggests, to be an example of a community binding itself together through its shared act of transgression and commemorating that communality formally with a photograph. Transgression is a common modality of symbolic law through which a community may become bound together in a specific mode of jouissance. Yet, as Sontag supposes, this does not seem to be the case with the Abu Ghraib images. Whether they were the result of a few bad apples or evidence of generic interrogation techniques, the pictures do not appear to depict the austere formality of a community bound together in transgression, nor of individuals excited by the jouissance of forbidden acts. There is little Sadean darkness to the pictures featuring Charles Jenner and Lynndie England stacking Iraqi bodies up into the shape of a bouncy castle or gleefully pointing to the genitals of naked men. But perhaps that is what makes them even more appalling. Sontag writes that

> The meaning of these pictures is not just that these acts were performed, but that their perpetrators had no sense that there was anything wrong in what the pictures show. Even more appalling, since the pictures were meant to be circulated and seen by many people, it was all fun. And this idea of fun is, alas, more and more—contrary to what Mr Bush is telling the world—part of the "true nature and heart of America." (Susan Sontag, 2004: 3)

The images are consistent with the 'fun' that Americans take during their leisure time, the fun to which work that is not abject has been transformed, the fun that is determined by the joy of the spectacle. Crucially, Sontag notes, these are not simply events that have been photographed as souvenirs—they are scenes that have been precisely arranged for the camera. The events are "designed to be photographed" (3).

In *Homo Sacer*, Agamben gives the Marquis de Sade a privileged place in the history of the politicization of bare life at the origin of modernity. Sade is our contemporary because of his "incomparable presentation of the absolutely political (that is, "biopolitical") meaning of sexuality and physiological life itself" (1998: 135). But it seems to me unlikely that the politics in *Philosophy of the Bedroom*, Agamben's point of reference, are anything other than ironic. There is no attempt at, or desire for, any serious politics or program of power evident in that text; it is self-evidently a joke. Which is not to say that Sade is frivolous—on the contrary. There is no positive conception of sensuality or perversion in Sade, in contrast to the positivity that characterizes the history of sexuality for Foucault. Rather, there is an austere negative philosophy that seeks the extermination of life in the experience of the greatest pleasure. Sade's philosophy is the rigorous expression it seems, of a thirst for annihilation. Bodies are generated simply for the purpose of annihilation in orgies of nonproductive sexual violence. Sade's biopolitics, if such it is, is directed to the ecstatic annihilation of nature in the name of Nature, even as "it is beyond our capacity to achieve the scale of destruction it desires" (Sade, cited in Lacan, 1992: 211). Nature ensures that there is always more nature to be destroyed. In Sade, it is not politics, or even the exposure of politics, just a human fantasy of nature in which life is never bare enough because of the metonymy of desire and has to be stripped and torn to nothing. This is not what is going on in Abu Ghraib according to the digital photographs.

The "shamelessness" (Sontag) of the images implies that there is no sense of transgression about them, no sense in which they are exceptional and therefore exemplary of the sovereign operation. The bouncy-castle images recall the theme park as much as the concentration camp. They depict not Sadean jouissance or industrial slaughter, but all-American fun, its pranks and japes playing with the life and death of Iraqi bodies for the pleasure of being photographed. In a strange way this is not the jouissance of negation but more the joy of affirming and recording the singularity of one's own life and pleasure. Is this not a case of the masters' joy at being masters, affirming their difference through their power and pleasure? In the case of the Abu Ghraib photographs perhaps it was, in the form of Jenner or England, an American body taking its chance to construct "an assemblage of forces, to dominate, subjugate and therefore 'affirm itself with more joy'" (Deleuze, 1983: 121). If so, perhaps Deleuze's concept of joy and the affirmation of a-life has something to contribute to the analysis of biopolitics or biopower, but in a way different to Agamben.

Perhaps it is possible to compare the life whose bareness offers the image of the nakedness of sovereign power with Deleuze's conception of a-life, the power of immanence. That is to say, compare Deleuze's a-life with the life of a, where a marks the object immanent to biopolitical desire. Or rather, since it is not an object, a marks the point of the singularity of desire's process, its joyful process of desiring. Is a-life simply another deviation on the horizon of biopolitics, does it promise its transformation, or does it belong to an altogether different plane? To address this, it is necessary to look a little more closely at the etiology of Deleuze's concept of life and its relation to desire.

LOVE LIFE

In an essay entitled "Dead Psychoanalysis: Analyse" collected in the book *Dialogues* with Claire Parnet, first published in 1977, Deleuze revises somewhat the discourse of *Anti-Oedipus*. The phrase "desiring machines" is officially given up and replaced by the notion of assemblages made up of different fluxes (2002: 101). These assemblages are still assemblages of desire, but sexuality no longer has preeminence and is just one flux among others. Desire itself is redefined in very similar terms to those of *a*-life. It is a process that both constitutes and inhabits a field of immanence (100). "Desire is not internal to a subject, any more than it intends towards an object: it is strictly immanent to a plane which it does not pre-exist" (89). Similarly, Deleuze's conception of *a*-life does not concern the life of a subject that would be defined in relation to its objects. Nor is *a*-life liberated by production; it is immanent to a plane of consistency that it inhabits and unfolds. "It is a question of life, to live in this way, on the basis of such a plane, or rather on such a plane" (2002: 92–93). In *Pure Immanence a*-life is defined as the immanence of immanence, absolute immanence: it is complete power, complete joy. In "Dead Psychoanalysis," desire is a process that 'unrolls' a plane of consistency (89), and "the process of desire is called 'joy', not lack or demand" (100). Joy, the immanent process of desire, replaces both "sovereign" authority and the pleasure principle defined as the pleasure-interruption (orgasm). A-life, then, is not established as an effect of the sovereign operation of exclusion that hollows out the lack intrinsic to its desire. Nor is it the natural life akin to *zoē*, which has been transformed by its politicization into bare life. However, the desire immanent to *a*-life does require the technical transformation of the desire predicated on lack or exclusion. Indeed, the goal of this technical transformation is also exclusion; it is to exclude the exclusion. The desire of *a*-life "requires a great deal of artifice to exorcise the internal lack," writes Deleuze. The exclusion of the exclusion, then, is an effect not of discipline but ascesis. "Ascesis has always been the condition of desire not its disciplining or prohibition" (100–101).

If desire's condition is neither discipline nor prohibition, what kind of regime is it, and what kinds of self-denial does it imply? Ascesis traditionally has a religious reference, but Deleuze cites the case of courtly love, another of Lacan's favorite examples. The example raises the suspicion that through revising some of the terms of *Anti-Oedipus*, Deleuze is also revising his critical appropriation of Lacan. Courtly love was an important example for Lacan in 1960, featuring prominently in Seminar VII, published as *The Ethics of Psychoanalysis* (1992). But Lacan revisited courtly love again in Seminar XX (1999). This seminar was held in 1972, the same year of the publication of *Anti-Oedipus*. In this seminar, Lacan introduces a number of highly significant new formulations of sexuality and its relation to the real that could not have been taken into account by Deleuze and Guattari. In Seminar XX, Lacan famously defines courtly love as a "highly refined way of making up for the absence of a sexual relationship, by feigning that we are the ones who erect an obstacle thereto" (1999: 69). That is, that for Lacan, courtly love elegantly effects the exclusion of the exclusion, exorcising the lack in the art of love. The ascesis of courtly love—the abasement, the service, the 'tests', the whole 'military service' of love—replaces the lack, the absence of a sexual relation.

In Deleuze's account, courtly love is constituted by the historical conjunction of two different fluxes that establish a field of immanence. Two movements are involved in this construction. First, chivalrous love is established through the combination of "the warrior flux and the erotic flux, in the sense that valour gave the right to love. But courtly love required a new demarcation in which valour became itself internal to love, and where love included the test" (101). In the ascesis of its ordeal, the process of desire inherent to courtly love is similar, for Deleuze, to masochism. But the organization of humiliation and suffering is not a means of playing out anguish or perversion, nor is its goal the attainment of forbidden pleasures. Rather, it is a "procedure . . . to constitute a body without organs and develop a continuous process of desire ['joy'] which pleasure, on the contrary, would come and interrupt" (101).

Deleuze's opposition between joy and pleasure seems to echo Lacan's distinction between pleasure and jouissance, a distinction that Lacan introduces into his teaching around 1959–1960, particularly in Seminar VII in which jouissance is located beyond the pleasure principle. In a very interesting text taken from one of Deleuze's seminars held in 1973 (2001b), he appears very curious about this distinction, but claims to be "unfamiliar with it" (97). Instead, he cites with displeasure Roland Barthes's *The Pleasure of the Text* (1975) where a similar distinction is deployed and which Deleuze correctly suspects has been appropriated from Lacan. But Deleuze uses Barthes's text to more closely relate jouissance to the *petit mort* of orgasm and the loss of self that establishes jouissance's "fundamental relationship with death" and its impossibility. "We can close the circle," he says: "desire-lack, desire-pleasure or orgasm, desire *jouissance*" (97). Certainly this version of jouissance is not foreign to Lacan, but it describes a version of phallic jouissance. Also known as the masturbatory jouissance, or the jouissance of the idiot, Lacan clearly seems to have as low an opinion of the jouissance of pleasure-discharge as does Deleuze. The jouissance of pleasure-discharge is always aiming at something else, and always misses.

In Seminar XX, however, a further nuance is introduced whereby phallic jouissance in Lacan is defined against the jouissance of the Other. This seminar was held in 1972, a year before Deleuze's seminar in 1973, so if he was unfamiliar with a distinction extant in Lacanian thought for thirteen years, it is unlikely that he would be aware of one made public for just a year or so. And yet, Lacan's seminars were by this time almost public events. Other jouissance (sometimes known as feminine jouissance) is located by Lacan beyond the phallus, but can be experienced by any gender, although for men under different conditions to women. Women have available to them both phallic jouissance and the jouissance of the Other, but for men it is one or the other. To experience the jouissance of the Other, men have to give up on phallic jouissance.

By the time he comes to formulate the essay "Dead Psychoanalysis" with Claire Parnet in *Dialogues* Deleuze seems to have some idea of Lacan's distinction between phallic and Other jouissance. Deleuze did not himself attend Lacan's seminars, but in the aftermath of the publication of *Anti-Oedipus* it is reported that he and Guattari asked Deleuze's wife Fanny Deleuze to attend to see what reaction, if any, Lacan would make to their book. So it is possible that the information concerning feminine jouissance was relayed to Deleuze by Fanny.

In his strategic return to courtly love, Deleuze suggests it has "two enemies"—not just "the hedonistic interruption that produces pleasure as discharge" but also the "religious transcendence of lack," suggesting further that they both "merge into one" (100). It is not obvious, but the latter could be a reference to Lacan's comment that the experience of the jouissance of the Other appears to have been an effect of the ascesis of religious ecstasy. This would be reinforced by Lacan's subsequent suggestion that it is possible to interpret "one face of the Other, the God face," as being based on feminine jouissance. However, Lacan argues that the jouissance of the Other does not lead to transcendence but rather immanence since it "puts us on the path of ex-sistence" (1999: 77). That is, it is to be located along the path to the real which, since it is unsymbolizable, does not exist but ex-sists. Since Lacan insists that existence always takes place, for speaking beings, in a world of symbolized reality, ex-sistence opens a transcendental (as opposed to transcendent) field immanent to reality. Since the jouissance of the Other is something one can experience without knowing anything about, it could be described quite precisely as a "transcendental empiricism in contrast to everything that makes up the world of subject and object" (Deleuze, 2001a: 25). Except that this is the description Deleuze gives to the experience of *a*-life from the first page of *Pure Immanence*. How close is "the path of ex-sistence" that is opened out by feminine jouissance to the plane of consistency "unrolled" by joy? There is no suggestion of a deliberate appropriation here because despite the implied recognition given to "the two enemies of courtly love"—religious transcendence and pleasure-discharge—that appear to map on to feminine and phallic jouissance, there is no further elaboration. Indeed, with his suggestion that they merge into one, Deleuze seems to move further away from an understanding of Lacan's concepts, always assuming that is his reference. The suggestion that they merge into one is wholly incompatible with Lacan's discourse. Phallic jouissance and the jouissance of the Other are poles apart; their relation is supplementary rather than complementary, although they both have something of a relation to the One. The libidinality of phallic jouissance forms a closed set based on an exception, while the jouissance of the Other is *pas tout* or not-whole, that is not wholly subjected to the phallus and therefore constitutes an open set.

If anything, it is Deleuze who merges something like phallic and feminine jouissance into the one concept of joy, particularly the joy of *a*-life, the immanence of immanence. They are merged into the concept of the One that is "the immanent contained within a transcendental field." But the "One is always the index of a multiplicity: an event, a singularity, a life" (2001a: 30). *A*-life "contains only virtuals," writes Deleuze, which is to say that it ex-sists. That which ex-sists does not lack reality except in so far as it cannot be symbolized, thereby providing symbolization with its principle. Similarly for Deleuze, "what we call virtual is not something that lacks reality but something that is engaged in a process of actualization following the plane that gives it its particular reality" (2001a: 31). This process of actualization, I would argue, is the same as the process of desire that is called joy. To pursue the analogy, it is also possible to hear this joy resonate with the Lacanian notion of ex-sistence as the echo of the *ekstase* of ecstasy that Lacan further conceptualized in the term "extimacy." The supreme example of extimacy is that immanent (non)object that both constitutes and inhabits the transcendental field of the Other, the *objet petit a*.

The Deleuzian definition of joy in "Dead Psychoanalysis" is the process of desire in pursuit of its principle. The *objet a* is extimate cause and principle of desire in Lacan. The *objet a* is not the property of a subject, but it is the means through which a desiring subject is actualized in relation to a series of objects that stand in for the Other with whom there is no relation. Lacan developed this concept out of the psychoanalytic theory of partial objects that he argues Freud discovered as the cause of desire—namely, the objects of sucking and excretion that Lacan himself extended to the voice and the gaze. It was precisely this multiplication of object-causes of desire, on the basis of the virtuality of *objet petit a*, that particularly impressed Deleuze and Guattari. As such, in *Anti-Oedipus*, it became the key component of desiring machines. A footnote makes this quite clear: "Lacan's admirable theory of desire seems to us to have two poles: one related to the 'object small *a*' as a desiring machine, which defines desire in terms of a real production . . . and the other related to the 'great Other' as a signifier, which produces a certain notion of lack" (Deleuze and Guattari, 1984: 27). In *Chaosophy* (1995), Guattari recalls how Lacan distinguished the *objet a* from partial objects, conceiving it as "detotalized, deterritorialized, and permanently distanced . . . from an individual corporeality." As such, it was "in a position to swing over to real multiplicities" (Guattari, 1995: 104). Deleuze and Guattari dispense with the Other in favor of the multiplicity engendered by the extimate virtuality of the *objet petit a*, that is, the multiplicity of the One. This is why the immanence of *a*-life can only be joyful—because there is no Other. The Other doesn't exist.

Contrary to the view of many of his followers, Lacan is in fundamental agreement with Deleuze in the suggestion that there is no Other, only the One. The One is the structure of the real that cannot be written but can perhaps be rendered topologically in the Borromean knot. "We proceed on the basis of the One," writes Lacan. "The One engenders science," but not, he quickly adds, in the sense of measurement, that is not what is important. Rather, "what distinguishes modern science . . . is precisely the function of the One, the One in so far as it is only there, we can assume, to represent solitude—the fact that the One doesn't truly knot itself with anything that resembles the sexual Other" (1999: 128). We proceed on the basis of the One, then, but only on condition that it is desexualized. Sexualization, or sexuation as Lacan terms it, depends on the function of the Other. The Other is the 'One-missing' (1999: 129). But since there is only the lonely One, the Other functions through its felt absence, as an effect of the solitude of the One. Therefore the One imaginarily engenders the two, that is defined by a third, the term that denotes the reality of their difference, the *objet petit a* that becomes the principle of multiplicity.

Therein, of course, lies the fundamental difference between Lacan and Deleuze: sex. There is no sex in Deleuze: no sexual fantasy, no sexual organs, no orgasms. There is joy, but no sex. *A*-life is asexual, then, and an index of multiplicity on condition of the radical desexualization of the plane of immanence, all planes of immanence. Deleuze's own specific examples illustrate this quite clearly. Where 'an erotic flux' combines with a 'warrior flux' to constitute a plane of immanence in courtly love, it is desexualized in an ascesis. It is not at all a question of sublimation, but the assemblage of a process of desire (joy) that is undisturbed by sexual pleasure (Deleuze and Parnet, 2002: 101). The plane of immanence is *horsexe*, outside-sex, like the [under-erasure] Woman who for Lacan does not exist. And yet perhaps it is this woman through whom all men and women must pass on the path of ex-sistence to other becomings. Becoming-woman in Deleuze and Guattari is prior to all other becomings.

ODE TO ANOREXIA

One of the curiosities of Deleuze's essay "Dead Psychoanalysis: Analyse" is that no sooner has he concluded his example of courtly love, than he pays 'homage' to his wife. The tribute could easily be located in the courtly tradition of epideictic love poetry, that is, the poetry of praise. Like a courtly lover, Deleuze praises his beloved's beauty and elegance specifically as an effect of her anorexia. Like courtly love itself, anorexia is a combination of two fluxes: a food flux and a clothes flux that constitute the plane of anorexic elegance. Far from being a question of deprivation or denial, the ascesis that marks anorexia is a paradoxical one. It is festive. That is, it does not have a relation to consumption but to expenditure. "The alternation of stuffing and emptying: anorexic feasts, the imbibings of fizzy drinks" (Deleuze and Parnet, 2002: 110)

Anorexia does not imply a refusal of the body, but the body's organisms, a refusal of what the organism makes the body undergo. And therein lie its politics and its resistance to the norms of social organization. Specifically, anorexia is a means of "escaping the organic constraint of lack and hunger at the mechanical mealtime" (110). It is a mode of micropolitics that enables one to "escape the norms of consumption" (110). And "the subjection of the family meal and a whole family politics of consumption" (110). In place of the tyranny of family mealtimes, the anorexic constructs a kind of conceptual persona, the "Cook-Model" who deterritorializes consumption from its domestic regime of feminine oppression.

> She will turn consumption against itself: she will often be a model—she will often be a cook, a peripatetic cook, who will make something for others to eat, or else she will like being at the table either without eating, or else multiplying the absorption of little substances. (Deleuze and Parnet, 2002: 110)

As so often with Deleuze, his examples raise many questions. Does this cook-model persona really constitute an escape from consumer society, or is it rather perfectly consistent with it? As a 'regime of signs' how close is the food flux and the clothes flux to the haute cuisine flux and the haute couture flux that seemed to come together in the anorexic elegance of nouvelle cuisine in the 1980s. Nouvelle cuisine consisted almost entirely in "the absorption of little things, little substances" (110). More radically, this persona is evident in the deterritorialization of the domestic space of the family mealtime. The emergence of the supermarket ready meal endorsed by the cook-model in the form of innumerable celebrity chefs has contributed to the destruction of the family meal as a scene of disciplinarity. One thinks of Nigella Lawson, for instance. Maybe this was not the case in 1977, when perhaps there was still such a thing as the family mealtime in France. But, if so, I would speculate that in Britain at least the rise of the ready meal and the celebrity chef is just another example in which the century is becoming Deleuzian. It could be argued that more often than not, the family meal is simulated by these cookery programs and media campaigns and sustained as a simulacrum, an object of nostalgia for a domestic idyll that never existed. But the figure of the cook-model is a trickster par excellence. "I'm starving," she says, "grabbing two slimming yoghurts" (111). "Let's have a family meal," she says to the camera or on a packet of Micro Chips.

The revenge of the anorexic cook-model on the society of consumption lies in the epidemic of obesity that is engendered by the peripatetic deterritorializations of her slimming yogurts, Diet Cokes, and ready meals that establish a plane consistent with Big Macs, pizzas, and bargain buckets of Kentucky Fried Chicken. But there is always the possibility, as Deleuze suggests, that these lines of flight are liable to end in disaster, in the destruction of the organic body, and death. This question is raised by Deleuze not of obesity, but anorexia itself: "why does the anorexic assemblage come so close to going off the rails, to becoming lethal?" Characteristically, he does not answer the question, but suggests instead that any answer must not be sought in psychoanalysis or origins. "We must try to find out the dangers that lie *in the middle of* a real experiment" (111).

It seems to me that the significant term in Deleuze's description of anorexia is "involution." Anorexia is "not regression at all, but involution, involuted body" (110). Involution has various meanings deriving etymologically from the Latin term *involutus*, past participle of *involvere*, to enwrap. To be enwrapped is also to be involved, of course, but sometimes involuntarily. It is also to be involved in something complex, intricate, and convoluted. In embryology, it is the ingrowth and curling inward of a group of cells. In mathematics, it is an operation, such as negation, which, when applied to itself, returns to the original number. In medicine, however, such enwrapping and convolution also seem to imply atrophy or withering away. It describes the decrease in size or degeneration of an organ, such as a uterus.

This process of involution can be seen in Deleuze's description of the anorexic as a trickster, betraying hunger in a "double-turning away" (110). "Trick-the-hunger, trick-the-family, trick-the-food" (111). The involution of betraying hunger (the hunger of the mechanical mealtime) by going hungry is similar to Lacan's formulation that anorexia is "the desire not to desire." It is not a lack, therefore, not the absence of desire, but an involution of desire: a desire not to desire. Anorexia, for Lacan, betrays or tricks desire.

Since desire in Lacan is always desire of the Other, it involves a rejection or confounding of the Other. As in mathematics, it is the negation of a negation that returns to the one, to one's self. One escapes the controlling power of the Other's desire by confounding it through the controlling power of one's own desire-negating desire.

Recent neo-Lacanian commentators have characteristically seen anorexia-bulimia as a symptom of consumer society or the hyperreality of hypermodernity. Gabriella Ripa di Meana, in *Figures of Lightness* (1998) notes "how it is that anorexics and bulimics—who adhere to the point of coinciding with the surrounding culture and environment appear as hypermodern, yet unhappy, creatures" (1998). In a correlation that recalls Fanny Deleuze's passion for fizzy drinks, Slavoj Žižek connects anorexia with products like Diet Coke and the suspension of taste and value that characterizes consumer products generally. With Diet Coke we "drink nothing rather than something" in a way analogous to the anorexic who does not simply "eat nothing"—but rather "actively wants to eat the Nothingness (the void) itself that is the ultimate object-cause of desire. So, along the same lines, in the case of the caffeine-free Diet Coke, we drink the Nothingness itself, the pure semblance of a property that is effectively merely an envelope of a void" (Žižek, 1999).

A void here, it should be insisted with Deleuze, that is not the originary condition of being, but itself a product, "the anorexic void has nothing to do with a lack" (Deleuze and Parnet, 2002: 110), but is a means of escaping the "organic lack and constraint of mealtimes." This is still consistent with Žižek's suggestion that the anorexic is the ideal subject of convenience foods, however, the enjoyment of which has been subtracted in the form of harmful substances. Enjoyment would thereby consist precisely in not eating caffine or drinking alcohol or smoking and so on. This is the involution of consumer society through which an intensive desire to consume the anorexic void produces an epidemic of obesity.

The problem of pathological forms of consumption is of course one of the major means through which biopower seeks to control populations in the name of life. And toward the end of his life, Deleuze reaffirmed the rights of *a*-life, however destructive of the organism it might be. "Better death than the health which we are given" (Deleuze, 1998a: 160). If the *nomos* of biopolitical life, in the shadow of the camp, is the reduction of human beings to consumers and human society to mere *oikonomia*, then the refusal of the anorexic to consume takes on a heightened significance. The immanence of the eater and the eaten is collapsed into the self-consuming immanence of the One that refuses to eat the Other. The emaciated image that results strikes an uncanny resonance with those figures that emerged from Belsen in 1945, or more recently in Omarska.

JOY BEYOND SOLAR DEATH

In *Homo Sacer*, bare life is the object in the desire of the posthistorical machine that governs in its name. For Jean-François Lyotard, in *The Inhuman* (1994), this machine is called "the techno-economico-scientific megalopolis in which we live (or survive) [that] employs the same ideals of control and saturation of memory, directed towards goals of efficiency" as those that informed Nazi Germany. The main difference being that, for Lyotard, there is less "recourse to an aesthetic, ideological, and political mobilization of energies" (Lyotard, 1994: 147). This qualification is not inconsiderable. Jean-Luc Nancy precisely identifies the totalitarian dangers of immanence in a community informed by aesthetic or political ideas that ultimately "contains no other logic than that of the suicide of the community governed by it" (Nancy, 1991: 12). But the goals of efficiency are not necessarily commensurate with the goal of racial purity, historical destiny, or the work of art. When those goals of efficiency incorporate the aneconomic, anorganic joy of *a*-life as its principle of immanent creativity, then efficiency opens on to multiple becomings.

This book has argued that a new order of joy subsumes the goal of optimal functioning. Joy is the name of the image, the experience, the expression, and the process of efficient life regulation and governance. It is a joy of pure immanence that remains a joy before death, a joy playing with death. Joy plays with death, sustaining it along multiple planes of intensity, establishing planes of consistency to the point where death no longer has any significance but is simply part of the process of desire and becoming, coextensive with joy. As such, joyful immanence places humanity on a path of ex-sistence out of existence. But it does not involve collective suicide because death has been abolished. "Death does not authenticate human existence. It is an outmoded evolutionary strategy. The body no longer need be *repaired* but simply have parts *replaced*. Extending life no longer means 'existing' but rather of being 'operational'" (Stelarc, 1997: 246). Further, the total prostheticization of *a*-life means that human organs can be done away with completely. Even the brain is no longer necessary since thought becomes anorganic, the effect of an acentered and probabilistic system or network, a network linking up a multitude of brain-screens. But that does not mean that *a*-life can be sustained totally in nonorganic forms such as rock and metals, steel and glass. Neither can it be understood as pure nonconscious mechanism.

An immanence of immanence requires the minimal maintenance of *a*-life in all its singularity. It is not a question simply of the life of the Mechanosphere; it is only the presence of *a*-life that indicates that the One is composed of a multiplicity. It is not thought that betrays the presence of *a*-life, but joy. Joy playing with death that is no longer its defining opposite or end point. Instead of marking an end point, death becomes a purely functional, immanent principle of becoming that can evolve anorganic life to such a degree that it can survive the death of the sun. This absolute death is "the sole serious question to face humanity today" and, according to Lyotard, informs both scientific and imaginative work in the biotech, information technology and new media industries (see Lyotard, 1988–1989).

One of Deleuze's favorite scientists is the microbiologist Lynn Margulis. In her book with Dorion Sagan, *Microcosmos* (1997), she envisages the (non)future of humanity as a kind of cyborg fusion in which "diaphanous nervous-system fragments of humanity, evolved beyond recognition as the organic component parts of reproducing machines [that] might survive the inevitable explosion and death of the sun" (Margulis and Sagan, 1997: 19). Perhaps some time in the future, some hard-bodied, hard-wired assemblage self-designed to survive the lifeless expanses of time and space will sense the soft sweetness of *a*-life penetrating it. With the incorporation of death as a mechanism of becoming, new forms of anorganic life may endure and prevail in the inhospitable space of the cosmos, bringing it joy.

Notes

CHAPTER 1

1. Félix Guattari called this dogmatism "a monstrous symbiosis between Maoism and Lacanism" (Guattari, 1995: 8).

2. According to Roudinesco, this section of Seminar XX was dedicated to Bataille's representation of feminine sexuality as a heterological combination of sacred and profane elements, embodied in Madame Edwarda. (See Botting and Wilson, 1997).

3. Also spelled jouisance; joyssance; jouyssance.

4. Most notably in the form of the East India Company. "A robust association of adventurers engaged in hazarding all in a series of preposterous gambles," some of which paid off. See John Keay (1993: xx).

5. The East Indiamen was as much a warship as cargo carrier with thirty-eight guns plus space, if nor accommodation, for 200 men (see Keay, 1993: 14)

6. For example, Manovich suggests that one commercial system, Battletech center from Virtual World Entertainment, Inc. "is directly modeled on SIMNET (Simulation Network), developed by DARPA (Defense Advanced Research Projects Agency)" (Manovich, 1996: 184).

CHAPTER 4

1. Yet, ironically, the specific features Hobbes describes in his state of nature also seem to have been drawn from his low opinion of contemporary aristocrats. Although the state of nature is posited as prehistorical, the notional ground of society, Hobbes makes this judgment on the basis of his observations of seventeenth-century England and his reading of history. A turbulent decade, Hobbes actually wrote his text in the midst of Civil War, Hobbes's "principall causes of quarrell" perhaps surprisingly are not based in economy or in the struggle for subsistence. But they are recognizably aristocratic: "First, Competition; Secondly, Diffidence; Thirdly, Glory" (Hobbes, 1985: 185).

2. See also the opening of Agamben's *The Open* and the messianic banquet where the righteous are transformed back into animals devouring other animals (2004a: 1–3).

CHAPTER 6

1. I wish to leave aside the highly problematic idea that art, science, and philosophy are the only means through which to confront the chaos. Or indeed, the rigidity of a disciplinarity that suggests that there are no concepts in art, not even conceptual art, no feeling in philosophy, no art in science, and so on. Except perhaps in the people-to-come who may emerge from the chaos into which the brain plunges, with its three planes (218).

2. The Kantian cogito is cited in *What Is Philosophy* as an example of why "the concept belongs to philosophy and only to philosophy" (31–34).

3. *Hamlet* was first performed 1600–02, shortly after *Julius Caesar*. G.H. Hibbard notes that these lines suggest that it is likely that the actors Richard Burbage and John Heminges would have played the corresponding roles. (See Hibbard's introduction in Shakespeare 1987: 3–4).

CHAPTER 7

1. I mean nation rather than nation-state. Any discussion of national characteristics or identity, however light-hearted as here, runs into insurmountable problems, especially when it comes to those nations constituting the British Isles. Why have I chosen English rather than British? It is because *The Office*, set among the middle classes in middle England, seems to encapsulate the queasy, embarrassing quality of this new Englishness particularly well. Therefore the negative implications in this chapter regarding the English sense of humor do not apply to the Irish, Scottish, Welsh, Asian or Afro-Caribbean communities, although members of those nations and communities are welcome to disagree.

2. "Why is the goose-step not used in England? . . . It is not used because the people in the street would laugh" (George Orwell, 1957: 70). See also the episode of *Fawlty Towers* entitled "The Germans" in which a deranged Basil Fawlty performs the Nazi goosestep to comic effect.

3. "It's not just *being* stuck . . . it's *knowing* you're stuck . . . To be dissatisfied Socrates or the satisfied fool. . . . That's the dilemma: do you trade happiness for wisdom?" And what would be *their* answers to that tricky question? Gervais points to Merchant: "He's a dissatisfied fool" (403).

4. A pun on the motto of the Royal Air Force's elite Special Air Services (SAS): Who Dares Wins.

5. One middle manager even changed his name to David Brent in tribute to his own ironic idiocy.

Bibliography

Adorno, Theodor (1991) *The Culture Industry* edited by Jay Bernstein. London: Routledge.

Adorno, Theodor and Max Horkheimer (1979) *The Dialectic of Enlightenment.* London: Verso.

Agamben, Giorgio (1998) *Homo Sacer: Sovereign Power and Bare Life.* Stanford: Stanford University Press.

Agamben, Giorgio (2004a) *The Open: Man and Animal.* Stanford: Stanford University Press.

Agamben, Giorgio (2004b) "Interview with Giorgio Agamben—Life, A Work of Art without an Author: The State of Exception, the Administration of Disorder and Private Life," *German Law Journal* No. 5 (1 May)—Special Edition. www.germanlawjournal.com/article.php?id=437

Agamben, Giorgio (2005) *State of Exception.* Chicago: University of Chicago Press.

Ansell Pearson, Keith (2001) *Philosophy and the Adventure of the Virtual: Bergson and the Time of Life.* London: Routledge.

Badiou, Alain (1999) *The Clamour of Being.* Minneapolis: University of Minnesota Press.

Bagemihl, Bruce (1999) *Biological Exuberance.* New York: St. Martin's Press.

Ballard, JB (1995) "Anything Could Happen," *The Guardian.* 6 October: 10.

Barthes, Roland (1975) *The Pleasure of the Text.* Trans. Richard Miller. New York: Hill and Wang.

Bataille, Georges (1973) *Literature and Evil.* London: Marion Boyars.

Bataille, Georges (1985) *Visions of Excess: Selected Writings, 1927–1939*, ed. Allan Stoekl, trans. Allan Stoekl with Carl R. Lovitt and Donald M. Leslie, Jr. Minneapolis: University of Minnesota Press.

Bataille, Georges (1986) *Eroticism: Death and Sensuality.* London: Marion Boyars.

Bataille, Georges (1988a) *The Accursed Share* I: Consumption. Trans. Robert Hurley, New York Zone Press.

Bataille, Georges (1988b) *Guilty*, trans. Bruce Boone. San Fransisco: Lapis Press.

Bataille, Georges (1989) *My Mother / Madame Edwarda / The Dead Man.* London: Marion Boyars.

Bataille, Georges (1991) *The Accursed Share* II and III, trans. Robert Hurley. New York: Zone Books.

Bataille, Georges (1992a) *On Nietzsche*, trans. Bruce Boone. New York: Paragon House.

Bataille, Georges (1992b) *Theory of Religion,* trans. Robert Hurley. New York: Zone Books.

Bataille, Georges (1997) *The Bataille Reader*, ed. Fred Botting and Scott Wilson. Oxford: Blackwell.

Bataille, Georges (2001) *The Unfinished System of Nonknowledge*, ed. Stuart Kendall. Minneapolis: University of Minnesota Press.

Baudrillard, Jean (1975) *The Mirror of Production*. St. Louis: Telos Press.

Baudrillard, Jean (1981) *For a Political Economy of the Sign*. St. Louis: Telos Press.

Baudrillard, Jean (1987) *Symbolic Exchange and Death*. London: Sage.

Baudrillard, Jean (1993) *The Transparency of Evil: Essays in Extreme Phenomena,* London: Verso.

Baudrillard, Jean (1998) *Consumer Society*. London: Sage.

Baudrillard, Jean (2002) *The Spirit of Terrorism*. London: Verso.

Baudrillard, Jean (2005) *The Intelligence of Evil and the Lucidity Pact,* trans. Chris Turner. Oxford: Berg.

Baudrillard, Jean (2005) "War Porn," *Journal for Visual Culture* 5(1): 86–88.

Beer, Gillian (1996) *Open Fields: Science in Cultural Encounter*. Oxford: Clarendon Press.

Bergson, Henri (1911) *Matter and Memory*. London: George Allen and Unwin.

Bergson, Henri (1928) *Laughter*. New York: Macmillan.

Bergson, Henri (1960) *Creative Evolution*. London: Macmillan.

Berman, Paul (2003) *Terror and Liberalism*. New York: Norton.

Blum, William (2000) *Rogue State: A Guide to the World's Only Superpower*. Monroe, ME: Common Courage Press.

Botting, Fred and Scott Wilson (1997) *The Bataille Reader*. Oxford: Blackwell.

Botting, Fred and Scott Wilson (1998) *Bataille: A Critical Reader*. Oxford: Blackwell.

Botting, Fred and Scott Wilson (2001a) *The Tarantinian Ethics*. London: Sage.

Botting, Fred and Scott Wilson (2001b) *Bataille*. London: Palgrave.

Botting, Fred and Scott Wilson (2004) "Toy Law, Toy Joy, *Toy Story*," in Leslie J. Moran et al. *Law's Moving Image*. London: Glasshouse Press.

Boyle, Danny (Dir.) (1996) *Trainspotting*. Channel 4 Films.

Burroughs, William (1977) *Naked Lunch*. Harmondsworth: Penguin.

Burroughs, William (2002) *Junky*. Harmondsworth: Penguin.

Canning, Peter (2000) "The Imagination of Immanence: An Ethics of Cinema" in Gregory Flaxman (ed.) *The Brain Is a Screen*. Minneapolis: University of Minnesota Press.

Caygill, Howard (1996) "Drafts for a Metaphysics of the Gene" *Tekhnema* 3 / "A Touch of Memory" (Spring). http://tekhnema.free.fr/3Caygill.htm

Cebrowski, Vice Admiral Arthur K and John Gartska (1998) "Network-Centric Warfare" *Proceedings*. www.usni.org/Proceedings/Articles98/PROcebrowski.htm

Chomsky, Noam (2000) *Rogue States: The Rule of Force in World Affairs*. Cambridge: South End Press.

Coker, Christopher (2004) *The Future of War: The Re-Enchantment of War in the Twenty-First Century*. Oxford: Blackwell.

Critchley, Simon (2002) *On Humour*. London: Routledge, 2002.

Damasio, Antonio (2000) *The Feeling of What Happens: Body and Emotion in the Making of Consciousness*. London: Harvest Books.

Damasio, Antonio (2003) *Looking for Spinoza: Joy, Sorrow and the Feeling Brain*. London: Harvest Books.

Dawkins, Richard (1986) *The Blind Watchmaker*. Harmondsworth: Penguin.

Dawkins, Richard (1989) *The Selfish Gene*. Oxford: Oxford University Press.

De Landa, Manuel (1991) *War in the Age of Intelligent Machines*. New Rork: Zone Books.

Deleuze, Gilles (1983) *Nietzsche and Philosophy*, trans. Hugh Tomlinson. London: Athlone Press.

Deleuze, Gilles (1986) *Cinema 1: The Movement Image*, trans. Hugh Tomlinson. London: Athlone Press.

Deleuze, Gilles (1988) *Foucault*, trans. Sean Hand. Minneapolis: University of Minnesota Press.

Deleuze, Gilles (1989a) *The Logic of Sense*. London: Athlone Press.

Deleuze, Gilles (1989b) *Cinema 2: The Time Image*, trans. Hugh Tomlinson and Robert Galeta. London: Athlone Press.

Deleuze, Gilles (1993) "Ethics and the Event" in *The Deleuze Reader*, ed. Constantin V. Boundas. New York: Columbia University Press.

Deleuze, Gilles (1995) *Negotiations*. New York: Columbia University Press.

Deleuze, Gilles (1997) *Difference and Repetition*, trans. Paul Patton. London: Continuum.

Deleuze, Gilles (1998) *Essays Critical and Clinical*, trans. Daniel W. Smith and Michael A. Greco. London: Verso Press.

Deleuze, Gilles (2001a) *Pure Immanence*, trans. Anne Boyman. New York: Zone Books.

Deleuze, Gilles (2001b) "Dualism, Monism and Multiplicities (Desire-Pleasure-Jouissance)," *Contretemps* 2 May: 92–108.

Deleuze, Gilles (2003) *Desert Islands and Other Texts* (1953–1974). New York: Semiotext(e).

Deleuze, Gilles (2006) *Two Regimes of Madness: Texts and Interviews 1975–1995*. New York Semiotext(e).

Deleuze, Gilles and Claire Parnet (2002) *Dialogues II*. London: Continuum.

Deleuze, Gilles and Félix Guattari (1984) *Anti-Oedipus: Capitalism and Schizophrenia*. London: Athlone Press.

Deleuze, Gilles and Félix Guattari (1988) *A Thousand Plateaus: Capitalism and Schizophrenia* II. London: Athlone Press.

Deleuze, Gilles and Félix Guattari (1994) *What Is Philosophy?* London: Verso.

Dennett, Daniel C (1995) *Darwin's Dangerous Idea: Evolution and the Meanings of Life*. Harmondsworth: Penguin.

Der Derian, James (1997) "The Virtualization of Violence and the Disappearance of War," *Cultural Values* 1.2: 205–218.

Derrida, Jacques (1992a) *Given Time I: Counterfeit Money*, trans. by Peggy Kamuf. Chicago: University of Chicago Press.

Derrida, Jacques (1992b) *Acts of Literature*, ed. Derek Attridge. London: Routledge.

Derrida, Jacques (1994) *Specters of Marx*, trans. Peggy Kamuf. London: Routledge.

Derrida, Jacques (1995) *Points*. Stanford: Stanford University Press.

Derrida, Jacques (1998) "Economimesis" in Julian Wolfreys (ed.), *The Derrida Reader*. Edinburgh: Edinburgh University Press.

Derrida, Jacques (2001) in *Deconstruction: A Reader*, ed. Martin McQuillan. Edinburgh: Edinburgh University Press.

Derrida, Jaques (2005) *Rogues*, trans. Pascale-Anne Brault and Michael Naas. Stanford: Stanford University Press.

Diken, Bulent and Carsten Bagge Lausten (2002) "Enjoy your fight! *Fight Club* as a Symptom of the Network Society," *Journal for Cultural Research* 6.4: 349–367.

Dickens, Charles (1983) *Our Mutual Friend*. Harmondsworth: Penguin.

Downer, John (2002) *Weird Nature. Science is stranger than myth*. John Downer Production for BBC and Discovery Channel.

Economist, The (1999) "A quiet joke at your expense." 16.12.99. www.econo mist.com/diversions/displayStory.cfm?story_id=268955

Evans, Dylan (1996) *An Introductory Dictionary of Lacanian Psychoanalysis*. London: Routledge.

Fincher, David (1999) *Fight Club*, 20th Century Fox Home Entertainments DVD.

Fink, Bruce (1995) *The Lacanian Subject*. Princeton: Princeton University Press.

Fink, Bruce (2004) *Lacan to the Letter: Reading* Ecrits *Closely*. Minneapolis: University of Minnesota Press.

Flaxman, Gregory (2000) *The Brain Is the Screen: Deleuze and the Philosophy of Cinema*. Minneapolis: University of Minnesota Press.

Foucault, Michel (1971) *L'Ordre du discours*. Paris: Gallimard.

Foucault, Michel (1972) *The Archaeology of Knowledge*, trans. A. M. Sheridan. London: Tavistock.

Foucault, Michel (1980) *The History of Sexuality, Volume 1*, trans. Robert Hurley. Harmondsworth: Penguin.

Foucault, Michel (1984) *Language, Counter-Memory, Practice*, trans. Donald Bouchard and Sherry Simon. Ithaca: Cornell University Press.

Foucault, Michel (1985) *The Use of Pleasure*, trans. Robert Hurley. New York: Vintage.

Foucault, Michel (1986) *The Order of Things*. London: Tavistock Press.

Foucault, Michel (1987) "Maurice Blanchot: The Thought from Outside" in *Foucault/Blanchot*, trans. Brian Massumi. New York: Zone Books.

Foucault, Michel (1988) *Politics, Philosophy, Culture: Interviews and Other Writings 1977–1984*, ed. Lawrence D. Kritzman. London: Routledge.

Foucault, Michel (1989) *Foucault Live (Interviews 1966–84)*. New York: Semiotext(e).

Foucault, Michel (1991) *Remarks on Marx*. New York: Semiotext(e).

Foucault, Michel (2003) *Society Must Be Defended,* trans. David Macey. London: Penguin.

Freud, Sigmund (1927) "Humour" Standard Edition of the *Complete Psychological Works of Sigmund Freud*, Vol. 21, trans. James Strachey. London: Hogarth Press: 161–166.

Freud, Sigmund (1984) *Beyond the Pleasure Principle*. On Metapsychology: The Theory of Psychoanalysis, trans. James Strachey. Harmondsworth: Penguin.

Freud, Sigmund (1989) *Civilization and Its Discontents*, trans. James Strachey. New York: Norton.

Freud, Sigmund (1995) *The Freud Reader*, ed. Peter Gay. London: Vintage.

Gay, Peter (1988) *Freud: A Life in Our Time*. London: Dent.

Gervais, Ricky and Stephen Merchant (2003) *The Office*. Complete first series. BBC DVD.

Gervais, Ricky and Stephen Merchant (2004) *The Office*. Complete second series. BBC DVD.

Gibson, William (1984) *Neuromancer*. London: HarperCollins.

Gibson, William (1987) *Count Zero*. London: HarperCollins.

Gilder, George (1981) *Wealth and Poverty*. New York: Bantam Books.

Goldman, Robert and Stephen Papson (1998) *Nike Culture*. London: Sage.

Goux, Jean-Joseph (1990) *Symbolic Economies: After Marx and Freud*, trans. Jennifer Curtiss Gage. Ithaca: Cornell University Press.

Goux, Jean-Joseph (1992) "The Phallus: Masculine Identity and the 'Exchange of Women,'" *differences: A Journal of Feminist Cultural Studies* 4.1: 72.

Goux, Jean-Joseph (1993) *Oedipus Philosopher*. Stanford: Stanford University Press.

Goux, Jean-Joseph (1997) "The Stock Exchange Paradigm," *Cultural Values* 1.3: 159–177.

Goux, Jean-Joseph (1998a) "'General Economics and Postmodern Capitalism," in Fred Botting and Scott Wilson (eds), *Bataille: A Critical Reader*. Oxford: Blackwell: 196–213.

Goux, Jean-Joseph (1998b) "Subversion and Consensus: Proletarians, Women, Artists" in Jean-Joseph Goux and Philip R. Wood (eds.), *Terror and Consensus: Vicissitudes of French Thought*. Stanford: Stanford University Press.

Guattari, Félix (1992) *Chaosmosis*, trans. Paul Bains and Julian Pefanis. Sydney: Power Publications.

Guattari, Félix (1995) *Chaosophy*. New York: Semiotext(e).

Hardt, Michael and Antonio Negri (2000) *Empire*. Cambridge: Harvard University Press.

Hardt, Michael and Antonio Negri (2004) *Multitudes: War and Democracy in the Age of Empire*. New York: Penguin.

Hirschman, Albert O (1977) *The Passions and the Interests: Political Arguments for Capitalism before Its Triumph*. Princeton: Princeton University Press.

Hobbes, Thomas (1985) *Leviathan*, edited by C. B. Macpherson. Harmondsworth: Penguin.

Hodge, John (1996) *Trainspotting*. London: Faber & Faber.

Hollier, Denis (ed.) (1988a) *The College of Sociology 1937–39.* Minneapolis: University of Minnesota Press.

Hollier, Denis (1988b) "January 21," *Stanford French Review* XII, 1: 31–47.

Houellebecq, Michel (2001) *Atomised,* trans. Frank Wynne. London: Vintage.

Hume, David (1978) *A Treatise of Human Nature,* ed. L. A. Selby-Bigge and P.H. Nidditch. Oxford: Clarendon Press.

Hume, David (1993) "Of the Delicacy of Taste and Passion" in *Selected Essays,* ed. Stephen Copley and Andrew Edgar. Oxford: Oxford University Press.

Hunt, Lynn (ed.) (1993) *The Invention of Pornography: Obscenity and the Origins of Modernity.* New York: Zone Books.

Joxe, Alain (2002) *Empire of Disorder.* New York: Semiotext(e).

Kay, Lily. E. (2000) *Who Wrote the Book of Life?* A History of the Genetic Code. Stanford: Stanford University Press.

Kelly, Kevin (1998) *New Rules for the New Economy: Ten Ways the Network Economy Is Changing Everything.* London: Fourth Estate.

Keay, John (1993) *The Honourable Company: A History of the East India Company,* London: HarperCollins.

Kincaid, James (1998) *Erotic Innocence.* Durham: Duke University Press.

Kittler, Friedrich (1997): *Literature, Media, Information Systems,* trans. John Johnson. Amsterdam: G+B Arts.

Klein, Naomi (2000) *No Logo.* London: Flamingo.

Kristeva, Julia (1982) *Powers of Horror.* New York: Columbia University Press.

Lacan, Jacques (1976) *Four Fundamental Concepts of Psychoanalysis,* trans. Alan Sheridan. Harmondsworth: Penguin.

Lacan, Jacques (1977) "Desire and the Interpretation of Desire in *Hamlet,*" *Yale French Studies* 55/56: 11–52.

Lacan, Jacques (1982) "Seminar of 21 January 1975" in Juliet Mitchell and Jacqueline Rose (eds.), *Feminine Sexuality.* Basingstoke and London: Macmillan.

Lacan, Jacques (1986) *Ecrits: A Selection,* trans. Alan Sheridan. London: Routledge.

Lacan, Jacques (1988a) *The Seminar of Jacques Lacan: Book I: Freud's Papers on Technique 1953–1954,* trans. John Forrester. Cambridge: Cambridge University Press.

Lacan, Jacques (1988b) *The Seminar of Jacques Lacan: Book II: The Ego in Freud's Theory and in the Technique of Psychoanalysis,* trans. John Forrester. Cambridge: Cambridge University Press.

Lacan, Jacques (1990) *Television.* New York: Norton.

Lacan, Jacques (1991) *L'Envers de la psychanalyse.* Paris: Editions de Seuil.

Lacan, Jacques (1992) *The Ethics of Psychoanalysis:* Seminar VII, trans. Dennis Porter. London: Routledge.

Lacan, Jacques (1993) *The Psychoses: The Seminar of Jacques Lacan* Book III 1955–56, ed. Jacques Alain Miller, tr. Russell Grigg, London: Routledge.

Lacan, Jacques (1999) *Encore:* Seminar XX, trans. Bruce Fink. New York: Norton.

Land, Nick (1992) *Thirst for Annihilation.* London: Routledge.

Land, Nick (1993) "Machinic Desire," *Textual Practice* 7.3: 471–482.

Lotringer, Sylvere (1988) *Overexposed.* New York: Pantheon.

Lowe, Shannon E. (2002) "Miskinetic Neuropoliticology: The Politics of Constructing and Disciplining the Organism of the Brain," *Culture Machine* 4. http://culturemachine.tees.ac.uk/Cmach/Backissues/j004/Articles/Lowe.htm

Lyotard, Jean-François (1984) *Postmodern Condition*, trans. Geoffrey Bennington. Manchester: Manchester University Press.

Jean-François Lyotard (1994) *The Inhuman*, trans. Geoffrey Bennington and Rachel Bowlby. Stanford: Stanford University Press.

Lyotard, Jean-François (1988–1989) "Can Thought Go On Without a Body?," *Discourse* 11.1: 74–87.

Manovich, Lev (1996) "The Labor of Perception" in Lynn Hershman Leeson (ed.), *Clicking in Hot Links to a Digital Culture*. Seattle: Bay Press.

Margulis, Lynn and Dorion Sagan (1997) *Microcosmos*. Berkeley: University of California Press.

Marx, Karl (1976) *Capital: A Critique of Political Economy*. Harmondsworth: Penguin.

Maté, Gabor (1999) *Scattered Minds*. London: Knopf Canada.

Meana, Gabriella Ripa di (1998) *Figures of Lightness. Anorexia, Bulimia, Psychoanalysis*. London: Jessica Kingsley.

Miller, Jacques-Alain (1988) "Extimité," *Prose Studies*, 11: 125–36.

Miller, James (1993) *The Passion of Michel Foucault*. London: HarperCollins.

Milton, John (1983) *Milton Poetical Works*, ed. Douglas Bush. Oxford: Oxford University Press.

Nancy, Jean-Luc (1991) *The Inoperative Community*. Minneapolis: University of Minnesota Press.

Nietzsche, Friedrich (1968) *The Will to Power*, ed. Walter Kaufmann. New York: Vintage.

Nietzsche, Friedrich (1969) *Thus Spoke Zarathustra*, trans. R. J. Hollingdale. New York: Vintage.

Nietzsche, Friedrich (1984) *Beyond Good and Evil*, trans. R. J. Hollingdale. Harmonsdworth: Penguin.

Nietzsche, Friedrich (1989) *The Genealogy of Morals*, trans. Walter Kaufman. New York: Vintage.

Nolan, Christopher (2000) *Memento*. Special Edition DVD. Pathe Distribution Ltd.

Orwell, George (1957) "England, Your England" in *Selected Essays*. Harmondsworth: Penguin.

Palahniuk, Chuck (1997) *Fight Club*. London: Vintage.

Pieterse, Jan Nederveen (2004) "Neoliberal Empire" in *Theory, Culture and Society* 21(3): 119–140.

Poole, Steven (2004) *Trigger Happy: Videogames and the Entertainment Revolution*. London: Arcade.

Prendergrast, Mark (1994) *For God, Country and Coca-Cola*. London: Orion.

Ridley, Matt (1993) *The Red Queen: Sex and the Evolution of Human Nature*. Harmondsworth: Penguin.

Ridley, Matt (1997) *The Origins of Virtue*. Harmondsworth: Penguin.

Risen, Clay (2006) "The Danger of Generals as CEOs. War Mart," *The New Republic* online. 04.03.06. www.tnr.com/doc.mhtml?i=20060403&s=risen 040306

Rodowick, D. N. (1997) *Gilles Deleuze's Time Machine*. Durham: Duke University Press.

Rose, Gillian (1996) *Mourning Becomes Law: Philosophy and Representation*. New York: Cambridge University Press.

Rothschild, Michael (1995) *Bionomics: Economy as Ecosystem*. London: Owl Books.

Roudinesco, Elisabeth (1990) *Jacques Lacan & Co: A History of Psychoanalysis in France 1921–1985*, trans. Jeffrey Mehlman. London: Free Association Books.

Roudinesco, Elisabeth (1997) *Jacques Lacan*. Cambridge: Polity Press

Rousseau, Jean-Jacques (1992) *Confessions*, ed. P. N. Furbank. London: David Campbell.

Shakespeare, William (1987) *Hamlet*, ed. G. R. Hibbard. Oxford: Oxford University Press.

Smith, Adam, (1976) *An inquiry into the nature and causes of the wealth of nations*; general editors R. H. Campbell and A. S. Skinner. Oxford: Clarendon Press.

Sontag, Susan (2004) "The Photos Are Us," *The Guardian* G2 24.05.04: 1–5.

Spinoza, Benedict de (1996) *Ethics*. Harmondsworth: Penguin.

Stelarc (1997) "From Psycho to Cyber Strategies," *Cultural Values* 2:1: 241–249.

Terranova, Tiziana (2004) *Network Culture: Politics for the Information Age*. London: Pluto Press.

Thompson, Ben (2004) *Sunshine on Putty: The Golden Age of British Comedy from Vic Reeves to The Office*. London: Fourth Estate.

Virilio, Paul (1989) *War and Cinema*. London: Verso Press.

Weinstein, Michael A (2001) "Virtual Bataille," *parallax* 18: 76–80

Welsh, Irvine (1993) *Trainspotting*. London: Minerva.

Wilson, Scott (2004)"The Joy of Things" in Ivan Callus and Stefan Herbrechter, *Post-Theory, Culture, Criticism*. Amsterdam: Rodolpi Press.

Wilson, Scott (2008) *Great Satan's Rage: American Negativity and Rap/Metal in the Age of Supercapitalism*. Manchester: Manchester University Press.

Wolfe, Tom (1988) *Bonfire of the Vanities*. London: Picador.

Wordsworth, William (1975) *Selected Poems*, ed. Walford Davies. London: JM Dent.

Žižek, Slavoj (1999) "The Superego and the Act." *European Graduate School*. www.egs.edu/faculty/zizek/zizek-superego-and-the-act-1999.html.

Index